C000140403

DEFENDING ESSEX

DEFENDING ESSEX

The Military Landscape from Prehistory to the Present

MIKE OSBORNE

The History Press

First published 2013

The History Press
The Mill, Brimscombe Port
Stroud, Gloucestershire, GL5 2QG
www.thehistorypress.co.uk

© Mike Osborne, 2013

The right of Mike Osborne to be identified as the Author
of this work has been asserted in accordance with the
Copyrights, Designs and Patents Act 1988.

All rights reserved. No part of this book may be reprinted
or reproduced or utilised in any form or by any electronic,
mechanical or other means, now known or hereafter invented,
including photocopying and recording, or in any information
storage or retrieval system, without the permission in writing
from the Publishers.

British Library Cataloguing in Publication Data.
A catalogue record for this book is available from the British Library.

ISBN 978 0 7524 8834 9

Typesetting and origination by The History Press
Printed in Great Britain

Contents

Acknowledgements

Mike Bardell of RFCA, Chelmsford; Alec Beanse and Wayne Cocroft of English Heritage; Simon Brand DSM, DCM, late of 2 Para; Fred Nash; Ivor Crowson; Major Tony Kriehn and WO1 Bruce Dickson, respectively 2i/c and RSM of 101 (EOD) Engineer Regiment at Carver Barracks; Colin Alexander; Paul Francis; Mrs Bygraves; owners and tenants at Bowaters Farm and Stow Maries airfield for allowing access.

All illustrations are by the author unless otherwise credited.

Abbreviations

AA	anti-aircraft
AAA	anti-aircraft artillery (US Army)
AAOR	anti-aircraft operations room (ROTOR system)
ACF	Army Cadet Force
ADGB	Air Defence of Great Britain (1924 scheme)
ARP	Air Raid Precautions
A/S	anti-submarine
AT	anti-tank
ATS	Auxiliary Territorial Service (forerunner of WRAC)
BD	Bomb Disposal (Unit)
BEF	British Expeditionary Force
BHQ	Battle Headquarters
BL	breech-loading (gun)
CASL	Coast Artillery Searchlight (Second World War)
CBA	Council for British Archaeology
CD	Civil Defence
CH	Chain Home (radar)
CHEL	Chain Home Extra Low
CHL/CD	Chain Home Low/Coast Defence
CRE	Commanding Royal Engineer
DEL	Defence Electric Light (Coast Defence Searchlight to First World War)
DEMS	Defensive Equipping of Merchant Ships (Second World War)
DFW3	Directorate of Fortifications and Works, Department 3
(E)(R)FTS	(Elementary) (Reserve) Flying Training School
EH	English Heritage
EOD	explosive ordnance disposal
EXDO	Extended Defence Officer (minefield control)
FIDO	Fog Information and Dispersal Organisation (on airfields)
FUSAG	First US Army Group (spurious formation in D-Day deception)
GCI	Ground-Controlled Interception (radar/fighter system)
GDA	Gun-Defended Area (Second World War AA defences)
GHQ	General Headquarters (as in GHQ Line)
GL	gun-laying (as in radar for AA artillery)
HAA	heavy anti-aircraft

HT	Horse Transport
IAZ	Inner Artillery Zone (London Second World War AA defences)
IFF	Identification Friend or Foe
KRRC	Kings Royal Rifle Corps
LAA	light anti-aircraft
LADA	London Air Defence Area
LCM/LCT(1-8)	Landing Craft Mechanised/Tank (eight sizes)
LDV	Local Defence Volunteers, later Home Guard (HG)
lmg	light machine gun
LST	Landing Ship Tank
MFV	Motor Fishing Vessel (for RN service)
MGB/L/TB	Motor Gun-Boat/Launch/Torpedo-Boat (RN)
(M)M/S	(Motor) Minesweeper
MOD	Ministry of Defence
MU	Maintenance Unit (RAF)
NOIC	Naval Officer in Charge
NZEF	New Zealand Expeditionary Force
pdr	pounder (as in weight of projectile)
PF	position-finding (cell) for ranging Coast Artillery
PSP	pierced steel planking (for runways and hard standings)
QF	quick-firing (gun)
RAAF	Royal Auxiliary Air Force (until 1957)
RAC	Royal Armoured Corps
RAF	Royal Air Force (from 1 April 1918)
RAFVR	Royal Air Force Volunteer Reserve
(R)AOC	(Royal from 1918) Army Ordnance Corps
(R)ASC	(Royal from 1918) Army Service Corps
RCHM(E)	Royal Commission on the Historical Monuments of (England)
RCM	radio counter measures (Meacon, Bromide, beam-bending etc.)
REME	Royal Electrical and Mechanical Engineers (from 1942)
RFC	Royal Flying Corps (up to 31 March 1918)
RFCA	Reserve Forces and Cadets' Association
RGA	Royal Garrison Artillery
RHA	Royal Horse Artillery
RML	rifled muzzle-loader (Victorian cannon)
RN	Royal Navy
RNAS	Royal Naval Air Service (up to 1918, Fleet Air Arm from 1938)
RN(V)R	Royal Naval (Volunteer) Reserve
(R)OC	(Royal from 1941) Observer Corps
SAS	Special Air Service
S/L	searchlight
SOE	Special Operations Executive
TA	Territorial Army (from 1920 to 1939 and 1947 to present)
TAC	Territorial Army Centre (drill hall post-1947)

TAF	Tactical Air Force (to support ground operations)
tb	temporary brick (single brick with buttresses in RAF buildings)
TF	Territorial Force (from 1908 to 1918)
UKWMO	United Kingdom Warning and Monitoring Organisation
UP	unrotated projectile (as in Z battery, AA rockets)
USAAF	United States Army Air Force (Second World War)
USAF(E)	United States Air Force (Europe) (post-Second World War)
VAD	Voluntary Aid Detachment (First World War)
VTC	Volunteer Training Corps (First World War Home Guard)
WAAF	Women's Auxiliary Air Force
WRAC	Womens' Royal Army Corps
WRNS	Women's Royal Naval Service (Wrens)

Introduction

Essex can thank the wide stretch of the North Sea as a natural defence against invasion – for otherwise, its 300 miles (480km) of coastline, the longest of any English county, much of it flat and inviting, would have seen countless invaders. Granted, the Vikings landed at Maldon and Mersea Island, and the Dutch raided Harwich, but Claudius the God, William the Conqueror and the future Louis VIII of France chose the Channel route, subsequently working their way north. Napoleon and Hitler planned Channel crossings, but missed the boat. The sea was not, however, sufficient protection in itself, and fixed defences were required to secure the landing places, especially in the Thames Estuary, representing the gateway to London. Medieval castles, Tudor forts, Napoleonic Martello Towers, Victorian casemates, and twentieth-century batteries and pillboxes all stand testimony to this vulnerability. Much of the Essex landscape is flat and, unsurprisingly, some 800-odd medieval moated sites, many of them with at least a nod to defence, have been identified, the highest total for any historic English county. In his survey of more recent times Fred Nash, working for an enlightened Essex County Council, has recorded 2,700 sites of Second World War defences. This has taken him nearly twenty years to date, and he recently estimated around a further 800 sites remain to be identified and recorded. A number of important survivals such as the defences of Chappel Viaduct have been scheduled as ancient monuments.

No county can be a discrete entity and both fixed geography and managed boundary changes demonstrate this. The wider defences of Essex straddle the Thames in the south and Harwich Haven in the north, so there are references in the text to sites in, respectively, Kent and Suffolk. Greater London's 1968 reorganisation turned a large slice of Essex into six new London boroughs, and whilst many of the monuments in those boroughs were covered in the London volume of this series there will remain a degree of overlap.

Despite much of Essex lying in the path of the developers, much of its defence heritage remains. Moreover, as plots are cleared for redevelopment, land use changes or road-layouts are altered, archaeologists and individuals alike continue to make discoveries such as that of the Napoleonic Bathside coastal battery in Harwich.

Any readers who might be lucky enough to uncover items of interest are asked to observe three principles: to respect private property and privacy; to take appropriate care in potentially hazardous locations; and to report discoveries to local authority Historic Environment Officers or museum staff. The landscape changes overnight and I suspect that few of those watching or participating in the Olympic mountain-biking at Hadleigh Country Park will know that they are in the middle of a Second World War anti-aircraft site.

It has been a pleasure to reacquaint myself with places well-known to me and to discover others less so. In the 1990s I walked the Outer London Line and the southern sections of the Essex GHQ Line with Colin Alexander. Soon after that, my wife and I walked the rest of the GHQ Line and the Eastern Command Line, as well as much of the coast, but in the last twelve months we have revisited many of those sites as well as taking the opportunity to visit some that are new to us. The county has a rich defensive heritage from many periods and it is the intention of this book to chart its development and to place it in its social and historical context.

Mike Osborne,
July 2012

one

Prehistoric to Saxon Essex

Prehistoric Fortifications

There are upwards of twenty or so prehistoric sites in Essex which could be described as defensible. Amongst the earliest is the Neolithic causewayed enclosure at Orsett, whose purpose is still not fully understood. Two millennia on and Bronze Age sites at Springfield Lyons, Great Totham and Mucking, none of them much larger than half an acre (0.2ha), comprise small groups of structures, often round-houses, surrounded by banks, palisades and external ditches. These defences were probably intended as much to protect the inhabitants and their stock from wild animals, as to defend against hostile neighbours or to control private space.

By the time of the Iron Age the size of social groups had increased and so settlements became bigger, often with more significant defensive features. Regardless of the terrain, such settlements are usually known as hill forts, and there are a number in Essex. Danbury Camp occupies a hill-top site, but many must have relied solely on the strength of their defences. One such was Wallbury, a pear-shaped fort sited on a spur over the Stort valley, and covering 30 acres (12ha). It has ditches 50-70ft (15-22m) wide, and a double rampart 7ft (2m) high. The rampart, constructed as a hollow timber framework, revetted with timber or rubble and filled with the spoil from the ditch, would have been topped by a timber palisade with a fighting-platform. The entrance would have been a dog-legged passage through the rampart, with a timber tower above it. Often this entrance was placed in a re-entrant so that the approaches could be flanked by fire from the defenders' slings and arrows. Most camps were less impressive than Wallbury, many – such as Ambresbury Banks, Ring Hill Camp at Littlebury, and Prittlewell Camp in Southend – being univallate with a single bank and ditch. Examples of the more substantial bivallate camp can be found at Chipping Hill, Witham, and Pitchbury Ramparts. These camps ranged in size from the 7 acres (3ha) of South Weald Camp to the larger Wallbury. Ditches could be up to 180ft (55m) wide, as at Pitchbury, and the 10ft (3m) depth of the ditch at Ambresbury Banks, combined with its banks, 7ft (2m) in height, would have created a formidable obstacle to the attacker, crossing under a hail of missiles. The situation of camps such as Wallbury and Loughton Camp on spurs would also have added to their defensive properties by limiting the number of possible approaches. At Ardleigh is the unusual occurrence of a single isolated round-house, surrounded by a deep rectangular ditch, ringed with a timber palisade.

Much larger than the usually compact hill forts were the much rarer Celtic oppida, of which there were only a handful in the whole of Britain. One such oppidum, or tribal centre, was that of the Trinovantes at Camulodunum, or modern-day Colchester, named for Camulos, the Celtic god of war, and dating from the early first century BC. It was characterised by its sprawling site, its extensive, but disjointed, systems of surrounding dykes, and the presence of many of the activities associated with towns. These included artisans' workshops, a mint and evidence of trade, particularly in food and pottery. The dykes at Camulodunum added up to a total of 18 miles (29km) of discontinuous lengths, and may not have been defensive in conventional terms, but intended to define space, to control movement and, it has been suggested, to limit the manoeuvrability of chariots, the Celts' most favoured tactical strike force. The earliest dyke was Heath Farm Dyke, dating from c. 100 BC, and the latest, Gryme's Dyke, from after the town's destruction by Boudicca in AD 60. Most of the ditches face west and are V-shaped, up to 13ft (4m) deep, with a bank behind. Heath Farm Dyke is on a slightly smaller scale, measuring 10ft (3m) from the bottom of the ditch to the crest of the bank. The earlier dykes may have faced west against the encroachments of the expansionist Catuvellauni. The oppidum appears to have occupied a significant area of up to 20 square miles (5,000ha) between the Colne and the Roman river, with its epicentre at Gosbecks, south-west of the modern town centre.

Roman Invasions

Following an armed reconnaissance the previous year, Caesar landed in Kent with five legions and 2,000 cavalry, in 54 BC. The forces of Cassivellaunus initially managed to avoid serious contact, drawing the Romans ever deeper into inhospitable country. However, the Romans were aided by the Trinovantes, and allied tribes, who bore deeply-felt resentments against Cassivellaunus. His forces, possibly based on the substantial hill fort of Wallbury with outposts at Uphall, Ambresbury Banks and Loughton, were defeated by the Romans. Although Caesar had gained the upper hand he was forced to hurry back to Gaul, where a rebellion was breaking out, leaving orders for Cassivellaunus to stop bothering the Trinovantes. In the following years, the Catuvellauni and the Trinovantes combined into a successful trading partnership, and under the powerful leadership of Cunobelinos, Shakespeare's Cymbeline, they thrived by balancing the influences of the three major power-blocks: Rome, the Gallo-Belgic immigrants of the first century BC, and native British tribes like the Iceni. In AD 43 the Romans returned, led by Plautius under the orders of the Emperor Claudius. Landing unopposed at Richborough (Kent), the Roman army marched inland, defeating the tribes under Caratacus on the Medway, in a particularly hard-fought battle lasting two days. Survivors of the British army retreated across the marshes, possibly crossing the Thames at Mucking or East Tilbury. The Roman army, now accompanied by Claudius in person, crossed the Thames at London and advanced towards Camulodunum. Some skirmishes were fought on the way, providing the emperor with military success for home consumption, and complementing the glory of the British leaders' swift submission.

Roman Consolidation

Following this military success, the Romans embarked on a campaign to conquer the whole country. The earliest Roman roads began at London and fanned out across the country with forts being built at regular intervals, usually a day's march apart, to secure the route, to provide accommodation for officials in transit, and as permanent garrisons in newly occupied areas. These garrisons would have ranged from cohorts of legionaries down to detachments of auxiliaries, depending on local circumstances. Stane Street, the road from London to Camulodunum, had at least three forts along its length. One would have been on an as-yet undiscovered site near Billericay, with others at Kelvedon and Chelmsford, the route terminating at a fort at Stanway, very close to the tribal oppidum itself. Chelmsford was named Caesaromagus, which may imply some significance for Claudius himself; perhaps it was the site of one of his famous victories. These interval forts were roughly square with sides of around 400ft (120m), defended by a bank and the characteristic V-shaped military ditch. Huts housed the garrison with grander structures serving as the commandant's house and unit HQ. The fort at Stanway has only three sides, with the Heath Farm Dyke forming the fourth. In Chelmsford the fort was next to a bridge over the river Can where a ditch, turf rampart and timber buildings have been excavated. At Kelvedon, Roman Canonium, the fort straddled the main road to Romanised Camulodunum. Other camps have been identified at Orsett and Hadleigh, possibly serving as signal stations on Thames crossings. By using the known Roman road network it is possible to infer the existence of further forts at the river crossings of Great Dunmow and Braintree on the route west from Camulodunum, and at Wixoe on the road which ran to Cambridge and on through Godmanchester into the Midlands.

Each of the four legions involved in the conquest of Britain was provided with a substantial depot, whose location shifted as the occupation proceeded. The XXth Legion's base at Camulodunum was established 2 miles away from the original fort, next to the river Colne, surrounded by a turf rampart built on a raft of planks, and a ditch 16ft 6in (5m) wide, the circuit extending to just under 2,000 yards. Barracks were built of clay blocks on oak ground-plates themselves resting on mortared plinths, preserved by Boudicca's conflagration. The discovery of Claudian coins at Fingringhoe Wick has led to suggestions that supplies for the legion were brought in by ship. Moreover, a Roman camp has been identified at Wick Farm. Within a few years the legionary base, whose street plan can still be traced in the town's modern layout, had outlived its usefulness and was replaced by a colonia for retired legionaries, occupying the site of the fortress, its eastern annexe, and as much land again to its east. The defences were levelled right down to the log foundations, and the buildings themselves adapted for civil use. A few years later, when the Boudiccan revolt broke out, the town was graced by the unfinished, but already imposing, temple of Claudius, but was otherwise virtually unprotected.

Boudicca's Revolt

The revolt in AD 60 was caused by a combination of, on the one hand, Roman arro-
gance, complacency and insensitivity, and, on the other, British naivety and pride. On
the death of her client-king husband, Boudicca, neglecting to read the small print,
expected to succeed him. The Romans, regarding the Iceni lands as theirs to bestow on
whomsoever they pleased, took them back under imperial management – ignoring, as
Boudicca herself must have known they would, her late husband's wish that his daughters would inherit alongside the emperor. The widowed queen and her daughters were
brutally and publicly punished for their presumption. At the same time that this was
happening, a Roman army was crushing the Druids on Anglesey, the defeats of the last
fifteen years were still smarting, taxes were being levied, foreign merchants were cream-
ing off the tribes' wealth, and this latest humiliation must have come as the final straw
for the Iceni, who determined to destroy the Romans before they were completely
crushed or enslaved. As news of the uprising spread, the Roman Governor gathered
together a scratch force of legionaries and cavalry, marching down from Longthorpe,
the legionary depot on the Nene, west of Peterborough. This expedition, premature
but at the same time lacking in urgency, was ambushed by Boudicca's army and effectively destroyed, leaving no significant Roman force within several weeks' march, and
a clear run for Boudicca to march her army south. Her intention was to eradicate all
traces of Roman power by utterly destroying Colchester, St Albans and London – the
buildings and everyone in them, collaborators all. Barely reinforced by a few troops
from London, the Colchester veterans, their families and the rest of the town's inhabitants were slaughtered by the Iceni, and the settlement razed to the ground, a last stand
in the hated Temple of Claudius marking the death throes of Roman Camulodunum.
Boudicca moved on, meting out the same treatment to St Albans and London, before
being defeated by the Roman army returning from its campaign in Wales, and committing suicide. Around the time of Boudicca's revolt the Roman settlement at Ardleigh, a
few miles north-east of Colchester, received defences in the shape of a deep V-shaped
ditch and a timber palisade with gates. Although there is no evidence of these defences
suffering assault, they appear not to have lasted very long.

The Defence of Britannia

The aftermath of the Boudiccan Revolt saw the rebuilding of Camulodunum as a
centre of Roman government, accompanied by a strengthening of the Roman military presence. Camulodunum was given a circuit of town walls, of 3,000 yards, slightly
increasing the area of the first colonia to some 108 acres (43ha). These walls, constructed between AD 65 and AD 80, were 9ft (2.8m) thick and up to 20ft (6m) high,
standing on foundations going down a further 4ft (1.3m). It was built of septaria, the
nodules found in the local clay, Roman tile and mortar, laid in bands and courses.
There were six gates, a tower at each corner, and rectangular interval towers built up
against the interior face of the walls. Around AD 50, the veterans of the colonia had

built a triumphal arch on their western boundary, on the site of the West Gate of the legionary fortress. This line still marked the western limit of the walled area and so the arch was incorporated into the defences as the Balkerne Gate.

The arch became two carriage arches and a quadrant-shaped tower, containing a pedestrian arch, was built each side. The whole structure extends to 107ft (33m), projecting 30ft (9m) into the field. The only other surviving gate, Duncan's Gate, consisted of a single archway 11ft (3.4m) in width. These imposing fortifications were not only some of the earliest, but also the strongest in Roman Britain, and still represent some of the best-preserved. Another immediate response to the Boudiccan Revolt was the expansion of the network of forts protecting the road system. There may have been a fort at Great Chesterford, guarding the Cam crossing on the road north from St Albans prior to the revolt, but it was most probably strengthened after AD 60 as a base for punitive operations into East Anglia, the Iceni heartlands. With the Cam forming its western defences, it had a double ditch 15ft (4.5m) wide, and a bank with a timber palisade, all enclosing an area of 24 acres (10ha), and appears to date from Nero's time.

During the third century the activities of sea-borne barbarian raiders prompted an overhaul of the Roman defences. At Colchester it would appear that the gates were blocked, limiting access through the walls; the Balkerne Gate reduced to just one of its pedestrian archways. A more pro-active response was the creation of the Saxon Shore,

a coastal defence system based on a string of forts supporting a fleet, the *Classis Britannica*. Forts and signal towers were built around the eastern and southern coasts of Britain and also on the Continent.

There were two forts in Essex, at Walton-on-the-Naze, its site now under the North Sea, and at Bradwell-juxta-Mare, or Othona. These forts were built of stone with surrounding ditches. Othona, much of whose fabric was either stolen to build the Saxon chapel of St Peter-on-the-Wall, possibly incorporating the Roman West Gate, or eroded by the sea, appears to

1 Colchester: the Roman Balkerne Gate, showing one of the entrances.

2 Colchester: the Roman wall and the projecting face of one of the quadrant-shaped gate-towers.

Figure 1 Colchester: the Balkerne Gate, reconstructed plan and front elevation, showing the central triumphal arch flanked by later quadrant-shaped towers containing footways.

have been roughly square in shape. The west wall, uncovered by excavation, was 525ft (89m) in length and about 13ft (4m) in thickness. It had an external ditch 25ft (8m) wide and 8ft (2.5m) deep. There was a C-shaped bastion at the north-west corner, and more along the wall itself. This would suggest a strong similarity, in both size and form, to Burgh Castle (Suffolk), the next fort in the chain. At some time the original fort at Chelmsford was replaced by a stronger structure, but still consisting of earthwork defences and was only small in area. In the fourth century, Great Chesterford was given an oval-shaped circuit of stone walls with a ditch, enclosing an area of 36 acres (15ha). By the time the Romans finally withdrew their forces in AD 410, many of these defences would already have been crumbling.

Saxon and Danish Fortifications

After the collapse of the Roman administration the Romano-British inhabitants of Essex strove to continue their previous way of life, initially in the face of voracious raiders from northern Europe, and ultimately of land-hungry settlers. As in other Roman towns it is likely that occupation continued in Colchester but only a small number of Anglo-Saxon dwellings have been discovered inside the walls, and there is no evidence that the town was a burh, although examples of Roman towns being adopted as burhs are known elsewhere in England. It has been suggested that the Roman temple site had some significance as a some-time royal dwelling, known as King Coel's Palace, and there is masonry in the blocked-up Balkerne Gate which could as easily be Saxon, as late Roman or post-Conquest. The remains of an apsidal chapel, probably late Saxon, have been excavated near the entrance to the castle keep.

Burhs were communal fortifications erected by Anglo-Saxon kings to defend against Danish or Viking attacks, and usually comprised earthwork and timber defences, not dissimilar to those employed by their British predecessors, and in fact hill forts were sometimes adapted as burhs. There was a close relationship between the size of burhs and the number of armed peasants available to man them. In Wessex, this relationship has been quantified to show that every four hides of land would gener-ate enough troops to man 5 yards of defensive perimeter. There are two known burhs in Essex, both built by Edward the Elder, at Maldon and at Witham, in around 916. At Maldon, there is archaeological evidence for the site, marked by banks on the west-ern edge of the town centre (TL846071), probably the angle of a rectangular enclosure of 22 acres (9ha), overlooking the river and the hythe. At Witham there is no such certainty. It has long been assumed that the concentric banks and ditches of the Iron Age Chipping hill fort were re-used as the burh, but nothing has ever been proved and there are apparently two other possible sites at Wulvesford (TL821142) near the river and, some way away to the north-east, at Burgate Field, Rivenhall End (TL838164). Chipping Hill is an oval measuring 1,200ft by 1,000ft (360 x 300m) with a ditch up to 30ft (9m) wide. Interestingly, eighteenth-century descriptions of both these burh sites mention inner enclosures, linked to the outer ones by cross-walls. One other possible site from this era is Danbury where the church stands in the middle of what is gener-ally accepted to have been a hill fort. The place-name, however, casts some doubt, so this may be a re-used Iron Age site, or a new ninth-century site – or neither.

Saxon and Danish Conflict

Wherever these burhs might have been located, it could be argued that they came a bit late to be a solution to Danish aggression, for the county had been a battleground for many years. While the various Saxon kingdoms had feuded amongst themselves for centuries, they found themselves faced with an external threat. The Viking incursions began in 793 with a raid on Lindisfarne (Northumbria), but within forty years, these raids became attempts at permanent settlement, initially signalled by their fleets over-wintering, often around the Thames Estuary. These expeditions soon escalated into a full-fledged invasion of East Anglia in 865, followed by another, five years later, in which Mercia was conquered, and King Edmund killed. By 878 Alfred ruled Wessex and Mercia, whilst the Danes held eastern England, the Danelaw, but were not averse to marauding over their neighbours' lands.

In 885 Alfred's ships won a sea-battle off Shotley, and in 893 his troops defeated a Danish army led by Hasten who had laagered at Benfleet on the Thames. Catching the Danes unawares, the army of Wessex, reinforced by locals, completely destroyed the Danish fleet. The Danes withdrew to Shoeburyness, building a new camp there and re-grouping. There was also a Danish base on Mersea Island, providing a jumping-off point for raids round the coast as far as Chester and the Wirral. These camps were usually simple half-moon-shaped enclosures of bank and ditch with the riverbank as the straight side, allowing the long-ships to be drawn up into a protected space for the winter. If, as happened at Benfleet, the camp could be stormed, then the long-ships would be fired, and raiding curbed, providing a breathing-space until a new fleet was constructed.

Operations of the Saxon army in 917 illustrate an unusually successful campaign. Following a victory at Tempsford, on the Ouse in Bedfordshire, which was stormed with the death or capture of the Danish leadership, Edward's army marched on Colchester, besieging it and then storming in and expelling the Danes, some of whom only escaped by going over the walls. The Danes were quickly back on the offensive, laying siege to Maldon, but a relief force joined up with the defenders, bringing the Danes to battle and defeating them. Periods of relative peace alternated with periods of outright war, but by 980 the Danes had regained the upper hand with their tactics of renewed raiding of the coastal communities. By 991 the Saxons under Aethelred decided to make a stand against a raiding force with over ninety ships which, so the story goes, landed on Northey Island, separated by a causeway from the mainland. Unwisely, the Saxon leadership agreed a truce, allowing the Danes to avoid what would have been the extremely dangerous manoeuvre of crossing the narrow causeway under fire. The Danes made their crossing unmolested and the subsequent Battle of Maldon resulted in a disastrous defeat for the Saxons. So began the payment of Danegeld in enormous quantities to buy them off, a catastrophic policy which merely encouraged the Danes to come back for more. Essex was totally ravaged in 1009 by Swein and Cnut, and the whole of East Anglia by 1011. In 1014 Swein died, as did Aethelred two years later, and, although his successor Edmund enjoyed early success, he was brought to battle by Cnut at Assingdun, generally thought to be Ashingdon near Canewdon, and defeated, thus bringing to an end the resistance to Danish domination, and leaving a Danish king on the throne of England.

two

The Early Medieval Period

The Norman Conquest brought William I to the throne of England but some of his compatriots had already been in the country for a while previously, enjoying the patronage of Edward the Confessor. Some of them are reputed to have built examples of the new private fortress which came to be known as the castle, one example in Essex being Clavering, first mentioned in 1052 as 'Robert's Castle'.

Norman Earthwork Castles

Apart from immigrant castle-builders such as Robert, at Clavering, native examples are not totally unknown. In some parts of the country Saxon church-towers, built of stone, have been suspected of having secular functions, both ceremonial and practical. But Essex is not a stone county – retaining, incidentally, the country's only surviving timber church, at Greensted by Ongar, constructed of split logs which have been dated to 1063 at the earliest and 1100 at the latest. Notable exceptions apart, the Norman castles of Essex were going to be constructed of earth and timber.

The Conquest, one way or another, heralded a period of prolific castle-building, and most of these new castles took one of two forms: the motte, and the ringwork. The motte was a mound of earth either raised from ground-level by digging a deep circular ditch and piling the spoil into the middle, or else the adaptation of an existing natural hillock which might be scarped to accentuate the steep sides so necessary defensively. The ringwork was larger in area, possibly a low moated platform, usually circular or ovoid, with a bank and timber palisade round the lip, and a ditch round the outside. Both forms could have one or more outer courts, or baileys, themselves defended by banks, ditches and palisades. Depending on the size of the motte-top, there might be merely a palisade around the edge or, more generally, a centrally placed timber tower. At Rayleigh there are three rows of post-holes around the edge of the motte suggesting a substantial palisade with a fighting-platform. Access to both forms would represent weak points receiving stronger defences – gate-towers and drawbridges, for instance. At Pleshey the bridge had a retractable section, and the outer gate at Rayleigh is suspected of having a barbican. If a motte appeared unstable, then it might be terraced, or layered with clay or gravel, or the central tower might be mounted on stilts standing on the natural surface with the mound heaped up around them or, as at Rayleigh, the motte might be strengthened with stone revetments. At Mount Bures the motte was encased in clay to stabilise the sandy soil of which it was composed. As to the question of why one should be chosen over the other, both models enjoyed advantages and disadvantages. The motte was probably stronger and more imposing, dominating the area around, but lacked comfortable accommodation in what, in all but the largest, was a restricted space. The less dominant ringwork could hold more structures in the inner-most enclosure but also needed a bigger garrison to defend its longer perimeter. Given that the incidence of castles undergoing assault was fairly rare, then it is likely that the occupants' other needs – domestic, judicial or administrative – would win out against the purely military demands. King lists twenty-five early medieval castles in Essex, recording sixteen as mottes, and six as ringworks, which compares with a national ratio of 22:6. Very often, we must assume, the military characteristics of the castle projected an image more symbolic than practical. That is not to say that castles were not seen as 'burdening the poor people of the country with forced labour' and worse, as the *Anglo-Saxon Chronicle* told it, but castles were seldom called upon to fulfil what could be assumed as their prime function, that of protecting their occupants from attack.

Clavering, the county's precocious castle, seems to have been quite low profile and particularly reliant on water defences, its moat being 75ft (23m) wide and 18ft (5.5m) deep, and connected to the river Stort. Mottes in the county range from the highest, Canfield, Ongar, Pleshey, Purleigh and Rayleigh, all around 50ft (15m) high and between 230ft and 300ft (70-90m) in diameter, to the much lower Bocking and

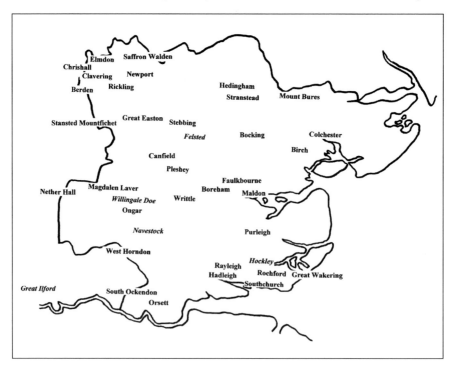

Figure 2 Map to show castles and other fortifications in Essex (1050-1500) (*see* Appendix 2 for details).

3 Stebbing: the large motte with its surrounding wet ditch.

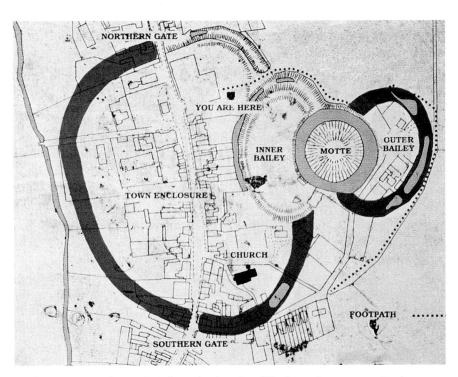

4 Chipping Ongar: the on-site information board usefully shows the motte, nestling between its two baileys, as well as the village enclosure.

Great Easton. Some, like Felsted – thought to be more likely a mill-mound – or Lavender Mount in Ilford, Plumberow Mount, probably a barrow, or Navestock, are unlikely even to have been mottes. Rayleigh, Pleshey and Ongar represent the classic motte-and-bailey layout, with the kidney-shaped bailey wrapped around the motte. The latter two also have outer enclosures taking in their dependent villages. Just as the motte-and-bailey castles vary widely in size, so do the ringworks. The Crump, at Berden, with a diameter of 123ft (38m), whilst admittedly larger than its neighbour the Rookery, thought to be an unsuccessful trial-run, is still considerably smaller than Elmdon's diameter of 165ft (61m) or that of the even larger Bishop Bonner's Palace at Orsett, which measures 200ft (62m) across. Very often the earthworks of a castle were just the beginning, as the site evolved into something more permanent.

Norman Stone Castles

One of the first, and largest, of the Norman castles built after the Conquest was Colchester. Built around the podium of the Roman temple, within a ringwork raised over the ruins of the Roman temple court, it was probably intended to meet symbolic as well as more concrete criteria. The donjon measured 151ft by 110ft (46m by 34m), a larger footprint than the Tower of London. Following the sack of Colchester by the Danes in 1071, it was begun on the king's orders either in around 1076, coinciding with the aftermath of Robert of Norfolk's rebellion of the previous year, or in 1085, when another Danish invasion was expected. Whenever it was started, work soon stalled with only the ground floor being built over the Roman vault and finished off with temporary corner turrets and battlements. It was to be twenty years, and several reigns, before work resumed under Eudo, steward to Henry I, to complete the massive four-storey keep. On Eudo's death in 1120, the castle reverted to the Crown.

Interpretation of the keep has been hampered by attempts to demolish it for its stone in the 1680s. Its great width meant that two spine walls, one of them possibly an arcade rather than a solid wall, were necessary to carry the floors, but the sheer floor-area available necessitated more partitioning than was normal, providing a greater provision of discrete spaces. Latest thinking suggests the following functions and allocation of space.

As the Roman sub-structure raised the ground floor above ground level, it was practicable in defensive terms to site the main entrance here, accessing a vestibule from which led the exceptionally wide spiral stair. The two vaulted spaces under the chapel and its projecting apse may have acted as strong-rooms, with the rest of this floor, once those above had been added, acting as storage. The first floor contained the hall and chapel, both of double height, another arcaded spine-wall increasing the size of the hall by adding an aisle. The blocked doorway next to the north-west turret could have led onto a balcony, used for appearances and ceremonial events. The remaining space would have provided private audience chambers and assembly space. The second floor had two mezzanine floors directly above those lower chambers, giving more private space, accessed via wall-passages or galleries reached by the second stair in the

5 Colchester: the imposing Norman keep, originally two storeys higher. (Photograph by Pam Osborne)

6 Hedingham: the Norman tower keep, showing the batter at the base of the wall, and one of the surviving corner turrets. (Photograph by Pam Osborne)

north-west turret. The entrance was protected by a fore-work entered between two small, solid, D-shaped towers and a route to the main door with its portcullis negotiating two dog-leg turns. There was an inner bailey with a gatehouse and wall towers, and an outer bailey between the keep and the Roman town wall. As well as the supposed Saxon chapel in the inner bailey, a hall and possible apartments have been excavated, suggesting that the majority of domestic accommodation was outside the keep. The keep is about to undergo a major redevelopment project and will be closed from Easter 2013 for a year.

The other major Norman stone castle in Essex is Hedingham, built some time after Colchester. The great 100ft (31m) high, four-storey tower of around 1140 was built by Aubrey de Vere, Earl of Oxford, within a ringwork, possibly raised in the late eleventh century. The ground floor or basement, entered only from the floor above, served as store-rooms, with the base of a fore-building butted up against its western wall, the spiral stair in the north-west turret nestling in its angle. This fore-building contained stairs leading up to the main entrance protected by a portcullis. The floor above is supported on an arch which bisects this single large space with its recesses, large enough for small chambers, in the thickness (11ft, 3.3m) of the wall. The floor above this lower hall contains a double-height hall with galleries halfway up, at normal ceiling height. This too has a Norman arch, one of the biggest in Britain, with a span of around 30ft (9m) and a similar height. Originally the fourth level was simply a screen wall, with elaborate windows, masking the pyramidal roof, but a floor represents a later inser-

tion. Two of the original four-corner turrets survive, making this one of the most striking Norman donjons in England. Since there was no living accommodation in the keep, the inner bailey contained the domestic buildings, of which a hall with vaulted under-croft, and a chapel have been excavated. Vestiges of double ditches excavated in 1976 suggest that there may have been

7 Hedingham: the entrance at the top of a staircase which was originally encased in a fore-building whose lower floor housed a dungeon. (Photograph by Pam Osborne)

8 Hedingham: the double-height hall whose roof is supported on a massive Norman arch, one of the biggest in the country. (Photograph by Pam Osborne)

a fortified village enclosure as at Pleshey and Ongar. This would have contained the church, market-place and several tenements, all to the south of the castle's outer bailey.

It was normal for castles to start out as wholly earth-and-timber structures and then subsequently to be rebuilt, often only partly, in stone. Pleshey received a stone building on its motte in the late twelfth century, probably built by William de Mandeville (who was allowed to re-fortify the castle in 1170, Henry II having ordered its demolition in 1158). It measures 67ft by 56ft (21m by 17m) and may have been a hall. Although it is said to have had corner turrets, the walls were only thin with buttresses, so it was probably not a keep. A thirteenth-century stone chapel excavated in the bailey was found to overlay the stone foundations of two, probably late twelfth century, round towers, the larger of which, 17ft (5m) in diameter, could have been defensive, or the bell-tower of an earlier chapel. Until replaced by a later brick one, the bridge of around AD 1200, connecting the bailey to the motte-top, was lodged on substantial stone platforms. At Stansted Mountfitchet it would appear that a ringwork was walled in stone to produce a shell keep in the latter part of the twelfth century. A small vestige of rubble walling survives on the southern side, suggesting that this stone shell may have had one or more projecting towers. Ironically, the site is currently managed as a reconstruction of an earth-and-timber castle.

Geoffrey de Mandeville's other castle in Essex was at Saffron Walden. Here he built a square keep entered at first-floor level through a fore-building approached by a chalk ramp and steps. The keep, of at least three storeys, measured 38ft by 40ft (11.7m by 12.3m). The earthworks of the original motte and bailey have largely

9 Saffron Walden: the sad remains of a once-impressive Norman keep whose outer shell of dressed stone has long ago been robbed.

disappeared but traces of rubble walling have been found in the bailey. De Mandeville had been permitted to build here in 1140 but Stephen seized it two years later, and Henry II ordered its destruction in 1158. Excavations have uncovered both unfinished ditches and others deliberately back-filled in the late 1100s so, given the short timespan available for building, it would suggest that the great keep might never have been completed.

A century later than all these was Hadleigh, a quite different type of fortress, one of enclosure, its strength contained in the circuit of stone curtain walls linking mural towers. It was licensed to Hubert de Burgh in 1230, but probably retrospectively, the castle being finished by then, having been built on a green-field site to replace the outdated Rayleigh. De Burgh had been justiciar to John and to Henry III but had lost his influence by 1232, and been forced to surrender the castle to the king. Built on a bluff overlooking the marshes, it was always subject to erosion, and the fabric of the castle has suffered badly over the centuries. The original castle appears to have consisted of a single bailey surrounded by a curtain with rectangular towers on the south and west sides, and a large hall and solar block on the west. All of the southern works had been destroyed in landslips by the end of the thirteenth century, necessitating the rebuilding of the hall, but these buildings themselves collapsed, leaving the castle to deteriorate well into the next century.

The Castle in War and Peace

Castles were sited by Norman barons to protect strategic locations, Colchester Castle, for example, being built against a background of continuous threats to the security of the realm. These could be internal uprisings such as that of Robert of Norfolk in 1075, and the activities of home-grown rebels such as Hereward, finally defeated in 1071, or external invasions such as a Danish attack in 1071 and its anticipated repeat in 1085.

A relevant statistic here is that considering the entire range of medieval and Tudor fortifications in the county and extending the timescale to include the events of the Civil War in the seventeenth century, we arrive at a figure of just nine assaults on the thirty-three castles of Essex. For most of the time, life was peaceful.

The Anarchy, 1135 to 1154

The reign of Stephen has gone down in history as a time when wicked barons grasped the opportunity to oppress the poor while royal power was diverted into a struggle for the throne. One of the most excoriated of these nobles was Geoffrey de Mandeville. King Stephen had acquired large estates in Essex on his marriage to Mathilda of Boulogne, the daughter of Count Eustace, and had chosen one of his loyal followers, de Mandeville, to be Earl of Essex and constable of the Tower of London. On Stephen's capture in 1141, de Mandeville, playing the pragmatic card, switched his allegiance to the Empress, Stephen's cousin and the designated heir of Henry I. She rewarded his new-found loyalty by confirming his appointment to the Tower, and making him sheriff of Essex, Middlesex and Hertfordshire. Once Stephen appeared likely to regain the ascendancy, de Mandeville switched back, no doubt expecting to be received with open arms by a grateful king, arguing that there had been little alternative to dealing with the Empress and that deep down he had always remained Stephen's man. However, a faction at Stephen's court, egged on by the citizens of London who never wanted him in the Tower from the beginning, and possibly envious of his power and accruing wealth, levelled charges of treason at him, accusations which Stephen chose to take seriously. De Mandeville was flung into his own prison, only to be released, having relinquished his castles, whilst his garrison at Pleshey was persuaded to surrender. Disappointed by this reaction to his undoubted loyalty, he took himself off to the Fens where he robbed and pillaged from an inaccessible base in Ramsey Abbey which he turned into a fortress. Stephen chose to blockade him by building a ring of castles around the fen-edge, and it was in an attack on the unfinished Burwell Castle near Newmarket in 1144 that de Mandeville took a chance hit from an arrow and died. Many of those castles which sprang up during this period were destroyed by Henry II whilst others, such as Great Easton, survived into the next century and beyond. Recent excavations at Mount Bures lead us to believe that the motte was raised during the Anarchy, was never permanently occupied, and bore no significant structure on its summit. If there ever was a bailey, it could have occupied what is now the churchyard. This small, temporary fort is thought to have functioned, in all probability, merely as a watchtower.

Barons in Revolt

Whilst Henry II managed to weather the threatened storm, in 1172, caused by his reduction of baronial power, and the ambitions of his sons, relations between king and nobility broke down entirely in John's reign. These events are reflected in the works carried out at castles. Rayleigh was put into a state of readiness against the threat of rebellion in 1172, and Colchester was strengthened by the addition of a new bailey by the king after those same troubles were past. A succession of disasters, both military and diplomatic, left John in a weak position as his barons, many of them holding John responsible for the loss of their French lands, combined to force a constitutional showdown. When the Pope declared the Magna Carta void, a number of barons invited Louis, Dauphin of France, to assume the throne of England, and a French army invaded England. During this time Colchester Castle changed hands several times. William de Lanvallei, John's constable, defected to the barons' party late in 1214, leaving his nominee in charge. John immediately despatched his own man, probably a Flemish mercenary, to take charge. Eight large catapults were installed, manned by siege engineers from London. After the signing of the Magna Carta, six months later, the castle was returned to de Lanvallei. By the end of the year a civil war was in progress and a detachment from the French expeditionary force occupied Colchester. One of John's captains, de Mauleon, laid siege to the castle, forcing the French to surrender after a siege of six weeks. Even then all was not over as a French force once more occupied the castle in 1217, only leaving after John's death secured the throne for his son as Henry III. A similar drama was played out at Hedingham, captured by John in 1216 after a lengthy siege, and then recaptured the next year by the French. Richard de Mountfitchet declared for the baronial party against John, who may have ordered the destruction of his castle of Stansted. Pleshey was besieged in 1215 by John and again in 1216 by the Dauphin. Many of these events were recorded by the Cistercian abbot Ralph of Coggeshall, who experienced the horrors of civil war at first hand when John's troops sacked his abbey, taking away treasure and livestock. Although very much a non-combatant, he had the misfortune to be located in rebel territory and thus became fair game for the marauding Royalist army, whose continuing ravaging of the barons' lands, as they retreated before the Royalist advance, Ralph reported in graphic detail in his chronicle.

Having restored order to the country, Henry III was to have his own troubles with the barons, reflected in local power struggles and shifts in allegiance. With the barons in the ascendant after the Provisions of Oxford, Henry's constable of Colchester was substituted for a baronial nominee in 1258, but following the defeat at Evesham, a royal candidate was back in residence.

In normal times castles had tiny garrisons, and if threatened with attack, troops would have to be gathered to man the defences, supplies of food laid in, and catapults firing 12in (30cm) diameter stone balls, or bows firing heavy bolts, would be mounted. Often wooden hoarding would be erected on the wall-head to allow the defenders to control the approaches to the base of the wall, discouraging mining operations. Sieges were often resolved by the defenders running out of food, but the defenders were just as vulnerable to starvation and particularly to disease. Psychology also came into it, and it is likely that after John had reduced Rochester by successfully mining one corner of the keep, word of this would have reached the defenders of Colchester and Hedingham, sapping their confidence and resolve.

The Castle in Peace

This present work is clearly intended to focus on the military aspects of the county's buildings, but it must be remembered that castles served a multiplicity of functions. The castle was a mix of town hall, law court, estate office, country house, hunting lodge, trophy home as well as fortress. People inherited, forfeited, bestowed and confiscated castles. As well as often being jealously guarded as the family heritage, they were exchanged and traded within the narrow, intimate and possibly incestuous elite of royalty and nobility which owned or controlled pretty much everything at this time. During the Anarchy, Colchester was granted to the de Veres by the Empress Matilda, and it was at the de Veres' Hedingham that the other Matilda, Stephen's queen, died.

Other Defensible Structures

Whilst castles may most overtly represent a tangible response to conflict, there were other ways in which individuals and communities sought to protect themselves.

Town Defences

At Colchester, the Roman circuit of walls survived into medieval times. Both Ongar and Pleshey included village enclosures. Pleshey represents a new town founded by William de Mandeville at the same time that he refortified his father's castle in 1178. Another de Mandeville foundation was Saffron Walden, where Battle Ditches, a thirteenth-century bank and ditch, mark an extension to the town's defences.

Strong Houses and Moated Sites

A common feature of the medieval landscape, particularly in low-lying or marshy areas, was the moated site. At its simplest this was a ditched platform possibly occupied by a house or farmstead. At its most complex this could mean a series of interlinked moated platforms surrounding a grand fortified house and its attendant domestic offices. There are many motivations for digging a ditch around one's real estate, and defence is but one of them. There are practical factors such as drainage, for producing fish for the table when the church calendar included so many non-meat days, or for fire-fighting when most of the county's houses were wooden and many were thatched. Security could be an issue when stock had to be protected from predators both human and animal, and cash crops such as orchards from the light-fingered. There are also considerations of actual or perceived status, social mobility, delusions of grandeur and keeping up with the de Mandevilles.

Essex is largely a low-lying area with plenty of flowing water, if little rainfall, an ideal landscape for moats. There are 548 – some say nearer 800 – moated sites in Essex, by far the greatest density of any English county, and even on the lower figure, representing 10 per cent of the total for England. Only Suffolk exceeds 500, and the next two highest are Cambridgeshire (270) and Lincolnshire (297). In size they range between 400 square metres and 14 acres (6ha), but the most common area is around half to 1 acre (0.2ha). Most of the county's moats appear to date from the later medieval period but there are notable exceptions. King John's Palace or Hunting Lodge at Writtle was built in 1211 with hall, kitchen and gatehouse within a rectangular moat, 50ft (15m) wide and 8ft (2.5m) deep, enclosing an area 320ft by 200ft (97.5 x 60m), or 1.4 acres (0.3ha). All the buildings were of timber with thatched roofs. Access was across a bridge and through a gatehouse. Along one side of a cobbled courtyard was a hall, joined on to the kitchen with the buttery and pantry in between. Here the timber framework of the buildings shows as post-holes and timber-slots bedded in clay. Beyond the hall were detached chambers and a chapel. The hunting lodge was built by King John and maintained for that purpose throughout the thirteenth century, being visited by Henry III and Edward I. Here there were clearly considerations of defence and security at work.

The absence of good building stone in Essex has led to a proliferation of medieval timber houses, but there are several in stone. Little Chesterford is an early thirteenth-century manor house, possibly a two-storey solar-block; the upper door was probably served by an external stair. It was built with thick walls of flint rubble. The present hall dates from a century later and may have replaced an earlier timber-framed hall, either attached or free-standing. This house would have provided its occupants with secure accommodation. More common is that exemplified by Tiptofts. Here a timber hall with a cross-wing, whose timbers have been dated to 1282-1329, stands within a moat.

10 Little Maplestead: the much-restored round church of the Knights Templar.

Monastic Houses

As the experience of Coggeshall shows, monasteries were not exempt from attack, and many were surrounded by crenelated precinct walls entered through secure gate-houses. Most of these structures belong to the later medieval period but there are nevertheless a number of earlier examples. Stretches of the twelfth-century precinct wall of St John's Abbey, Colchester, have survived along Mersea Road and elsewhere. As a military order the Templars always had an eye on security, and Cressing Temple is a fine example of a monastic moated site. Queen Matilda granted Cressing to the Templars in 1137 and they developed the site as a market, a farm and a store for the produce from their lands. The two great barns have been dated, using tree-rings, to between 1205 and 1235 (Barley Barn), and 1257 and 1280 (Wheat Barn). The Templars had a number of properties in Essex, memorialised in such names as 'Knights Templar Terrace' in Kelvedon, and at Little Maplestead is the much-restored round church which replaced an earlier church of a Templar preceptory of 1185. The Kelvedon site is thought later to have become a house of the abbots of Westminster and there may once have been a Templar connection. Monastic granges and the houses of wealthy church-men were often moated for the same reasons as secular sites. At St Aylotts, Saffron Walden, is a moat of 1248, surrounding a later house of the abbot of Walden. The scanty remains of Latton Priory, near North Weald Bassett, and dating from 1200, stand within a moat, possibly contemporary with the monastic foundation or belonging to a post-Dissolution farm.

three

The Later Medieval and Tudor Period, 1300–1600

The Development of the Stone Castle

Some stone castles of the earlier medieval period, such as Stansted Mountfitchet and Saffron Walden, had already been demolished by this time, but others survived and some of these actually thrived, enjoying an increased importance by serving new functions. Colchester remained in use as a centre of administration and as a prison throughout the later medieval period, but there is no evidence that it was kept up for any military purposes, and certainly appears never to have undergone improvements to its fortifications.

Having come into royal ownership after the fall from grace of Hubert de Burgh in 1239, mainly patching-up was carried out by Edward II at Hadleigh. As walls collapsed, fences were substituted, and the main gate, then on the eastern curtain, was underpinned and bolstered with ditches and stakes, essentially temporary repairs which were never consolidated. Little was done for the thirty years after Queen Isabella surrendered the castle to Edward III, for whom extensive works were finally carried out during the decade 1360-70. At a cost of over £2,000, work amounted to a radical rebuilding. On the eastern side, the gate was taken out and two large rounded towers, those remaining today, were built. On the north side a larger round tower, whose foundations survive, was built next to a new main gate with its barbican, and a semi-circular tower to its east. The south side, which had suffered most from the instability of the land, was completely rebuilt with a new range of domestic apartments including royal chambers and a chapel, with another semi-circular tower built to the east of it. On the west, it would appear that the earlier rectangular towers were left, along with the decaying hall block which may have been refurbished.

Pleshey was acquired by Henry V in 1420, becoming part of the Duchy of Lancaster's holdings. A new chapel was built over the existing one early in the fourteenth century. Throughout the fifteenth century the structures on the motte were maintained, with the gatehouse to the donjon being reconstructed in 1482. Chambers, kitchens, and the chapel all received attention, as did the separate lodgings of the constable. The existing brick bridge appears to date from this century but is not recorded in the accounts which survive from 1440 onwards, so may be earlier than this date, some authorities even dating it as early as 1380 to 1397. There is a tradition that a stone castle existed at Newport, its hall later serving as a gaol.

11 Hadleigh: the south-east tower built as part of Edward III's refurbishment of the castle in the late fourteenth century.

12 Hadleigh: a view of the southern towers with the stump of the high tower or keep in the centre.

Hedingham continued to serve through this period as the main seat of the Earls of Oxford, but only after 1485 was work carried out by the 13th Earl to transform this forbidding fortress into a comfortable Tudor palace. John de Vere had fought beside Henry VII at Bosworth and now became Lord Chamberlain and Lord High Admiral of England. He clearly needed a residence to match his reputation and status. A brick gatehouse with octagonal angle-turrets was built, accessed by the contemporary brick bridge over the moat. There was a great brick tower, possibly like the king's new donjons at Richmond and Greenwich, a solid mass of chambers and galleries offering prospects over his landscaped estates, and providing privacy for the lord and his family. A new range of domestic buildings included a great hall, chapel and chambers. The existing great tower remained as the centrepiece of this new ensemble providing a setting for ceremonials in the great audience chamber, and also as a reminder of the de Veres' ancient lineage. Henry visited in 1498 and, as ever, failed to prevent his paranoia getting the better of him. De Vere fell foul of Henry's livery and maintenance statutes and was fined for the size of his private retinue – for which he was probably grate-ful, seeing as others were executed for similarly ostentatious behaviour. He was still around to officiate at the coronation of Henry VIII, who restored Colchester to him, it having been granted to his forbears nearly 400 years before.

13 Hedingham: the bridge which was built across the moat of the ringwork in the late fifteenth century to provide access to the new brick gatehouse.

Social Unrest

The fourteenth century had been a time of particular insecurities. The 'Little Ice Age' affected both livestock and crops leading to scarcities, rising prices and in many cases starvation. As if this were not enough, the Black Death reduced the population by around 40 per cent, leaving flocks untended and crops un-harvested. In addition, bands of armed peasants who had lost their livelihoods, and discharged soldiers with little to return home for, roamed the countryside perpetually threatening the peace. Twice in the mid-fourteenth century Colchester was besieged and held to ransom by John Fitzwalter, an Essex gang leader. Then came the Poll Tax and the Peasants' Revolt. It is hardly surprising that those with wealth and property wished to protect themselves against at least the casual offender. In the next century the country was subjected to the struggle between the royal houses of York and Lancaster, known to us as the Wars of the Roses. Whilst most of the activity was confined to set-piece battles, there was still an atmosphere of lawlessness, and bands of medieval soldiery were not generally noted for their sympathetic approach to community relations.

The Peasants' Revolt of 1381 was the result of legislation which tried to limit the independence of peasants who, after the great reduction in the labour force caused by the Black Death, had attempted to apply market forces to ease their hardships. Coupled with the hated Poll Tax, the Statute of Labourers was enough to push not only peasants but small landowners and artisans into armed insurrection. One of the flashpoints for the revolt was Fobbing, where tax-collectors, attempting to gather in the Poll Tax, were sent on their way empty-handed. The Chief Justice was quickly despatched to sort out the problem, only to be attacked in Brentwood. By now the die was cast and the first of several armed peasant bands marched on London, linking up with the Kentish men under Wat Tyler. Another gathering of Essex men assembled at Great Baddow, sacking Cressing Temple along the way, and also then marching on London. Southchurch Hall was attacked and the manorial records seized and burnt. After the Templars had been suppressed, their property had passed in 1312 to the Hospitallers whose leader, Sir Robert Hales, as the king's Treasurer, was held responsible for the Poll Tax. Hospitaller properties became targets for the peasants' anger – hence the attack on Cressing Temple. When the peasants later ran amok in London, both the Hospitaller headquarters at Clerkenwell and the Grand Master himself felt the wrath of the mob, the priory being burnt and Hales killed, his head ending up on a spike on London Bridge.

There was also an external threat from both pirates, raiding coastal communities, and from foreign powers. Harwich had been raided several times after 1320 by the French, and in 1340 Edward III assembled his ships in the Haven prior to the expedition which culminated in the defeat of the French fleet at Sluys. In 1380 a Franco-Spanish fleet sailed into the Thames, making landfall on both sides of the Thames, seizing livestock and taking prisoners for ransom, looting and burning what could not be removed. Such hit-and-run raids were impossible to defend against, despite the fact that Hadleigh Castle was maintained partly for that very reason. The best people could hope for was to see the beacons lit and to retreat inland with any portable wealth until the danger had passed. In 1450 Harwich was burnt by the French, the culmination of over a century of raiding.

The Wars of the Roses

The de Veres of Castle Hedingham, supporters of the house of Lancaster, raised an unsuccessful rebellion against Edward IV in 1461. Old Lord Oxford, Sir Aubrey de Vere and John Montgomery of Faulkbourne were among those who were messily executed. Edward IV sought to diminish the de Veres' standing in the region still further by creating Lord Bourchier, the Archbishop of Canterbury's brother, Earl of Essex. In 1464 the young John de Vere was allowed to re-occupy Castle Hedingham and Wivenhoe as Lord Oxford, standing in as Lord Chamberlain at Queen Elizabeth's coronation in 1465. He then began to rebuild support in Essex with his brother Thomas organising a resistance to Yorkist landings on the coast. After defeat at the Battle of Barnet, John fled to France and sought French support for his attacks on Calais and the Pale. He then took to the seas, engaging in piracy from a base on St Michael's Mount in Cornwall. He was captured, imprisoned and had his estates forfeited to the Crown, whilst his wife spent two years in sanctuary, but still forced to relinquish her own property, her house at Wivenhoe. John de Vere was to survive the times, regaining his title of Earl of Oxford and the offices of Great Chamberlain and Admiral of England.

Licences to Crenelate

Over the whole medieval period there are extant records of only between 500 and 600 instances of the Crown granting a 'licence to crenelate' to the builder of a castle, fortified manor house or monastic precinct across the whole country. Given that the number of fortified sites over a 400-year period runs into thousands this would suggest that gaining such a permit could not have been mandatory. A number of possible explanations for this discrepancy have been advanced but the most plausible suggest that a subject could petition for a licence which might then be held as a public manifestation of the Crown's high regard for that subject. Conversely, if the Crown disapproved of particular subjects' architectural adventures, then they could be ordered to be destroyed on the basis that no licence had been sought or granted. This may have been the stance adopted by Henry II after the Anarchy. Seeking a licence retrospectively for work already completed may indicate the builder's apprehension knowing that he may not currently be the monarch's favourite subject. Successful petitioners in Essex range from the powerful magnates Hubert de Burgh in 1230, for Hadleigh, or Humphrey de Bohun in 1347, for a number of sites including Saffron Walden and Writtle; to the townsmen of Harwich in 1352, and again in 1405 for the fortifications of the town; to the abbot and convent of Waltham in 1366 and 1369 for the abbey's precinct and gate; to Lewis Johan, esquire, in 1414 for Old Thorndon Hall, West Horndon, a fortified house. If the hypothesis above is tenable, then none of these people need have obtained a licence to implement their building plans but for whatever reason, possibly no more than their own peace of mind, they felt it right to do so. One of the advantages for us of licences being issued is that it makes it very much easier to date properties. Conversely, without a licence, one has to rely on stylistic or circumstantial evidence.

Fortified Manor Houses

One of the earliest licences from this period was granted to Humphrey de Bohun in 1347, permitting him to crenelate his house at Saffron Walden, possibly in the bailey of the old castle, as the keep had long been slighted. Southchurch Hall represents the mid-fourteenth-century timber-framed service-block and hall of a manor house which stands on a raised mound inside a late twelfth-century moat. The foundations of a stone gatehouse, possibly furnished with a drawbridge, were found, accessed by a timber bridge which rested on stone abutments. Some of the water-logged timbers from this bridge have been excavated from the moat. Also within the moated area were detached buildings likely to have included a kitchen, a brew-house, a chapel and lodgings. An outer courtyard appears to have enclosed barns and other agricultural buildings. Old Thorndon Hall, West Horndon, licensed in 1414, consisted of a massive brick central block with turrets, set within an outer wall with bastions, extended out over the moat in around 1450. Rochford Hall was extensively rebuilt around 1430 within its existing moat, as was Faulkbourne Hall, licensed to Sir John Montgomery, a Welsh soldier of fortune and administrator who had become rich campaigning in France. In 1439 he transformed a timber manor house into a palatial residence by adding not only a brick skin, but a four-storey strong-tower, crenelated and buttressed, and adorned with a wealth of architectural detail including false mâchicoulis. The effect is exotic and designed to demonstrate the builder's familiarity with Continental style and his sophistication in using this comparatively new building material, even incorporating details, traditionally rendered in stone, but here fashioned in brick.

14 Southchurch Hall, the excavated gatehouse now providing the base for a modern bridge over the twelfth-century moat; the house in the background dates from the middle years of the fourteenth century and the gatehouse is probably slightly earlier.

The house might not have been impregnable, but its belligerent appearance should have persuaded potential assailants to seek out one of the many softer targets nearby. The masons may have been the same ones who worked on Oxburgh Hall in Norfolk – similarly designed spiral stairs, for instance, appearing at both sites. Later in the century the house was enlarged by Sir Thomas Montgomery, a highly successful public servant who managed to serve not only Edward IV, who had demanded his father's execution, but also Richard III and Henry Tudor. The majority of these fortified houses were in the countryside, but in Maldon stands the only surviving example in Essex of an urban strong-tower. The Moot Hall is a plain brick two-storey tower of 1435 with an adjoining solar now incorporated in the adjacent building. A third storey was raised later in the century, with a small annexe at the north-west angle and a higher, octagonal stair-turret. This was the fortified townhouse of the Darcy's. Fortified houses were built by the old nobility and the newly enriched soldier. Nether Hall, Roydon was built by Thomas Colte, a Yorkshire lawyer who flourished under the patronage of Edward IV. Here is a quadrangular moated house in brick with corner turrets, and a particularly dominant gatehouse, 70ft (21.5m) high, flanked by two polygonal towers with higher stair-turrets, and containing comfortable apartments, decorated with wall-paintings. One of the flanking gate-towers is ruined but it has left behind the garderobe turret and the stair-turret, formerly attached to it. Thirty years later than Faulkbourne it, too, uses cleverly moulded bricks. The reign of Henry VII is noted for his crackdown on over-mighty subjects maintaining private armies in fortresses, but a number of licences were nevertheless issued during his reign. Thomas

Butler, Earl of Ormond, was a sometime owner of Rochford Hall, but in 1491 he was granted a licence to crenelate Walkfares at Boreham, now Newall Convent. From the same period comes Rickling Hall, a moated, quadrangular brick house built over an earlier Norman earthwork castle, from 1490, with a gate-arch of around 1500. At South Ockendon Hall, there is a moat with a brick bridge and ruins of a stone gatehouse, the site for a new house of 1862.

15 Faulkbourne: licensed to Sir John Montgomery in 1426 after he had returned from the French wars; the massive brick tower is intended to impress as much as it seeks to discourage intruders.

16 Nether Hall, Roydon: the gatehouse of a fortified house built by a London lawyer, Thomas Colt, who died in 1467.

17 Rickling Hall: the gatehouse range of a house built in around 1490, occupying the bailey of a medieval earthwork castle.

Moats

Moats gained in popularity in the later medieval period. At Writtle, King John's Hunting Lodge was rebuilt early in the fourteenth century; the buildings remaining very much as earlier, but their timber footings were replaced with new ones of cob. In the fifteenth century a much more radical rebuilding took place. A new timber-framed building on brick footings replaced the old kitchen, the chapel was replaced by a cloister, on the adjacent site, a new great chamber was built on brick footings with a wine-cellar, and a new bridge and porter's lodge were built on the south side of the moat. Killigrews at Margaretting is a moat with its original brick revetment with ornamental brick turrets at two angles, all that survives of the late fifteenth-century house. At Little Braxted the detached kitchen which once served a now vanished manor house within a moat has been dated by tree-rings to 1398 to 1410.

The abbots of Walden continued to occupy their moated house at St Aylotts, a chapel being recorded in 1444, and a rebuilding of the house itself in 1500. Many moats survive simply as earthworks, mainly simple rectangles crossed by one or more causeways. Most of those which are apparently empty will have contained a dwelling of some sort, and many will now present as a later house in an ancient moat. It must also be remembered that moats might have originated as serving one purpose – defence, perhaps – but as that function diminished, might have been converted into, say, garden features.

18 Colchester: one of several semi-circular bastions added to the rebuilt Roman town wall in Priory Street.

Town Defences

Town defences are present at several locations in Essex. Colchester preserved its Roman walls right through the medieval period without much improvement; in fact, records of the theft of stone from the walls in the early 1400s exist. Later in the century the town commuted the expenses of its MP into cash for maintaining the walls, preferring security over democracy. It was at this time that eight semi-circular bastions were added to the walls, of which three survive on Priory and Vineyard Streets. Harwich received murage grants in 1338 and petitioned successfully for licences to crenelate in 1352 and 1405. These defences consisted mainly of banks with palisades and ditches, particularly on the north and west, but had a stone wall on the seafront and the south with, from the evidence of a later plan, a gateway on the south, a circular south-east angle tower with a second tower to its north. The north-east corner was occupied by the castle, which appears to have been little more than a stone, D-shaped tower at the angle of the town walls. The fact that the strongest defences were to seaward would suggest that they were intended to counter raids by French pirates, similar to those that plagued the South Coast prior to and during the Hundred Years War. At some stage, possibly before 1500, the castle tower was adapted to carry gunpowder artillery. At East Tilbury, permission was granted for a rampart and towers in 1402, and warning beacons had been in place there, and at Shoebury, from some decades earlier.

19 St Osyth's: the priory gatehouse of the late fifteenth century which became the entrance to
Lord D'Arcy's conversion of the bishop's lodging into a grand Elizabethan manor house.

Monastic Precincts

Both monastic precincts and estates were made secure against the same threats that
disturbed the laity right up until the Dissolution. Cressing, transferred in 1312 to the
Hospitallers, stayed protected by its moats until its suppression in 1540, when a house
was built on the platform. Similarly, Boblow Hall, at Helions Bumpstead, was built on
the site of a Hospitaller estate. Waltham Abbey was granted a licence to crenelate in
1369, and the existing gateway and bridge appear to correspond to that date, with the
existence of part of a turret on one side of the outer arch, suggesting the presence of
a substantial gatehouse. However, Essex does retain two of the country's most lavishly
decorated monastic gatehouses. At St Osyth's Priory, the great gatehouse of 1475 has a
tall carriage arch flanked by two pedestrian arches, with half-hexagonal turrets on one
side, and square ones on the other. It is built in stone and covered in flush-work, but set
in an earlier embattled range which contains a blocked arch of the thirteenth century,
probably the original entrance. The priory's precinct wall survives on the west, south
and east sides. Abbot Vyntoner built a grand house in 1527 within the precinct, north-
west of the church. It is of brick with three arches below and a hall above. Colchester's
St John's Abbey has just as magnificent a gatehouse of the late fifteenth century with
a tall carriage arch and a single pedestrian one, and flanking polygonal angle turrets.
Again, it is stone-built with flush-work adornment on the outer face.

Tudor Buildings

The structures here fall into two main categories. Firstly, the measures taken through successive reigns to counter the threat of foreign invasion; and secondly, the houses built by both the nobility and the new men, to proclaim their importance to the world, using an architecture which employed selected vocabulary from the language of chivalry, to produce showy, but ultimately defensible, grand houses.

Henrician Fortifications

Faced with the likelihood of an invasion by the French around 1540, Henry VIII's response was to build a chain of forts around the English coast from Hull in the north to Milford Haven in the west. Many of these forts, his 'Great Castles' such as Deal or Pendennis, were designed for artillery mounted on tiered bastions, often to the plan of the Tudor rose. On the East Coast, however, the works were much more modest. Harwich already possessed town walls; the tower of its castle may already have mounted guns, and the townsfolk had dug two earthen batteries by 1539. But there was still much more to be done to secure the town against attack, especially after Henry designated it a royal naval base in 1543, as part of his programme to expand the navy.

Instead of the two forts proposed for Beacon Hill, and Landguard Point across the estuary in Suffolk, three smaller blockhouses were built. One was on the Beacon Hill position, another on the point by the castle tower, probably utilising what was already there, and the third, Middle House, midway between the two. The two south of the town appear to have been little more than earthwork batteries reinforced with gabions, and hardly more effective than the townsfolk's earlier efforts. Within a decade they had been abandoned. The mouth of the river Colne was defended by three blockhouses built of earth and timber. One was at the extreme east end of Mersea Island. With sides of 100m and with a circular bastion at each corner, it was surrounded by a moat crossed by a drawbridge. The other two were at Brightlingsea and St Osyth, and were no more substantial. Like the Harwich blockhouses they had fallen into dereliction within a few years. On the Thames, the direct route to London, the installations were a little more durable. Plans of 1539 introduced the notion of five blockhouses, three on the south bank and two on the north, being sited in order to cross their fire. The two on the Essex bank were at The Hermitage, West Tilbury (the future site of Tilbury Fort), and a couple of miles downstream at East Tilbury, to the south of the future site of Coalhouse Fort. Each blockhouse consisted of a two-storey D-shaped tower, with an open semi-circular platform. Guns were mounted in the lower storeys in casemates, and on the open platform above. The tower stood within an irregular polygonal enclosure, surrounded by a wet ditch fed by the river, forming a platform from which guns could fire across – and downriver – through embrasures. Timber palisades were erected as revetments for the riverbank and to form an obstacle against enemy landings. Traces of these can still be detected at Coalhouse Point. The permanent establishment is listed in 1540 as comprising of two soldiers and four gunners maintaining the cannon which, seven years later, numbered nearly thirty assorted weapons ranging from an impressive demi-culverin through to fowlers, serpentines and harquebuses. In the dank conditions of the foreshore these iron weapons must have deteriorated very quickly. Although gunpowder weapons had not been standardised at this time, a demi-culverin would most likely have been capable of projecting a shot weighing 10lb (4.5kg) with an effective range of around 850 yards. Serpentines, falconets and falcons, all listed in the East Tilbury inventory, fired shot ranging from 0.5lb to 3lb (0.25-1.5 kg) over effective distances of 250-400 yards. These guns would have been expected to fire at more-or-less point-blank range at passing ships. At times of national emergency, once the beacons at the mouth of the estuary had been fired, the permanent gunners would have been reinforced by local militiamen who would have received a rudimentary training in the drills necessary to operate the guns. At the same time, Tilbury town was defended by banks and ditches, a renewal of the earlier town banks.

The Spanish Armada

By the time that a new threat of foreign invasion had appeared the defences of Harwich had collapsed and new works were needed. Once more, ambitious plans were produced, this time a reinforcement of the existing walls with four arrow-head bastions, one on the point by the castle tower, one midway down the seaward curtain, and one at each of the south-east and south-west angles. Instead, the Earl of Warwick, Lord Lieutenant of Essex, was grudgingly given £1,000 to improve what was there already, building a bulwark at the south-east angle, and a demi-bastion at the south-west corner. Guns were mounted – but after the Armada's defeat, it was all left to rot.

On the Thames, the Earl of Leicester arrived to find the older works in disrepair and set about constructing additional batteries at Purfleet and Grays, and building a new star-shaped bank and ditch round the West Tilbury blockhouse. An Italian engineer, famous for his floating mines, constructed an unsuccessful boom, strung across the river between Tilbury and Gravesend. Next, a boom fashioned from ships' masts and chains from the Royal Dockyard at Deptford was more successful. The Tilbury town defences were refurbished once again. The camp above West Tilbury contained an army of 23,000 men, poised to fight on either bank of the river as necessary. This army was assembled by mustering the county militias by the authority of an order in council of April 1588, granting the power to impress men to resist the Armada. Essex was expected to produce 6,340 men, but in fact could find only 4,000 armed men, only half of whom were trained, a figure only exceeded by London, Kent and Devonshire. Around 80,000 men answered the call and were organised into four roughly equal forces, of which that at Tilbury constituted but one. After the scare was over, the Italian engineer Genibelli was employed to provide new outworks for the West Tilbury blockhouse. These consisted of a new rampart, ditch and glacis, protecting the existing blockhouse and battery from landward attack.

Tudor Strong Houses

Throughout the sixteenth century, the grand country house underwent enormous design changes, but a number of such houses, such as Gosfield Hall, Horham Hall, Rochford Hall and Ingatestone, stuck with the traditional 'moat, gatehouse, courtyard and tower' formula. At Horham Hall, Sir John Cutte, privy councillor and treasurer of Henry VIII's household, began to rebuild an earlier house in 1502. Only one range of what was a courtyard house with a gatehouse now remains, and includes a tall hexagonal stair-tower added in 1572. Rochford, of around 1545 – and again represented by only part of the original house – had polygonal crenelated angle towers. This rebuilt house had five courtyards, within the moat, originally 200ft (62m) square, but now only the north-east corner survives as a golf club-house with an octagonal angle tower with polygonal stair-turret. Gosfield Hall, built after 1539 by Sir John Wentworth, is quadrangular with a gatehouse in the west front. Ingatestone, licensed in 1551, was built by Sir William Petre, a lawyer protégé of Thomas Cromwell who cut his teeth during the Dissolution, rising to serve as Secretary of State under three monarchs. The house consisted of three courts, only one of which remains, still entered through the original, but altered, gatehouse. Old Thorndon Hall was completely remodelled in 1570. Wickham Bishops was a moated palace of the bishops of London. New Hall at Boreham passed from the Butlers to Ann Boleyn's father and thence to Henry VIII in 1516. It was then rebuilt as a quadrangular mansion with a great gatehouse in the south range, with half-hexagonal turrets to the front, and octagonal ones to the rear.

Sir Richard Rich was a successful lawyer who, though a Catholic, served as Thomas Cromwell's assistant in dissolving the monasteries, as Chancellor of the Court of Augmentations, awarding himself Leez Priory and 100 Essex manors as his bonus.

As Solicitor General, he prosecuted Sir Thomas More, not allowing the small matter of his own perjury to get in the way. Later on in life he persecuted Protestants for Mary, and Catholics for Edward VI and Elizabeth I, clearly a man for all eventualities. Having owned Rochford Hall, he approached Leez Priory in 1536 with the idea of creating a great Tudor mansion. After demolishing the church and most of the conventual buildings, he turned the cloisters into an inner court, entered through an imposing three-storey brick gatehouse

20 Rochford Hall: the surviving north-east corner tower of a once quadrangular mansion built by Lord Rich, but previously owned by Anne Boleyn's father.

21 Ingatestone Hall: the south front of the inner court, one of three which formed the original house of 1548-60.

22 Leez Priory: the outer gate of the house built by Lord Rich out of the ruins of the priory, dissolved in 1536, much of which was itself demolished in 1753, leaving the inner gate standing in isolation.

with polygonal angle turrets, now standing in isolation. His great hall occupied the former nave, with other domestic offices ranged around the former cloister, occupying ranges with turrets at the corners. The outer courtyard was entered through a smaller gatehouse, of two storeys with higher octagonal angle turrets. Rich used a mixture of building materials, the stone from the priory providing dressings for the largely brick buildings.

The other great monastic prize eventually went, through a property exchange of 1553, to Lord D'Arcy, Henry VIII's Master of the Ordnance. He turned St Osyth Priory into a traditional late-medieval strong-house, building the Abbot's Tower, a solid four-storey block with angle-turrets two floors higher. A further octagonal tower

23 Horham Hall: the surviving range of an Elizabethan H-plan house. (Photograph by Pam Osborne)

and turrets on other ranges completed the image. Fifty years earlier was the gatehouse at Layer Marney, built by a privy councillor of Henry VII and his son. This building is so clearly for display yet employs the motifs of power and dominance. The three-storey gatehouse is flanked by four square and polygonal turrets of seven and eight levels. It would appear that the house, which was never built, would have been of the symmetrical courtyard type, and that the gatehouse was designed as servants' quarters. If Layer Marney demonstrates the extreme form, then Beckingham Hall at Tolleshunt Major is almost a pastiche of the grand Tudor house. Although the house has mostly disappeared, the gatehouse and walls surround an enclosure measuring 100ft (31m) square. The gatehouse of 1543 is little more than a symbol, with the angle turrets reduced to mere pinnacles. The defensive intent may have largely disappeared from domestic buildings by the end of the 1500s, but the wider message behind the style hung on, proclaiming the chivalric themes of power, influence and grandeur.

four

Stuart and Georgian Essex

The 200 years of this period include the internal strife of the Civil Wars, the twenty-year period of external threat posed by the wars with France, and the attacks on the East Coast carried out by Flemish pirates. Throughout the early 1600s the Flemish pirates, known as Dunkirkers, raided the coastal towns virtually paralysing East Coast trade. The numbers of ships holed up in Harwich Haven prompted some expenditure on fortifications and, in 1626, new batteries were built at the castle, and near the old Middle Blockhouse site, but within a few years these too had rotted. Mersea Blockhouse had also been patched up, being pronounced serviceable in 1631. The Tilbury defences were in a parlous state, and ironically these were the only ones needed in the forthcoming wars. Fortunately the fleet was committed to Parliament – otherwise the Thames approaches to London would have lain wide open. By the start of the wars, then, the defences were generally neglected and derelict, only the citizens of Colchester making the effort to patch up their town walls, later rather wishing that they had left them alone. The early-warning system of coastal beacons, established in the Middle Ages and revived in the Armada crisis, was still operating on the Essex coast in 1630, linked to the Kentish beacons via Stone near Dartford and Purfleet.

The Civil Wars

Essex was part of the heartlands of parliamentarian support embodied as the Eastern Association. These were the East Anglian counties which provided many of the troops for Parliament's armies, 2,000 from Essex alone by the end of 1642. Following the early, often inconclusive engagements of the war, the parliamentarian commanders realised that the then-current system of the short-term employment of amateur, largely untrained soldiers was so disruptive to campaigning that it was unlikely that a result could ever be forced. Their solution was the New Model Army, a permanent body of troops who could be properly trained, drilled and equipped, and around whom prolonged campaigns might successfully be planned and implemented. Many of the troops forming the New Model Army, such as the initial fourteen troops of cavalry, were already in being, but by the middle of 1643 conscription was being introduced to find the extra 20,000 men needed by Parliament from the eastern counties. Essex was additionally required to raise a force of 1,000 dragoons, mounted infantry, under the command of local captains. Most of these new recruits from the middling sort of folk were volunteers and one of their first tasks was to escort unwilling conscript infantry to mustering points. Impressment often led to desertion, particularly when men were encamped close to their homes, but conscription was seen as an unavoidable if unsatisfactory policy. The dragoons fought under the Earl of Manchester throughout the war, suffering losses that required consolidation into just five companies in spring 1644 – under Colonel Lilburne initially and then under Colonel Okey – but steadily gaining a reputation as one of Parliament's most reliable units. Parliament was fortunate that virtually all gunpowder production was located in the south-eastern counties, one such gunpowder works being in Colchester.

Not all Essex men fought for Parliament, however. William Maxey was one of three sons of Sir William Maxey of Bradwell-juxta-Coggeshall. At the beginning of the Civil War he was a professional soldier fighting in Leinster. He immediately went to join Sir Charles Lucas as a captain in the cavalry regiment which Lucas, himself a neighbour from Essex, had raised in Yorkshire. When Lucas was captured at Marston Moor, Maxey became Lieutenant Colonel commanding the remnants of his regiment. Almost immediately, he was captured at Malpas in Cheshire, but exchanged for a parliamentarian prisoner in December 1644. At the end of the First Civil War, he returned home, where his elder brother Greville had remained throughout the war to safeguard the family estate. In 1648, when Sir Charles Lucas was looking for support for his Royalist rebellion, William and his brother Henry flew straight to his side.

The Siege of Colchester

Having been spared the horrors of war throughout the First Civil War, Colchester was to find itself in the front line in the Second. In 1648 King Charles was imprisoned in Carisbrooke Castle on the Isle of Wight, and attempts were under way to free him and to secure London. The rebel forces in Kent, under the Earl of Norwich (Lord Goring the elder), having been defeated by Fairfax and the forces of Parliament, and also prevented from entering London, marched on Colchester hoping to raise an army for the king, arriving there on 9 June. Goring was joined by Arthur, Lord Capel, with troops from Hertfordshire, and Sir Charles Lucas with a contingent from the Essex Trained Bands, mainly from the Chelmsford area, who had defected to the Royalist cause, a total of 4-6,000 men altogether. Along with Sir George Lisle, Capel and Lucas had garrisoned the town, intending to use it as a temporary base for recruiting a Royalist army. On 13 June, however, Fairfax, who had quickly ferried his troops across the Thames at Tilbury, arrived unexpectedly outside the walls of Colchester and called on Goring to surrender.

Initially, the citizens of Colchester, who had supported Parliament and provided troops for the New Model Army, barred the gates against Goring, but they had reluctantly been forced to admit the Royalist army on the basis that it was going to be only a temporary and short-lived arrangement. Goring was therefore aware of how unwelcome a guest he was, but had a further problem. Lucas and Lisle were on parole, as they had been captured but not exchanged. To secure their release in 1646, they had recognised the authority of Parliament, and Lucas had paid a fine and given his word not to take up arms again. By initiating armed rebellion in Kent, and by holding a number of Parliamentary Commissioners hostage in Colchester, he was committing treason. Recognising that his colleagues would get short shrift for such flagrant mendacity, Goring determined to fight on.

Fairfax had already made arrangements to conduct a textbook siege, and Colonel Rainsborough, the parliamentarian army's siege expert, arrived – soon to be followed by some forty heavy cannon from the Tower of London for the bombardment. The fort at East Mersea, commanding the mouth of the Colne, was quickly captured by parliamentarian dragoons, enabling four warships to enter the river in order to prevent either escape or reinforcement. Rainsborough completed a blockade by digging lines of circumvallation around the town. A ring of five forts on the north bank – one of which, Fort Whaley, was centred on Greenstead church – and six more, joined by continuous banks and ditches on the south, completely sealed off the town from the outside world. No supplies or reinforcements could get in and no one could leave. Fort Bloyes was placed directly opposite the castle, which it could bombard at close quarters, while, in the south, as well as the forts, there were small redoubts and batteries, whose guns pounded away at the southern suburbs. All these eleven forts, along with another dozen or so batteries and redoubts, were constructed of earth with timber palisades, sharpened storm poles and gabions filled with rubble – basically fieldworks, but nonetheless effective. One of these unnamed redoubts has been located by archaeological fieldwork, as has Fort Suffolk north of Ipswich Road. Two batteries were pushed forward of the main encircling line to bombard specific weak points in the defences, one of them, Fort Ingoldsby commanding the two northern bridges.

While all this was going on, the defenders too had been busy, mounting guns on earth platforms behind the Roman and medieval walls. Snipers and artillery spotters used church-towers to overlook the besiegers, placing a small brass cannon up one (to the constant annoyance of the besiegers). A bastion was built at the north-east corner, near the castle, and St Mary's churchyard, in the opposite corner, was turned into a battery. In order to disrupt Rainsborough's stranglehold before it was too late, a large force of defenders attempted to force a passage across the east bridge on 6 July, in order to secure livestock and other food supplies. After a fierce fight, with casualties on both sides, the Royalists' ammunition ran short and they were forced back behind their defences. The Siege House nearby still bears scars from this encounter. A further such sally never got off the ground. One of the reasons for this lack of commitment was that most of the Royalist officers, particularly Lucas and Lisle, kept horses permanently saddled in the hope that they might make their escape, and their soldiers were less than enthusiastic about being abandoned to their fate. Fairfax had consistently offered fair terms of surrender but always excluded the officers from this clemency, thus driving a wedge between leaders and led. St John's Abbey, south of the walled area, had been fortified by the defenders, and this fell in hand-to-hand fighting. A siege battery was pushed forward at the south-east corner of the walls, bombarding the town and destroying St Botolph's Priory in the process. The townsfolk were now desperate to get rid of their uninvited lodgers, begging Goring to surrender, but without success.

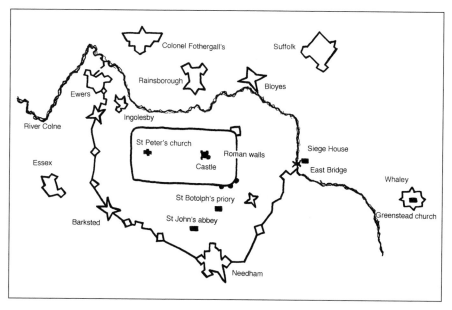

Figure 3 Colchester, sketch-map showing the siege-works and the defences from the 1648 siege during the Second Civil War. The Royalist defenders used the Roman/medieval walls as the basis of their defences, strengthened by earthen gun-platforms, a new north-west bastion, and St John's Abbey as an outwork. The besiegers surrounded the town with redoubts, linked by a continuous rampart south of the Colne, with four detached forts north of the river (and another, to the east, centred on Greenstead church). Batteries were pushed ever closer to the defences to force a breach prior to the town being stormed.

With food and other supplies by now almost exhausted, some starving women and children tried to leave the town, but Rainsborough, as was the custom with 'useless mouths', forced them to return inside the walls. Eventually, on 28 August, Goring had little choice but to agree to surrender unconditionally. Over 3,000 soldiers became prisoners, many of whom would be enslaved in the Caribbean. Lisle and Lucas, as they must have expected, were given a summary court martial and shot. Capel was imprisoned. He eventually escaped from the Tower of London, was recaptured, and beheaded at Westminster. Goring was spared. Even though the citizens had tried to keep the Royalists out, and had suffered extensive damage to their homes and livelihoods, they were fined £14,000 and forced to slight the walls they must have regretted renovating back in 1642. Local influence limited the damage to the walls, and the old Norman keep survived intact for a later generation to mutilate.

Essex men were involved in the final action of the Civil War which saw the future Charles II defeated at the Battle of Worcester on 3 September 1651. The three regiments of the Essex Trained Bands had been mobilised at Dunstable in mid-August, and marched on Worcester, which was held by the Royalists. Standing up well under enormous pressure they withstood the Royalists' last desperate throw, and then successfully stormed Fort Royal, turning the captured cannon on the Royalist defenders. The victorious Essex Militia returned home, many of them spending the rest of their lives petitioning for financial aid as their injuries prevented them from working and

24 Colchester: a bastion on the medieval walls which were re-fortified by the Royalists prior to the siege of 1648 in the Second Civil War.

25 Colchester: St Botolph's Priory was retained as a church after the Dissolution and was described as in good repair right up to the siege of 1648, when it was reduced to ruins in the fighting.

supporting their families, many of their claims being rejected by the very men who had led them into battle. Those returning to Colchester had even more suffering to face when the town was devastated by plague in 1665, some 5,000 townsfolk dying during the outbreak.

War with the Dutch

Between 1652 and 1674 a series of three wars were fought with the Dutch, each lasting around two years. The first engagements were fought off the Essex coast and 'The Gunfleet', an anchorage off the coast south of Harwich used by the English fleet as a launching pad for sea-battles. It was from here in June 1666 that the English fleet under the Duke of Albemarle (formerly General Monck) and Prince Rupert of the Rhine joined the Four Days' Fight, a very costly moral victory for the English: they lost 6,000 casualties, three times those suffered by the Dutch, but stayed in contention to bounce back within a few weeks, destroying 150 merchant ships at anchor, and driving the Dutch fleet back to harbour. One result of the wars was the realisation that England's defences were very weak. In 1667 the Dutch fleet raided up the Medway as far as Chatham, but fortunately paid very little attention to the Thames, believing that the blockhouses crossing fire at East and West Tilbury were in good order, and confining themselves to raiding Canvey Island. This gave Charles II the chance to rectify things.

Harwich Dockyard had been closed by Charles II as an economy measure, but given its strategic location, war with the Dutch prompted its re-opening. In 1664 it was repossessed from its civilian owners, and Samuel Pepys appointed Anthony Deane as Master Shipwright. Within three years Harwich had launched vessels totalling over 2,000 tons, including the sixty-six-gun third-rate HMS *Rupert*. Under the supervision of Pepys, Harwich Royal Dockyard continued to construct sizeable warships, and received a second building slip in 1681, but by the end of the century Harwich had been eclipsed by Sheerness (Kent) which, despite its reputation for sickness, received the investment which allowed it to increase its facilities under the guns of a new fort.

Rebuilding the Coast Defences

The Restoration of the Monarchy in 1660 had prompted a survey of Britain's coastal defences, carried out by Sir Bernard de Gomme, who had been the chief Royalist engineer throughout the Civil Wars. Fortification during the Civil Wars had been very much on an extemporised basis, with little attention paid to the scientific and mathematical approach which had characterised Continental developments for a century and a half. Only at Oxford had de Gomme been able to bring his experience of the Dutch methods to bear, designing a classical fortress enceinte around what was Charles I's capital. Now de Gomme was commissioned by Charles II to make good the deficiencies uncovered by this survey. Along with the naval bases at Portsmouth,

Plymouth and Sheerness, de Gomme cited the Thames approaches to London as most in need of defences, suggesting West Tilbury as the best location for a fortress. From 1665 he submitted a series of plans for Tilbury Fort, one being selected prior to the start of building works in 1670. This plan was for a pentagonal fort with five bastions, that facing the river enclosing the existing blockhouse. The entire fort was encased in earthwork moats, ramparts, ditches and bastions, throwing out the defences as far as possible into the field. The main entrance was along the river frontage and through the Water Gate, with a secondary entrance through the Landport Gate reached by lifting-bridges over the wet moats, controlled by sluices so they could be drained if in danger of freezing in winter. One quite fundamental change was made to the plan when the Water Bastion was scrapped, even though thousands of piles had already been sunk into the foreshore to carry it. The fort's main armament would now be in the gun-lines along the river frontage, firing over a low parapet and mounted on stone diamond-shaped platforms, angled to point the guns downriver. The old blockhouse was adapted for use as a magazine, and one quite revolutionary idea was proper barracks for the officers and men of the garrison.

Once a general survey was under way, the 1650 re-establishment of the naval yard in Harwich prompted questions about the town's defences. Realising that nothing had been done since the Elizabethan improvements over a century earlier, de Gomme put forward a scheme to enclose the town within an enceinte with bastions and demi-bastions, and work began in 1665. De Gomme died in 1685, and was succeeded by Martin Beckmann. Strangely enough, a stone arch from Beckman's Hull Citadel of 1681 was brought to the garden of Lea Hall, Hatfield Heath, presumably as ornament.

In 1684 the Essex Militia had been assessed at a level of three regiments of foot, the Blew, the Earl of Oxford's (de Vere was the Lord Lieutenant), and the Green, making a total of 3,070 men. Additionally, 250 cavalry were organised in four troops of horse.

26 Tilbury Fort: the north-west bastion, west curtain and moat of de Gomme's pentagonal fortress of the late 1600s.

27 Tilbury Fort: the Water Gate of 1694, its baroque detail typical of the time, provided access from the river front.

Essex in the Eighteenth Century

The accession of William of Orange saw an increase in the traffic of troops along the road between London and Harwich, and Colchester became a convenient staging post on this route, seeing many soldiers billeted in the town, disrupting the inns' civilian patrons. In 1741 the War of the Austrian Succession further increased the numbers of troops being sent to Hanover, and camps were established on Lexden Heath and at Brentwood, to hold troops in transit, awaiting embarkation from Tilbury. Although these camps remained in use until the end of the century, there were no permanent facilities and the unpopular practice of billeting continued.

The coast defences, hardly touched since de Gomme's time, were once again in a state of dereliction, with the defence of Harwich centred on Landguard Fort on the Suffolk side of the harbour. In 1745, HMS *Winchester*, an obsolete frigate, was moored in the harbour as a floating battery to avoid the expense involved in updating the defences of Harwich itself.

During the Seven Years War, it had been realised that the facilities for the storage of gunpowder at Greenwich were inadequate and that a new depot was needed. An isolated site on the north bank of the Thames at Purfleet was chosen and work started in 1763 on the construction of five magazines, a proof house, storekeeper's house, barracks, cooperage, and a headquarters in Ordnance House. Purfleet, supplied with powder from Waltham Abbey after 1787, became the main distribution point for all the naval ordnance yards on the Thames and Medway, as well as the Royal Arsenal

28 Purfleet: the clock tower and gatehouse of the Powder Magazine complex, dated 1767.

29 Tilbury Fort: the Powder Magazines, built in 1717 on either side of the Landport Gate (the square structure with the pyramid roof); they were subsequently altered in Victorian times.

30 Harwich Naval House in Kings
Quay Street was built to house the
senior officers of the naval dockyard.

at Woolwich. Each of the five
magazines held 10,000 barrels of
gunpowder which, based on the fig-
ures for government consumption
between 1789 and 1810, provided
over eighteen months' reserves. The
Purfleet magazines were built to
a design similar to, but larger than,
those that had been built at Tilbury
Fort from 1716.

The French wars brought a
boom to the shipbuilding indus-
try, revealing that the established
Royal Dockyards were unable to
cope with the increased work-
load. Harwich, which had built
ships for the Commonwealth and
Restoration navies in the previous
century, but since then had been no
more than a gun-wharf for arming and provisioning passing ships, was among the
smaller yards pressed back into service to build ships for Nelson's navy. Shipbuilding
was still very much a manual operation, and the restored dockyard treadmill crane of
1667 on the quay represents the only concession to mechanisation available to the
shipwrights. Alongside the dockyard, the Ordnance Board maintained a cooperage
and a specialist cement factory, producing high-grade cement for use in fortifications.
The cement factory, whose boundary walls survive, was disposed of in around 1830.

Napoleonic Fortifications

In 1781, the War with America once again highlighted the vulnerability of the East
Coast ports and estuaries and temporary batteries were thrown up at Maldon and
Fingringhoe, but within two years the guns had been withdrawn. Tilbury Fort,
although it had undergone improvements in its accommodation, had lost most of
the assorted guns it had mounted, many of them either obsolete or mounted on rot-
ting carriages, and now mounted just thirty 42-pounders along the river front to
counter hostile ships, and a smaller number of 9-pounders defending the ramparts
against infantry assault. The annual military manoeuvres of 1780 had taken an assault
on Tilbury Fort by 5,000 infantrymen as their focus, but unfortunately with the main
emphasis being on the logistics of the river crossing rather than the efficacy of the
fortifications. Thus, they appear to have remained untested.

31 Tilbury Fort: the officers' quarters, built as part of the original fort but radically altered in 1772.

Little more than a decade later, Britain was at war with France, and the usual hurried appraisals of the defences took place. In 1794, works designed to defend the mouths of the Crouch, the Colne and the Blackwater, with further batteries between Clacton and Walton, were proposed, a total of fifteen land batteries and five afloat. In the event only nine were built: one on the north bank of the Crouch, another near Bradwell, one in the old fort at East Mersea, one at Brightlingsea and one at St Osyth, all armed with six 24-pounders, plus four further batteries covering the beaches between Clacton and Walton, and each armed with fewer guns. It was hoped that these defences would prevent an enemy force, sailing from Dutch ports, landing on the Essex coast, only three days march from London. An Ordnance Board inventory of 1805 lists the guns mounted at the river Colne mouths as comprising mainly 24-pounders, a grand total of seventy-two in all. Volunteer artillery units were raised on Mersea Island and at St Osyth in 1805. As a further precaution, field fortifications consisting primarily of an entrenched camp north of Chelmsford, astride the London-Ipswich road, were proposed in 1795, to bar the way to London, but were not built. The traditional East Tilbury position, Coalhouse Point, was also selected for improvement. A semi-circular earthwork battery with V-shaped gorge containing barracks and stores was built, mounting four 32-pounders on traversing carriages, with an oven for heating the red-hot shot which was so deadly against wooden ships. In 1803, an entrenched camp for 15,000 men and over 200 guns was eventually built south of Chelmsford, the lines running from Widford through Galleywood Common, and with a detached fort and two small redoubts at each end, all joined up by a continuous rampart and ditch. Earthworks from this scheme still stand on Chelmsford golf course. At Danbury there was another earthwork redoubt of 1803 and a weapons store of

32 Danbury: the reconstructed armoury, put up in around 1802 to store weapons and stores for the troops manning the earthwork redoubt whose remains can still be seen nearby.

1802, long-known as the Old Armoury, and now reconstructed following the destruction of the original in a fire in 1996.

Tilbury Fort

Although a number of improvements to Tilbury Fort were suggested in 1778, the only one implemented was a six-gun battery in the covered way near the eastern end of the river front, and no more was done beyond a re-arming towards the end of the century. There were now fourteen 42-pounders in the east gun-line and fourteen 32-pounders in the west. The new six-gun battery mounted 32-pounders and there were three dozen 9-pounders mounted in the bastions. In 1809 a hospital, a kitchen and a mess-room were added on the West Curtain rampart behind the soldiers' barracks. In the late 1790s, a 'stationary' unit, the Gravesend Volunteer Artillery, had been raised to man guns on both sides of the river. To ensure that the maximum possible firepower might be brought to bear on any enemy ships attempting to force the passage, ten armed hulks, manned by men of Royal Trinity House Volunteer Artillery, were moored across the Thames from Tilbury to Gravesend in 1803. Ironically, the only potential for action that the fort anticipated at this time was confined to internal security. In 1797 elements of the Fleet were in a state of mutiny. HMS *Lancaster* had been taken over by its crew upriver towards Woolwich and there was a fear that the artillery would be subverted. The Warwickshire Militia was marched from camp at Brentwood to Romford, and the guns at Tilbury and Gravesend were warned to prevent the mutineers from Sheerness from passing upriver to reinforce the Lancaster mutineers and to put more pressure on the hitherto loyal artillerymen.

Harwich

It was recognised by the planners at Horse Guards that if Napoleon were to send his invasion barges across the North Sea from Holland, their success would depend on easterly winds, the very same winds which would disperse the Royal Naval squadrons blockading the coast. These conditions, however, would make landing on East Coast beaches so hazardous in the resultant surf that the only alternative for the invading boats would be to head for the relative calm of Harwich Haven. This, in turn, raised the problem of the vulnerability to attack of Landguard Fort, and the military addressed this by proposing additional redoubts and batteries on the Point, but nothing on the Essex side. An added problem was that the entire reserve of ammunition for the Eastern (Military) District was kept in the fort under the guard of just one 'invalid company'. In 1804 the munitions were removed to the relative security of Chelmsford, and the invalids were replaced by militiamen. The 1805 inventory lists eight 24-pounders at Harwich, mounted in the Angel Gate and Bathside Batteries, the latter recently excavated prior to the opening of the new by-pass, and now with its trace marked in the ground. Three 24-pounder guns on traversing carriages were mounted to fire *en barbette* over a low wall, crossing their fire with Martello Tower 'L' on the Shotley peninsula (Suffolk). These heavier guns were supplemented by a battery of five 12-pounders on Beacon Hill, and only a short time later by the redoubt as well.

Martello Towers

Most of these measures were fairly traditional ones, often achieved by rebuilding or re-arming existing fortifications, but there was one quite innovatory element in the anti-invasion defences. The outer shell of the defence system, begun in 1804, was the chain of towers which extended from Seaford (East Sussex) around the south-east corner of England and up the East Coast as far as Aldeburgh (Suffolk). Seventy-four towers, numbered 1-74, from east to west, ran from Folkestone in Kent to Seaford. The twenty-nine East Coast towers, built between 1809 and 1812, and running south to north from Point Clear at St Osyth's to Aldeburgh, were lettered A-Z and AA-CC. There were eleven towers in Essex between Brightlingsea and Clacton, with a gap before the line picked up again on the Shotley Peninsula, a larger redoubt being built to defend the port of Harwich. The towers were designed to carry artillery and, especially on the East Coast, to act as keeps for their attendant batteries.

Whilst the circular South Coast towers carried a single 24-pounder gun, those on the East Coast were cam-shaped and larger in size, built to mount three guns on traversing platforms, a 24-pounder and either two 5.5in howitzers or two 24-pounder carronades. The towers were 30-35ft (9.2-10.75m) high and had three levels. The basement was used as a magazine; a vaulted main floor, with four windows, was entered through a door reached by an external ladder; and a gun-floor on the roof, reached by a stair in the thickness of the wall and supported by a vault and often a central brick pillar, carried the armament. The towers were wider at the bottom, 40-50ft (12.3-15.3m) in diameter, than they were at the top, 35-40ft (10.75-12.3m). Some towers were set in a ditch and these were entered, still at first-floor level, over a drawbridge. In Essex, towers B at St Osyth, F at Clacton and J at Walton-on-the-Naze were amongst those

33 Clacton: Martello Tower 'E' (TM167137), a typical example of an East Coast tower designed to carry three 24-pounders on its roof.

34 Harwich: the redoubt, a circular fort built in 1808-10 to supplement the Martello Towers and specifically to defend the Haven. It was armed with ten 24-pounder guns firing through embrasures on the upper roof level.

given moats. The towers were built of brick, each East Coast tower consuming some 500,000, and then covered in stucco. The redoubt at Harwich, built in 1808 to 1810, and similar to the three built on the South Coast, is 200ft (62m) in diameter inside a 20ft (6m) deep dry moat crossed by a drawbridge. The lower level consisted of rooms for use by the garrison, and magazines, while the upper floor, open to the sky, mounted ten 24-pounder guns firing through embrasures. If it was planned to have caponiers in the ditch as at Eastbourne, then they were never built. Each tower was garrisoned by an officer and two dozen men. Although the tower was considered to provide sufficient accommodation, most of the troops manning towers A-K were based at Weeley Barracks, east of Colchester. Virtually all the East Coast towers were supplemented by attendant batteries, with stone gun-platforms behind earthen breastworks.

Barracks

Barracks were quite a novelty to the British soldier, who was used to either tents in fields or billets in inns or private houses. The increase in the size of the army during the Napoleonic wars – from 40,000 to 225,000 men, supplemented by at least 100,000 militiamen, a number doubling by 1804 – meant that the government was forced to provide large amounts of dedicated accommodation. In 1793 the Board of Ordnance could provide barrack space for barely 200 men at Tilbury Fort, and another 400 at Landguard Fort. Temporary camps were set up in timber huts at Writtle outside Chelmsford, for 1,700 men at Widford, and for 2,700 men at Colchester in the well-established Lexden Heath Camp, and for 2,000 cavalry at Brentwood, but these were not sufficient to meet the escalating demands. Such camps were erected very quickly, huts for 2,400 men at Chelmsford being finished in five weeks in 1796. Timber barracks for infantry and artillery were built in Colchester from 1794. These were followed by more permanent barracks for infantry and cavalry in the area of the town still called Barrack Street and Artillery Street, built in 1799 by local builders. By 1805 the Commission of Military Enquiry reported accommodation for 200 officers, 7,000 NCOs and other ranks, and 450 horses. Weeley Barracks was in use throughout the wars until 1815, and as well as accommodating the coastal defence troops who would reinforce the skeleton garrisons of the Martello Towers it served troops in transit.

The 42nd Highlanders (Black Watch) passed through on their way to Gibraltar in 1802, where they stayed for three years before joining Sir John Moore's army where they fought at Corunna. Their 2nd Battalion stayed at Weeley Barracks and Lexden Heath Camp in 1804. The 79th Highlanders (Cameron Highlanders) spent barely six months at Weeley in early 1809 between returning from their service in Spain which had culminated in the Battle of Corunna (January) and embarking on the Walcheren Expedition (July).

Colchester grew and grew as a barracks town throughout the wars, by 1803 holding 7,000 men in hutments, and a 414-bed hospital. This rapid growth was a result of the resumption of hostilities in 1803 after the Peace of Amiens had collapsed. Orders were given for further temporary camps at Abberton and Thorrington near Colchester, and at Maldon. Despite being built of timber, some barracks were referred to by the Barracks Departments as 'Established', suggesting some degree of permanence.

The earliest of these in 1794 were the Chelmsford and Colchester infantry camps, and the camp at Romford, between Waterloo Road and London Road, for six troops of cavalry in 1795. Permanence is a relative term, however, and Romford Cavalry Barracks was demolished around 1825, the timber from its buildings being sold in 1829. Warley Barracks opened in 1805, later being used by the East India Company. In addition to the demands for space of the regular army and the militia, there were also tens of thousands of volunteers to cater for. Fortunately they lived, and more importantly ate, at home, but they still needed places to drill and to store arms and ammunition. Colchester Castle crypt was used as an armoury for the Colchester Volunteers, a force of 600 infantry and 200 cavalry, and retains a steel-lined door with three Chubb locks. Chelmsford had an Ordnance Store in 1815, storing weapons and ammunition for issue to the volunteers. Virtually all these establishments, whether regarded as permanent or temporary, were demolished soon after 1816, hitting the local economy hard.

Signals

The Admiralty was behind a number of schemes to cover the country, or at least those parts of the country that connected naval ports, by semaphore relay stations, and much of the South Coast system was complete by 1795. In 1803 a review of the beacons suggested a double line through the flat lands of Essex, primarily intended to warn of invasion and to hasten mobilisation of volunteer troops, but this was considered unnecessary and too expensive, it being proposed that large red flags should be flown from church towers instead. Also in 1803, it was reported that the military telegraph line had been extended from London to Norwich, and thence to Great Yarmouth (Norfolk), via Colchester and Diss. This may have used the portable system which, depending of course on the terrain, needed stations at intervals of roughly 5 miles (8km). This was well in advance of the Admiralty's own line of 1808, which was to leave London via Hampstead travelling on through St Albans, Dunstable and Royston. In 1812 the Admiralty also initiated a coastal link between Orford (Suffolk) and Great Yarmouth. It is evident that Essex already had several coastal signal stations using the old ball and flag codes, mainly useful for ship recognition, and these may have been based on the Martello Towers as the Board of Ordnance had given permission for signal masts to be erected so long as they did not interfere with the operation of the towers and batteries. Others may have been on church towers. The Admiralty now proposed that these existing stations be converted to the new Shutter Telegraph system. At Foulness, there remains a 'Signal House', formerly a semaphore station, thought to have been built around 1800, and this may represent a link in the chain joining up the north Kent semaphores with the East Coast ones.

The Army: Regulars, Militia, Volunteers and Yeomanry

The two regular regiments who would later constitute the Essex Regiment were the 44th (East Essex) foot and the 56th (West Essex) foot, formed respectively in 1741 and 1755. The 1st Battalion of the 44th served in Spain and North America, and the 2nd

Battalion served in the Peninsular campaign, covering itself in glory by capturing a French eagle at the Battle of Salamanca in 1812, and going on to fight at Waterloo. The 1st Battalion of the 56th served in the Caribbean and in Holland, and then with its two other battalions in India, being reinforced by a draft of militiamen, sent out in 1810 to form the garrison of Goa. At the end of the wars the 1st Battalion remained in Mauritius on garrison duties, the other two battalions being disbanded.

The militia had its origins in the Anglo-Saxon Fyrd, or citizen army, and had waxed and waned over the intervening centuries. The Act of Parliament championed by Pitt (1757) set about a reorganisation intended to produce a 'well-ordered and well-disciplined militia … necessary to the safety, peace, and prosperity of this kingdom'. Essex now had to produce 960 trained militiamen, less than a third of the total in 1684, but more efficient as soldiers. They were organised into two units, the East and West Essex Regiments of Militia. Both served during the French wars, the West Essex Regiment spending time on internal security duties policing Luddite disturbances in Nottingham in 1812, and then volunteering for three years service in Ireland until 1816.

Volunteer units – or military associations, as they were often termed – had emerged in the early 1790s as a response to the threat posed by the spread of revolutionary ideas from France. They were aimed primarily at preserving the *status quo,* particularly in urban industrial and mercantile quarters, and members were required to be householders. The Yeomanry were volunteer cavalry, usually recruited from amongst tenant farmers and small landowners, and officered by members of the squirearchy. Independent troops usually numbered under 100 men and were responsible to the Home Office, and could only be mobilised and deployed by the Lord Lieutenant. The invasion scare of 1803 to some extent democratised the volunteer movement cutting across the social divide, but it must be remembered that volunteers were exempt from the militia ballot. There were companies of Loyal Volunteers at Chelmsford, Colchester and Tendring, amongst others, that at Chelmsford being commanded by a prominent lawyer, a member of the professional classes rather than the landowners from amongst whom officers had traditionally been recruited. This was one of the aspects that Horse Guards disliked about the volunteers, who some regarded as an ill-disciplined rabble who would strut around like peacocks and then flee at the first shot. Colonel Crauford, the MP for Chelmsford, who commanded a body of local volunteers, considered military training a waste of time, in the absence of muskets equipping his men with pikes, and believed that an untrained, but well-led 'smock-frocked peasant horde' could be perfectly effective in a melee. The matter of volunteers armed only with pikes would, of course, return to haunt the military establishment in a future war. One of the consequences of this ambivalence regarding the value of the volunteers was that the militia, a constitutional body under proper military discipline, was built up at their expense, and the volunteers finished the wars 50 per cent below their notional strength.

There were six independent troops of Yeomanry Cavalry in Essex, including troops formed in Colchester in 1797, and Havering in 1802, their members responsible for purchasing their own uniforms and supplying their own mounts. These units only combined as the 1st Essex Yeomanry Cavalry Regiment in 1813, and unlike many such units which were disbanded in 1815, continued for another thirteen years. The 1804 Volunteer Return divided Essex between the Eastern and Metropolitan Districts. Essex volunteer cavalry units thus contributed to the undifferentiated total of 2,961 cavalrymen in the Eastern District, and met the Metropolitan's Essex quota of 138. The number of infantry volunteers was much higher, the Eastern District's 18,600 men including a sizeable Essex contingent, and the London total, a further 1,063 from Essex. Across the country there was a network of thirteen Assembly Stations, of which all but three were in the southern half of the country, where volunteers were instructed to gather as part of a general mobilisation. One of these was Brentwood, where 739 cavalry and 9,999 infantry from Hertfordshire and parts of Essex and Middlesex would gather.

Comprising a final category of volunteers were the Sea Fencibles. These were units of professional seafaring men, fishermen and the like, under Royal Navy officers. They were formed in seaside towns as part of the anti-invasion preparations, providing intelligence and local knowledge, and carrying out inshore patrols. They trained a few hours each week and were paid a small daily rate for operations which took them away from their normal occupation for any length of time. There were units of Essex Sea Fencibles at Brightlingsea, Maldon, Wivenhoe and a dozen other places.

five

The Victorian Age, 1815–1914

The nineteenth century saw accelerating progress toward the industrialisation of warfare. New technology, particularly in naval design, but also in artillery, gunnery control, materials and munitions, added to advances in military organisation and discipline, and particularly in the methods of production; all contributed to a realisation that war had become a more effective and efficient item in the politician's toolbox.

Coast Defences

The early part of this period is characterised by three bouts of invasion fears, mainly centred on France. The first lasted through much of the 1840s when inflated expectations of the offensive power of steamship technology allied to trivial disagreements were whipped up by the press to convince people that an attack was imminent. The Crimean War of 1854 to 1856 presented more opportunities for general insecurity (even though the French were allies and the Russians would have had great difficulty in invading Britain). By the end of the decade the threat had returned when France built iron-clads. These, for a while, were superior to anything the Royal Navy, Britain's traditional blue-water defence, could muster. Each of these three scares was reflected in programmes of fortification, and an official enquiry was set up in 1859 to survey, evaluate and improve the nation's defences. This was the Royal Commission to Consider the Defences of the United Kingdom, whose recommendations to build costly fixed fortifications would introduce the phrase 'Palmerston's Follies' into the national vocabulary. Then everything changed. After the comprehensive defeat of the French at the hands of Prussia in 1871, a perception grew that Germany would attempt to challenge the might of the British Empire, and could even become a potential protagonist in a European war. The focus of the country's defences suddenly switched from the English Channel to the North Sea, although it was only with the signing of the Entente Cordiale in 1904 that in some people's eyes France lost her status as the immutable enemy. Just to be on the safe side, the British Army's 1907 standard textbook on fortification has an appendix listing the armour and armament of all the capital ships belonging to the navies of France, Germany, Japan and the United States.

The Thames Defences

In 1847 the battery at Coalhouse Point was rebuilt as a more heavily gunned version of its predecessor, carrying seventeen 32-pounders. However, by the time it was finished it had already become due for a re-appraisal. The Commissioners, reporting in 1860, considered Tilbury too far upstream to remain the primary line of defence, proposing that Coalhouse should become the forward line with new powerful works on Coalhouse Point and on the Kent bank at Cliffe and Shornemead. These three forts were to be multi-level casemated works mounting heavy guns, with defensible barracks to the rear. Begun in 1861, Coalhouse Fort suffered numerous delays caused both by construction problems and the continual changes necessitated by improvements in artillery. The fort was finally finished in 1874, mounting the most effective guns available. Eleven 11in and four 38-ton 12.5in RMLs were mounted in the semi-circle of granite casemates with their iron-shielded embrasures, whilst a further three 9in 12-ton RMLs were emplaced in a battery a little way downriver.

Whilst this new building was going on, Tilbury Fort and New Tavern Fort at Gravesend were not only the sole guardians of the river, but also undergoing their own improvements. Although Tilbury had been equipped with a mixture of 68-pounders, 32-pounders and 10in shell-guns in the gun-lines of the river frontage, none of these had the armour-piercing capability so vital for taking on armoured ships. As well as replacing the guns, it was also necessary to render the fort's profile even lower, and to thicken the riverside defences. The bastions and curtain nearest to the Thames were buried under mounds of earth containing new magazines. The south-east corner now held eight emplacements for 9in RMLs, crossing fire with New Tavern Fort on the opposite bank, and five more emplacements, one mounting a 12in RML, in the north

35 Coalhouse Fort: iron-shuttered casemates of the Royal Commission fort, built of granite blocks in the 1860s; the searchlight position on the roof, one of a pair, was added later.

36 Coalhouse Fort: the two-storey caponier which flanks the main gate.

and west bastions, were similarly protected. The Commission's two suggested lines of defence were thus completed, presenting an impressive face to an enemy. The Royal Commission appointed ten years later to 'Enquire into the Construction, Condition and Cost of the Fortifications Erected' expressed satisfaction with all aspects of the operation. An advanced outlier of the defences fortuitously lay at Shoeburyness where the artillery ranges had relocated from Woolwich in 1859. Here there were guns firing out into the Thames Estuary for practice and proving purposes, but which could be equally useful as additional coast defence batteries if needed. The Royal Commission forts, despite their vast cost, were only to remain effective for around fifteen years, for by 1886 all these defences were considered obsolete, leaving London once more vulnerable to attack. A number of solutions, some traditional, others innovatory, were explored. Booms dated back to classical times but could be effective if supported by quick-firing guns and searchlights. The Brennan Torpedo was wire-guided and launched from rails on the riverbank. Minefields were electrically operated from elevated observation posts.

But the real solution lay in finding the right guns for the job. A reinvention of the earlier, disappearing Moncrieff mounting allowed guns to remain hidden except for a few seconds whilst they were firing. New batteries were located on low crests overlooking the river, and surrounded by low-profile earthworks and fences which could not be climbed, a design perfected at Chatham and known as the Twydall Profile. Such a new battery at East Tilbury, completed a short distance downstream from Coalhouse Fort in 1892, was armed with two 10in guns and four 6in guns, all on hydro-pneumatic disappearing carriages. The gunners' continuing debate over the outcome of duels between armoured ships and coast batteries now entered a new phase. Not only was the coast gun stable while the ship rolled, it was now also invisible. At the same time, to counter possible attack by fast torpedo-boats, a new battery of four 6-pounder QF guns was built a little way upstream from Coalhouse Fort.

Within a very short time all those massive RML guns had become redundant, and by 1900, all but a few had been replaced. Tilbury Fort, from 1894 to 1904 the HQ Thames District Establishment, now mounted two 6in BL guns and four 12-pounder QF guns. Coalhouse Fort underwent a radical reconstruction, alternate casemates being filled with concrete to take the weight of four new 6in BL guns mounted on the roof, along with four 12-pounder QF guns and two Defence Electric Lights, or searchlights. The increasing range of guns, whether mounted on land or sea, meant that heavy guns at the rivermouth could command the whole estuary, leaving the guns in the river to mop up anything which had penetrated these outer defences. Coalhouse Fort also had one of the new Position Finding Cells which was part of a new system of range-finding, enabling fire to be controlled accurately, still further tipping the balance toward the land-based battery. Four of the old 12.5in RMLs were retained at Coalhouse as what Peter Kent called 'giant blunderbusses' capable of firing grape-shot at short range to counter torpedo-boat incursions.

On the eve of the First World War, then, the Thames defences were formidable. Heavy BL guns at the mouth of the river and at East Tilbury and Shoeburyness could engage enemy ships at long range, holding them at bay for the maximum of forty-eight hours needed for the Dreadnoughts of the Royal Navy to arrive. Medium guns at Coalhouse and Tilbury Fort, along with others on the Kent bank, could stop anything heavy which had got past the outer defences. Light QF guns protecting booms and minefields could prevent smaller craft from getting upriver to the arsenals of Woolwich and Purfleet, and ultimately to the docks and the heart of Empire.

37 Coalhouse Fort: two of the four emplacements for 12-pounder QF guns in the battery which lies just upriver from the fort. In the background can be seen the Second World War radar tower.

38 Tilbury Fort: an emplacement on the river front with a 6in gun mounted.

The Harwich Defences

Whilst Landguard Fort on the Suffolk side of the Haven remained the major focus of the defences, attention was periodically paid to Harwich itself. Recommendations were made in 1853 to re-arm the redoubt but nothing was done, and Harwich was not even included in the Royal Commission's report of 1860. Eventually, in 1862, ten new guns were installed in the redoubt, and three more in Angel Gate Battery. In 1870, some of these obsolescent guns in the redoubt were replaced by three 9in RMLs. By 1887, however, Harwich was recognised as a possible invasion target, a dangerous jumping-off point for an expedition aimed at attacking London, and in need of more substantial defences. The Beacon Hill position was selected as the site for a brand-new battery, incorporating the most up-to-date guns, enclosed within Twydall Profile defences. Opened in 1892, there was a 10in and a 6in BL gun, both on hydro-pneumatic mountings, and two 4.7in QF guns, all supported by DELs and PF cells, and manned by a regular brigade of the Royal Garrison Artillery, supplemented by the volunteer artillery unit based in Dovercourt. The redoubt received three 12-pounder QF guns in 1890, and two more new batteries were added to the Landguard position in 1901. Over the years another 6in gun and four 5in guns in a practice battery had been added to an enlarged defensive perimeter on Beacon Hill, but in 1905 the Owen Committee decided that Harwich was of little significance and should be reduced to the status of a C Class port, losing many of its guns, and being left with only a pair of 6in Mark VII guns and the quick firers. The irony was that the Royal Navy regarded Harwich with its dockyard facilities as a strategically important naval base.

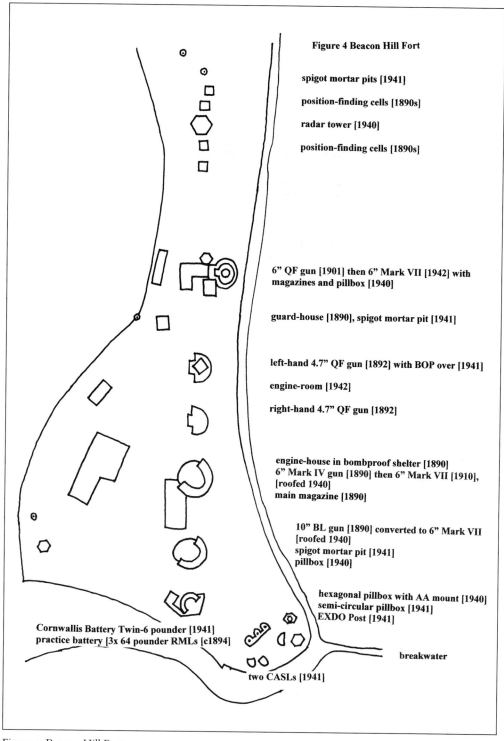

Figure 4 Beacon Hill Fort

spigot mortar pits [1941]

position-finding cells [1890s]

radar tower [1940]

position-finding cells [1890s]

6" QF gun [1901] then 6" Mark VII [1942] with magazines and pillbox [1940]

guard-house [1890], spigot mortar pit [1941]

left-hand 4.7" QF gun [1892] with BOP over [1941]

engine-room [1942]

right-hand 4.7" QF gun [1892]

engine-house in bombproof shelter [1890]
6" Mark IV gun [1890] then 6" Mark VII [1910], [roofed 1940]
main magazine [1890]

10" BL gun [1890] converted to 6" Mark VII [roofed 1940]
spigot mortar pit [1941]
pillbox [1940]

hexagonal pillbox with AA mount [1940]
semi-circular pillbox [1941]
EXDO Post [1941]

Cornwallis Battery Twin-6 pounder [1941]
practice battery [3x 64 pounder RMLs [c1894]

breakwater

two CASLs [1941]

Figure 4 Beacon Hill Fort.

39 Beacon Hill Fort, Harwich: right-hand emplacement for 4.7in QF gun of 1892 in the foreground and, beyond it, an emplacement for a 6in gun of 1890, upgraded in 1910, and given overhead protection in 1940. In the background the director tower of Cornwallis Battery may be seen beyond another 6in position hidden by bushes. The photograph was taken from the battery observation post built on the left-hand 4.7in QF gun emplacement in 1941.

Anti-Invasion Defences

Apart from the Thames and Harwich, there was no permanent provision for coast defences on the Essex coast. A review in 1870 suggested that extra Martello Towers should be built on Holliwell Point, at Clacton, Holland, and Frinton, but these were never built. Many of the original Martelloes had been disarmed by 1818, whilst Towers 'G', 'H' and 'I' had been sold and immediately demolished in 1819; Tower 'J', suffering from coastal erosion, met a similar fate in 1835.

In the 1880s the threat of enemy armies advancing on London across the Essex or Surrey countrysides again raised fears, as it had three generations previously. The planners realised that it would have been impossible in terms both of cost and of negative public opinion to build permanent fortifications ringing London. One unrealised proposal was to build entrenched camps around the capital, to be occupied by field armies as and when necessary. The two sites in Essex were to be Brentwood and Epping. The final answer lay in an arc of secure storehouses, to be connected in wartime by trench systems. These stores, or redoubts, known as London Mobilisation Centres, would hold arms and ammunition to be issued to newly mobilised units, as well as the picks and shovels to be used in digging the trench-lines. The line ran along the crest of the North Downs and then up the Darenth Valley to the Thames. North of the river, two more redoubts at Epping, only eventually an advanced depot, and North Weald, would anchor the line as it ran down to Holehaven Creek, backed up by the ordnance stores at Tilbury Fort and Warley Barracks, both housing cartridge-filling

40 Tilbury Fort: the gun store of 1868.

stations by 1892. North Weald Redoubt, planned as one of only four artillery redoubts, consists of a roughly semi-circular rampart over casemates holding several thousand shells for 20-pounder field pieces, and 300 barrels of cartridges. Although described at the time as redoubts, or even forts, these centres were intended as defensible rather than defensive, possibly a very narrow distinction but one meant to avoid the complacency that fixed fortifications were thought, at the time, to engender. On the rampart were six notional gun-platforms which could have been improved prior to use as necessary. The shells were for a gun which was obsolete when the redoubt was completed in 1888, let alone when the *London Defence Position Handbook* was issued to the Volunteer Force in 1903. The regular Royal Artillery were resistant to the notion of volunteer field artillery, but those that struggled to serve were mainly equipped with the 15-pounder Ehrhardt gun, so why North Weald's shell-stores were stuffed with shells for 20-pounder guns is a mystery, as very few could still have been in service by the end of the century. The *Handbook* was directed at the volunteer element of the army, the source of the 2,000 men needed for each of the 70 miles of lines, with their thirteen redoubts.

The Victorian Army

The reign of Victoria witnessed major reforms to the regular British Army, a re-birth of the militia and the establishment of a Volunteer Force, all overseen by burgeoning bureaucracies at Horse Guards and the War Department.

The Regular Army

As ever after a war, the army was drastically reduced in numbers by 1818, with whole sectors, such as the Royal Wagon Train, being disbanded, and valuable expertise, accumulated over twenty years of fighting, lost. Parliament, with its usual distaste for a standing army of any size, continued to cut budgets, allowing the militia to wither and die. Some of the volunteers, such as the West Essex Yeomanry Cavalry, remained, periodically being called on to police agrarian or civil disorder, and to protect government property such as the Purfleet Magazine against perceived threats from politically inspired mob action, particularly at the time of Chartist activism. It took the chaos of the Crimean War in 1854 to highlight the army's weaknesses, both operational and organisational. The experience of the Indian Mutiny of 1857 to 1859 simply repeated these failings, forcing them to be addressed.

Major reforms were therefore implemented relating to supplies, welfare, uniform, recruitment and living conditions, but one of the most important, effected by Cardwell, Gladstone's Secretary of State for War, was the localisation programme. Hitherto regiments may have had an area designation such as the 56th Foot's notional attachment to West Essex, or the 44th's to East Essex, but this generally held little meaning as the regiment and its depot could be posted anywhere at home or abroad, sometimes for ten years at a time. Cardwell's intention was to tie regiments to specific localities, thus encouraging a consistent supply of recruits, and fostering a sense of pride in the community's relationship with the regiment. A proper depot would also remove the problem of billeting, going some way to severing soldiers' institutional links to public houses, and thereby promoting a public perception of soldiering as a reputable occupation. In 1872 the country was divided up into sixty-six military districts, each

41 Warley Barracks: the Essex Regimental Depot officers' mess of 1878, now Blenheim House, part of the present Territorial Army Centre.

forming a depot for one or more Line Regiments. The 44th Military District was based on Warley, becoming the depot for the 44th and 56th Foot who, in 1881, would combine as the Essex Regiment, together with their affiliated militia and volunteer battalions. The regulars became respectively the 1st and 2nd Battalions, the Essex Rifles Militia and West Essex Militia became respectively the 3rd and 4th (Reserve) Battalions and the volunteers became the 1st-4th Volunteer Battalions, and from 1908, after the former militia element had been reduced to a single battalion, the 4th-7th (TF) Battalions. Whilst the two regular battalions would alternate between home and overseas postings, the reserve battalions would provide depot facilities, training recruits and supplying drafts to the battalion serving overseas. The volunteers were scattered around the county in company-sized units, only meeting up in strength for annual camps. On the eve of the First World War, the 1st Battalion was in Mauritius, the 2nd Battalion on garrison duties at Chatham and the 3rd Battalion in the depot at Warley.

The Yeomanry Cavalry

The West Essex Corps of Yeomanry Cavalry reformed in 1830, serving from 1838 to 1843 without pay, rather than being stood down. In 1877 it was disbanded but a cadre remained as the Essex Troop of the Suffolk Hussars. Companies of yeomanry cavalry were raised during the South African wars, and this provided the opportunity for lapsed regiments to reform, the Essex Yeomanry being re-raised in 1901. The HQ was at 17 Sir Isaac's Walk in Colchester with the four squadrons centred on Colchester, Braintree, Waltham Abbey and Southend-on-Sea. Each squadron had three or four drill stations where troops or smaller units could meet for evening drill without having to travel great distances after a day's work. Some of these drill stations could have been inns which would have had stables and tack-rooms, whilst others would have been the farms or country houses from which many of the personnel were recruited.

The Militia

With the effective rebirth of the militia encapsulated in War Office Circular No. 954 of December 1845, the quota for Essex was set at 1,244 men. The precedence of the militia regiments had been decided at a conference called by William IV in 1833, and they were consequently organised into the 14th East Essex Regiment of Militia, later the Essex Rifles Militia, with their HQ in the old County Gaol on Ipswich Road, Colchester, and the 19th West Essex Regiment of Militia with their HQ in Market Street, Chelmsford. There had been an attempt to renew the unpopular militia ballot, but it was defeated in Parliament and new legislation in 1852 set up the framework for voluntary enlistment with a national ceiling of 80,000 men. A number of specialist militia units were also raised, two of which would form part of the Harwich defences. The Harwich Division of the Royal Engineers Militia Submarine Miners had their base in the Ravelin of Landguard Fort and was responsible for controlling and main-taining the minefield which protected the harbour entrance. The Suffolk Artillery Militia was formed in 1853 with headquarters in a purpose-built defensible barracks in Great Gipping Street, Ipswich, and was tasked with manning Landguard Fort and the other batteries on the Point and at Shotley. At the time of the Crimean War the majority of militia regiments had volunteered for overseas service in order to relieve regular units from garrison duties in Ireland and the Mediterranean, both Essex units serving abroad. In 1881 the two Essex infantry militia regiments were combined into the 3rd (Reserve) Battalion of the Essex Regiment.

The Rifle Volunteers, 1859-1908

By 1859 a number of factors combined giving impetus to a public demand for a National Volunteer Force which might act as local support for the regulars and the militia in the event of a foreign invasion. The day-to-day demands of Empire and crisis events such as the Crimean War and the Indian Mutiny had shown the politicians' notion of the appropriate strength of the regular army to be a gross under-estimate. At one stage only fourteen battalions remained in Britain. There were also concerns that Britain's enemies had vastly more men under arms – and this at a time when a French invasion once more seemed possible. Furthermore, it was mooted, those troops that Britain did maintain in arms were not so well trained as they might be, as there had been suggestions after the recent conflicts that military skills as elementary as shooting had left much to be desired.

The foundation of the National Rifle Association went some way towards addressing these concerns but what Britons really wanted was a uniformed, locally organised military force. Rifle Volunteer Corps were formed by local initiative from 1859 onwards, the first of the Essex corps apparently being raised in Ilford in August 1859, closely followed by units in Brentwood, Chelmsford, Colchester and Witham, all by the year's end. In total there were over twenty-five corps raised in the county, organised in three Administrative Battalions initially based on Ilford, Colchester and Plaistow. Almost constant re-numberings and reallocations took place as some corps failed to thrive, and others grew and sub-divided. In the early days corps were entirely dependent on their own resources as the War Department regarded them as an undisciplined rabble. Units needed a sponsor who would provide money for uniforms, equipment, secretarial facilities and storage space. Money was always an issue and the 13th (Stour Valley) Corps, raised at Dedham in 1860, disbanded for lack of financial resources within a few years. Subscriptions to the 4th (Chelmsford) Corps and the 23rd (Maldon) Corps were payable by instalment. One solution was sponsorship by an employer and the 3rd (Brentwood) Corps was recruited from within the agricultural implement works which employed them, and the 22nd Essex Corps were all employees at the Royal Gunpowder Works at Waltham Abbey, later joining a Hertfordshire battalion. The 5th (Plaistow) Corps was recruited from the clerical staff of the Plaistow and Victoria Docks under the command of the manager. The 1st Essex Volunteer Artillery was originally recruited from a single workplace, a foundry, and the 1st Essex RE Volunteers may have formed in similar circumstances at Heybridge but had been disbanded by 1871.

Before long the War Office decided that they needed to exercise some form of control over the dozens of private armies springing up all over Britain, so a form of subsidy based on the numbers of trained personnel, or effectives, was introduced, but this was contingent on corps providing an orderly room for administrative functions, an armoury for storing arms and ammunition securely, spaces both indoors and out for drill, and access to ranges for rifle-shooting. Ultimately, optional but desirable, was accommodation for a permanent staff instructor or drill sergeant, usually a retired senior NCO who supervised training and acted as quarter-master. Although some of the initial enthusiasm, particularly of busy professionals, might have worn off, the great majority of corps continued, often carried along by civic or institutional pride. There was also some participation by the county's more influential citizens, Colonel Holmes, the Deputy Lord Lieutenant of Essex, raising a battery of the volunteer artillery in 1882. In 1881 the county's Rifle Volunteer Corps were reorganised into the four Volunteer Battalions of the Essex Regiment. The Volunteer Force attempted to mirror the developments in the regular army and in 1885 a Captain London of the 1st Volunteer Battalion convened a conference to explore the possibilities of raising dedicated volunteer transport units.

The Territorial Force, 1908

One of the problems which never left the volunteers was the absence of a definitive mission statement. The regulars and the Whitehall bureaucracy were sceptical of the volunteers' potential if it came down to actual fighting, so they were reluctant to allocate specific roles and responsibilities. It was generally felt that the incorporation of the Volunteer Battalions into the military family had benefited both parties, but also felt that this association should now go much further. The result of this thinking was the establishment in 1908 of the Territorial Force. The majority of volunteer units were absorbed into the TF but organised on a different basis. The new force was charged with home defence, organised at county level by Territorial Associations and organised into fourteen self-contained divisions. Most of the Essex units joined the East Anglian Division, with HQ at Warley Barracks, composed of a mounted brigade, three infantry brigades, and supporting field artillery with ammunition trains, RE companies which included signallers, supply and transport companies, and field ambulances. The Essex Yeomanry were brigaded with Suffolk and Norfolk as the Eastern Mounted Brigade with its HQ at 8 Head Street, Colchester. Its accompanying Royal Horse Artillery unit was provided by Essex with its HQ at Market Road, Chelmsford and its Ammunition Column split between Chelmsford and Colchester. The Yeomanry Stores in Waltham Abbey were in a chapelesque building next to the Lloyds Bank in Church Street. The brigade was also now allocated its own supply and transport units and a field ambulance. Four of the five Essex infantry battalions, now the 4th-7th Battalions of the Essex Regiment (TF) with HQs at Brentwood, Chelmsford, West Ham and Walthamstow, formed the Essex Infantry Brigade. By 1914, the unattached 8th (Cyclist) Battalion had been raised, functioning as reconnaissance and communications troops. Essex supplied one of the East Anglian Division's four field artillery brigades, based on Stratford, Grays and Romford.

Separate from the divisional organisation but still part of the TF were units committed to coast defence. The 1st Essex Volunteer Artillery was reformed in 1908 as the Essex and Suffolk Royal Garrison Artillery with five companies in Harwich and Felixstowe, one at Southend, and two at Stratford. These units manned the Coast

Artillery guns alongside the regular gunners and, in some cases, the Militia Artillery. A unit of Fortress Royal Engineers, No. 1 Electric Lights Company based in Association Buildings, Market Road, Chelmsford, manned the searchlights of the Harwich defences, and an Essex RE Signal Company had a parent unit based in Bedford.

Cadet Units

For some time there had existed cadet units based on schools, the Boys' Brigade, the Church Lads' Brigade and volunteer battalions of the Essex Regiment. Felsted had been one of the very first School Volunteer Corps in 1860, and others, such as Chigwell and Forest, also maintained companies of the Junior (Officer) Training Corps. Many other schools including Colchester RGS and King Edward VI's Chelmsford, had cadet units affiliated to particular battalions of the Essex Regiment. The Warley depot had its own cadets alongside a company of the Boys' Brigade.

Training and Weapons Development

As artillery got more powerful it became dangerous to continue to use Plumstead Marshes for testing new weapons produced at Woolwich Arsenal, or for providing firing practice for the cadets at the nearby Royal Military Academy. From the 1840s, the desolate wastes of the Thames Estuary were therefore developed as artillery ranges.

Shoeburyness and Foulness

Working in conjunction with the Ordnance School and the Repository (the school of gun-mounting) at Woolwich, Shoeburyness was established between 1856 and 1859 as an artillery proving-ground and the School of Gunnery. Experimental case-mates were built to trial the mountings used for the 43-ton, 12in BL gun prior to its installation in the Spithead sea-forts off Portsmouth, whose arc and yoke fittings survive. These casemates were also used for the 38-ton, 12.5in gun which was mounted, amongst other places, in Coalhouse Fort. A pier for heavy guns next to the casemate, with railway lines linked to the track serving the whole site, was used to unload 9.2in BL guns, for instance. An 80-ton gun-platform on the foreshore below the Repository, excavated in 1983, was built in the early 1870s, and known as the Repository Berth. There were also pits for Moncrieff Disappearing guns. The barges *Gog* and *Magog* were used for bringing in the heavy guns such as the enormous 110-ton, 16.25in BL gun for test-firing, unloading at Gog's Berth beside the pier. Other guns, such as the Zalinski 15in Pneumatic Dynamite gun, were mounted in 1890-1 inside the western boundary of the Foulness New Ranges. Four pits for QF guns formerly occupied the site of the later Drill Shed. At the turn of the century the Heavy Experimental QF Battery with two 6in and two 4.7in QF guns was built. There was a 9.2in Mark X on Mark V mounting in a pit between the QF Battery and the officers' mess. A Light QF Gantry in front of the experimental casemate was converted from an old hydraulic gantry of around 1860, mounting four 12-pounders and four 6-pounders. An additional 9.2in Mark VII and two 6in guns on towers,

42 Shoeburyness: the pier with its railway track, used for unloading heavy ordnance for testing on the ranges. The barges *Gog* and *Magog*, which also served Coalhouse Fort, would berth alongside the pier.

similar to those at Sheerness (Kent) and the Humber defences, completed the provision available for practice and active defence.

However powerful the Coast Artillery might appear, defence against invasion still hinged on the ability to get large numbers of infantry in a position to oppose a landing as quickly as possible. The War Department manoeuvres of 1908 centred on such an enemy landing at Shoeburyness and the army's response. The task facing the defending force was to transport troops there from Warley Barracks using vehicles supplied by the London General Omnibus Company, the first time such an operation had been attempted. The exercise was adjudged a success, discovering the flexibility of transporting troops by road, against the rigidities of rail.

Purfleet and Rainham Ranges

As the numbers of regulars and volunteers requiring practice in outdoor rifle-shooting increased, new ranges were needed as existing provision at Bisley (Surrey), Hythe (Kent) and elsewhere was insufficient and not always easily accessible. In 1906 the War Office purchased land at Purfleet next to the Powder Magazine with its existing 200-yard proofing range on the east bank of the Mardyke. The new complex consisted of three blocks of 1,000-yard ranges, graduated in increments of 100 yards from firing positions to stop butts, the most commonly used distance being 400 yards. The five ranges containing seventy numbered targets could accommodate more riflemen at a time as required. Purfleet is different from all contemporary ranges in that, owing to the marshy nature of the ground, the butts, rather than consisting of the normal massive earth banks, are built of open brick boxes supporting a stepped concrete platform carrying the conventional sand layer, all reinforced by brick buttresses. The Musketry Camp opened in 1914, and troops were delivered by railway, whilst a tramway served the cordite store inside its earth embankment, continuing on to the Powder Magazine. A second tramway served the Butts, allowing the use of moving targets.

Colchester Ranges

As Colchester developed as a garrison town, training facilities were needed, such as the rifle ranges at Middlewick, eventually extending to Fingringhoe. Colchester retains two fine examples of training buildings dating from the developments of the early 1860s. One is the Riding School of the Cavalry Barracks with its spectator gallery at one end, and the other is the garrison gymnasium, a similar example of the latter surviving at Warley.

Barracks

Horseshoe Barracks was begun on the marshes at Shoeburyness in the 1850s as an artillery training school, and retains an almost academic atmosphere. From 1860 to 1890, the eight barrack-blocks and the Reading-room/Institute were grouped around a horseshoe-shaped parade ground entered through a gateway surmounted by a clock tower with guardrooms to each side and a HQ building. The porticoed, five-bay hospital of 1856 has single-storey wings and is flanked by terraces of single-storey officers' cottages of 1871. The CO's mansion stands in its own grounds and the large officers' mess occupies a cliff-edge site with the REs' and laboratory sergeants' quarters along-side. The Repository or gun-mounting practice shed of 1859, nine bays by three, has a saw-tooth northern-light roof, and blocks of accommodation for officers attending

43 Colchester: interior of the Cavalry Barracks Riding School, recently converted into a health centre.

44 Shoeburyness: Horseshoe Barracks' hospital of 1856, with single officers' cottages alongside.

45 Shoeburyness: Horseshoe Barracks, the terrace, married officers' and surgeons' quarters on one side of what is now Warrior Square.

the One Year Gunnery Instructor Course stand next door to it. Detached houses for senior staff line one side of a cricket field, and married officers' quarters another. The church cum school of St Peter and St Paul dates from 1866. Three single-storey pavilions with verandas remain on the magazine site, as do officers' stables near the cottages. The site is now a housing development, and a combination of original buildings, conversions and infillings, all in a delightful setting, make this an outstandingly successful and sustainable restoration project.

Colchester's various and extensive barracks had been demolished in the years after the victorious troops had returned from Waterloo. After the Crimean War it was eventually realised that the country could not do without a properly organised and trained standing army. The return to billeting in the intervening years had totally destroyed any public confidence in the army, and had contributed to the contempt felt for both the army's rank and file and its leadership. Colchester was chosen for the site of a new hutted camp in 1855. This lay between Military Road and Mersea Road with the timber garrison chapel, dedicated to St Alban the Martyr, still marking its southeast corner. There were six blocks of huts, each accommodating an infantry battalion, and a hospital with ten wards off a central corridor, very similar to those designed by Brunel for emergency use in the Crimea. By 1864 permanent extensions were added in the form of the Cavalry Barracks on Butt Road, and in 1866 the HQ of the new

46 Colchester: an accommodation block in the Cavalry Barracks, with stables below and the troopers' quarters above.

47 Colchester: the officers' mess of the artillery or Le Cateau Barracks of 1873, subsequently known as the Cavalry Barracks.

Eastern District was established in Colchester on Napier Road. Ten years later the Le Cateau Cavalry Barracks, originally intended for the artillery, was built next door to its predecessor. These Cavalry Barracks were designed with blocks containing stables on the ground floor, and quarters for the men above reached by external staircases and open verandah corridors. The ten-year interval between the construction of these two barracks is reflected in the healthier approach to design shown in the later buildings with their better ventilation, higher ceilings, concrete floors and cast-iron columns, airier dormitories and separate quarters for NCOs. The officers' mess at Le Cateau is a very grand building, but even the humbler buildings, such as cart sheds, forges and hay sheds, are well built and substantial. The hutted camp lasted well into the 1890s but new permanent barracks were built steadily ringing the old Abbey Field drill ground, Meeanee and Hyderabad on the east, Goojerat on the west, and Sobraon and the military hospital on the south, all built between 1898 and 1904. In 1904 the War Office bought Reed Hall for future use.

Warley Barracks opened in 1805 as a development of the earlier hutted camp. After 1815 it was expanded to provide accommodation for two troops of horse artillery and a half-battalion of infantry. In 1842 the East India Company had outgrown Brompton Barracks at Chatham and bought Warley Barracks as its military training school. Space was found for 785 recruits and twenty sergeant instructors who were provided with married quarters. As well as new quarters for the officers, a chapel was built by 1857, the year that saw infantry recruitment increased in response to the Indian Mutiny, 1,000 infantry recruits a year now being trained and despatched abroad, particularly

48 Warley Barracks: the chapel built by the East India Company in 1857 which later served as the regimental chapel of the Essex Regiment. Part of the original plan, the campanile, was only added in 1956.

49 Warley Barracks: the gymnasium of 1859, now Keys Hall.

to India, and an additional 3,000 cavalry recruits also undergoing training. After the Indian Mutiny, the East India Company's European troops were absorbed into the British Army and Warley, now the property of the War Department, became a depot for the Royal Artillery and then the Guards. With the Guards move to Caterham (Surrey) in 1870, the barracks became available for use as a Localisation Depot. The Essex Regiment took over the chapel, which survives – along with Blenheim House, formerly the depot officers' mess of 1878, and now part of the TAC. The gymnasium of 1859 is now a dance and trampoline centre known as Keys Hall.

Drill Halls

As the volunteer units became more deeply embedded in the community then their need for dedicated premises grew more acute. Although the War Office had only demanded that corps provide the security of an armoury for the storage of weapons and ammunition, it made sense for units to have their own bases rather than the ad hoc arrangements of shared drill space in chapels and public halls, and orderly rooms lodging in the local solicitor's, but these arrangements appear to have continued for quite a long time in Essex. One exception may be the Essex Volunteer Artillery's base at Artillery House, Stratford Green, in use from soon after 1860. Until recently a number of stables with rooms over and adjacent possible gun sheds stood on the university campus, but their occupants sadly proved unresponsive to enquiries. These may represent the earliest purpose-built volunteer premises in the historic county. A drill hall was built by public subscription in Ongar High Street, opening in 1873. It stands behind the earlier Wren House and, though primarily a drill hall, it served the community as a venue for concerts and public meetings. The two militia storehouses both in use in 1855 appear later to have been devolved to the volunteers, probably after

50 Chipping Ongar: the drill hall behind Wren House on the High Street, built by local subscription in 1873.

the militia moved into Warley Barracks soon after 1881, but Colchester's new Stanwell Street premises were functioning as a volunteer drill hall from 1887, or as early as 1881 in some records, and Chelmsford's in Market Road were rebuilt in 1902, becoming (Territorial) 'Association Buildings' in 1908. Elsewhere it appears that existing buildings were bought for conversion or extension. Around 1890, the Cedars in Portway, the former home of Elizabeth Fry (*d*.1845), Lea Lodge in Church Road, Leyton and Walthamstow Lodge in Church Hill, were acquired as HQs for three of the Volunteer Battalions. The drill hall at Burnham-on-Crouch was a converted chapel, as it appears was Waltham Abbey's, whilst at Coggeshall, King's seed mill was converted for use. In Clacton the former Osborne Hotel (now Sandles Inn) incorporates a large hall with clerestory windows and is recorded as being used by the volunteers in 1902, when shooting took place there. Some units were fortunate enough to have an outdoor range like that on Danbury Common, but many were confined to small-bore rifles on a 25-yard range, the only alternative being to use a Morris Tube inserted into the barrel of their service rifle, reducing the bore, and allowing shooting on the shorter range to take place. Pitfield House in Chelmsford, a large detached house of around the turn of the nineteenth century, appears to have been the centre of a complex of buildings serving the Volunteer Forces, most recently the Royal Naval Reserve.

Between 1908 and the outbreak of war, there was a spate of building. Braintree had made do with the Corn Exchange for fifty years but a new purpose-built drill hall was opened in 1911, consisting of a compact block containing orderly room, messes and stores, with a hall alongside. On the opposite side of Victoria Street stands a pair of semi-detached houses with an Essex county crest over the front doors. These were provided for the permanent staff, probably the drill instructor and the quartermaster. Other drill halls from this period appear to include Ingatestone, Maldon and Manningtree, but village halls such as that at Little Waltham were still used in the absence of dedicated premises. Several of those drill halls demolished over the years, such as Saffron Walden, Witham and Grays, are likely to have dated from this period as they were in use prior to the First World War, as indeed were Prince Avenue and York Road in Southend-

51 Braintree: the drill hall
of 1911.

52 Dovercourt, Harwich:
the HQ of the Essex and
Suffolk Royal Garrison
Artillery, the volunteer
gunners who manned the
guns at Beacon Hill Fort.
It was built soon after
the establishment of the
Territorial Force in 1908.

on-Sea. The HQ of the Essex and Suffolk RGA is in Main Road, Dovercourt, and probably dates from very soon after 1908 when the unit assumed its new identity. Its Felixstowe element had built a new drill hall in Garrison Lane in 1901, so a shiny new HQ would have been in order, with an E-plan front block with an inscription carved into a stone pediment over the main door. This main block includes a small hall, a two-storey wing and various annexes. To the rear is a large corrugated-iron-clad hall which would have been where gun-practice took place, although the real thing at Beacon Hill Battery is only a short way along the coast.

The Royal Navy

In Victorian times Harwich was considered to be the fourth most important naval base in England. As attention turned away from France, in the last quarter of the nineteenth century, to focus on Germany as a potential enemy, the East Coast ports had grown in strategic significance. Despite a downgrading by the Owen Committee, Harwich became the base for a number of vessels, the dockyard being provided with a floating dock in 1903 for maintaining and repairing submarines and destroyers. HMS *Audacious* and a destroyer flotilla were based there from 1905, later, on the eve of war, being joined by submarines. The submarine berthing ship HMS *Camperdown* had been stationed at Harwich from 1908 to 1911 but the next year the 6th Submarine Flotilla, with the 1892 cruiser HMS *Bonaventure* as depot ship, arrived, staying until 1914 when they were moved to the Humber. Another old cruiser, HMS *Andromache*, served as a drill ship in 1904; it was replaced by HMS *Scylla*, which was sold in 1914.

Many of the navy's battleships were built by the Thames Iron Works at Millwall, the very last being the Orion class Dreadnought, HMS *Thunderer*, who fought at Jutland. This enormous vessel, displacing 22,000 tons and costing £1.9 million, mounted ten 13.5in guns in five twin turrets. She was completed in 1911 and fitted out downriver at Dagenham.

Munitions and Logistics

The Crimean War had required the Royal Gunpowder Mills at Waltham Abbey to develop new processes and techniques in order to meet the increased demands of the army and the navy. This involved radical technological change as new steam-powered gunpowder mills were brought into use and new types of building were developed to exploit these new processes. Five new gunpowder mills, T-shaped structures with central beam-engine, under-floor drive shafts and a boilerhouse with coalyard, had been built by the end of the century. These steam-driven mills were 50 per cent more efficient than the water-driven ones, improving the core task of milling gunpowder. Another innovation was introduced in the efforts to produce powders for use in specific weapons. Unless powder was presented in particular ways, the sheer volume that a heavy gun needed to propel its enormous projectiles could easily blow the gun apart.

The 38-ton, 12.5in guns at Coalhouse Fort, for instance, required a charge of 160lb (73kg) to propel their 802lb (365kg) shells to a distance of close on 4,000 yards.

The new layout at Waltham Abbey incorporated tramways, cranes and auxiliary engines. Large brick-vaulted magazines held the powder produced on site prior to its move by barge to Purfleet for storage and issue. Some of the facilities would over time be converted to produce the alternatives to gunpowder which began to appear, such as cordite and guncotton, and these new processes involved the conversion of existing buildings and the construction of new specialist ones. Waltham Abbey's output went mainly to Purfleet, with supplies also going directly to Woolwich Arsenal and to Shoeburyness. When the new explosives factory was opened by Kynoch's in 1895 at Kynochtown, south of Corringham, it was most likely powered by electricity. Whilst the factory had the traditional gunpowder section, it was really intended for cordite, for whose production it had secured a government contract; guncotton and nitroglycerine were also made here, and the complex included a factory producing 0.303in rifle cartridges. The works consisted of timber sheds and brick buildings all roofed in corrugated iron, with storage magazines surrounded by earth traverses. The site was made as attractive as possible by laying out gardens around the industrial buildings, and building a model village to accommodate the workers. The whole site now lies under the Coryton oil refinery.

Just as new explosives had brought radical changes to warfare, radio was to revolutionise the battlefields of the new century. In 1899 the Royal Navy had proved the effectiveness of Marconi's radio telegraph for communication between ships at sea, and the implications for command and control. That same year Marconi acquired a former silk mill in Hall Street, Chelmsford, for the production of wireless-telegraphy

53 Chelmsford Hall Street: the former silk mill of 1858 acquired by Marconi in 1899 and used as a wireless factory until 1912.

54 Chelmsford New Street, Marconi's purpose-built factory, opened in 1912.

equipment. In 1912 the first purpose-built radio factory in the world was opened by Marconi in New Street, Chelmsford. The town was already established as a centre for the production of electrical components, with Crompton's Arc Works, in Moulsham Street and Writtle Road, manufacturing arc lights, generators, electric motors and dynamos; Hoffman's, in New Street, made precision steel bearings, and Batcheller's Pneumatic Tube Company shared the Writtle Road site. Marconi's newly built premises, bounded by Glebe Road, Marconi Road and New Street, with the railway on the fourth side, included an office and a factory. The main façade of the complex was a neo-Baroque pedimented office building, typical of many favoured by the new technology-based industries of the period such as aircraft factories. Many of the contemporary buildings on the site maintain the aesthetic in their detail and scale.

If Chelmsford was the epicentre of one new technology with military potential, then Dagenham and Barking were central to another. The Aeronautical Society of Great Britain opened an airfield in Dagenham in 1909. It lasted barely a year but was used by Frederick Handley Page, and was home to a number of experimental aircraft. The sheds went to the Handley Page works at Barking Creek, Britain's first aircraft factory, also operating by 1909. Following a series of failures, the factory produced the two-seat HP5 in 1911, powered by a 50hp engine and capable of staying up long enough to cross London, flying from Fairlop to Brooklands. By 1912 the company had outgrown the site and removed to Cricklewood.

six

Essex in the First World War

During the First World War Essex anticipated being in the front line were the Germans to invade, but had not expected the aerial assault that actually ensued. Air defence, in the shape of not only anti-aircraft guns and searchlights but also fighter aircraft to intercept and destroy enemy aircraft, was an innovation, continuously evolving throughout the conflict. Essex was also an assembly area for the armies which were despatched, one after the other, to the Western Front, sometimes via other theatres on the way: first the regulars, then the territorials, then the four tranches of Kitchener's volunteers (K1-4), and finally, from early 1916, the conscripts, many of whom had been too young legitimately to volunteer earlier. Alongside all this were naval bases, training camps, experimental establishments and munitions plants and depots. Although there was never any real possibility of invasion at any time during the war, a perceived threat existed for the duration. This meant that large numbers of reserve and second- or third-line formations were maintained in the eastern counties. These might be based in permanent barracks at Colchester and Warley; garrisons such as Harwich; or in inland camps like Witham or Coggeshall.

Defence Against Invasion

Possibly stimulated by the considerable volume of literature pushed out in the early years of the century envisaging the Prussian army pouring across the North Sea, there was a permanent perception that invasion was imminent. Towards the end of the war these fears actually intensified as the enemy was thought to be planning an invasion as a way out of the deadlock of trench warfare. Therefore the defences were constantly being updated, and large bodies of troops tied up patrolling the coast, or waiting to counter the assault which never came.

The Thames Defences
As the Coast Artillery grew more efficient, increasing the range of its guns way out into the Thames Estuary, the number of guns mounted in the inner lines could be substantially reduced. In 1914 only Coalhouse Fort was armed, with four 6in guns, two of which were soon removed to Cliffe Fort on the opposite bank. Coalhouse Fort was the designated Examination Battery for the ports of Tilbury and London and was supported by the guard ship HMS *Champion*, which could supply boarding parties of blue-jackets and

55 Tilbury Fort: the riverside emplacements for QF guns, now mounting an assortment of 6- and 12-pounder models.

56 Shoeburyness: the heavy experimental QF battery mounted two 6in QF and two 12-pounder QF guns throughout the First World War.

marines should any suspect ship hove to under the fort's guns. In 1914 Tilbury Fort was garrisoned by the 2nd Battalion of the Royal Dublin Fusiliers, based in Gravesend, but these were soon despatched to France, leaving only second- and third-line troops such as the 1st (Reserve) Garrison Battalion of the Suffolk Regiment on garrison duties from early 1916 until the Armistice. To facilitate movement of troops across the Thames, a pontoon bridge with a removable centre section operated until 1918, probably protected by 12-pounder QF guns on Tilbury Fort's river front. There were two 12-pounder QF guns and a Maxim machine gun at Thames Haven, and further Maxims mounted to protect Tilbury Docks. There was so much movement in the river that it was vital to distinguish between friend and foe, especially at night, so searchlights were installed at Cliffe Fort, at Thames Haven and at Coalhouse Fort, where they were mounted on the roof. By 1916 the guns at Shoeburyness had been reduced to two 6in and four 12-pounders, all QF models. The wide expanse of artillery ranges were defended by a number of Boer War-style blockhouses, both circular and polygonal, consisting of two concentric skins of corrugated-iron sheeting filled with pebbles, and fitted with timber prefabricated loopholes, dismantled at the end of the war.

The Coast Defences

Harwich was strongly defended by the forts at Beacon Hill and Landguard. Beacon Hill had two 6in BL Mark VII guns and two 4.7in QF guns, with a pair of 12-pounder QF guns mounted on the old redoubt. The rest of the defences – with 4.7in QF guns on Landguard Point covering the harbour entrance, and a total of four 6in guns in the other Landguard batteries – were all on the Suffolk side. During the war barely twenty new coast batteries were constructed across the whole of Britain, with just one forming part of the Harwich defences. This was Brackenbury Battery, built to the north of Felixstowe with two 9.2in BL Mark X guns with a maximum range of over 20 miles (33km). Apart from these defences protecting the Thames and Harwich Haven, there were only sparse fixed defences on the rest of the Essex coast. Four 15-pounder field guns were emplaced at Clacton with four more at Frinton, but only fieldworks were constructed elsewhere. High up on the Naze is a brick-and-concrete building in the shape of an elongated hexagon. Its front face, overlooking the estuary, consists of a wide, wrap-around window-type space framed by the steel uprights which support the thick concrete roof. On the floor, against the middle of the front wall, is a large concrete plinth which may have supported an instrument or a gun. Local information dates the structure to the First World War, with a later remodelling.

The Harwich garrison was mainly composed of reserve battalions of regular infantry regiments. Some, such as those of the Essex, Bedfordshire and Suffolk Regiments, were there for the duration, the 2nd Garrison Battalion of the Suffolk Regiment being specially raised for garrison duties in Harwich in May 1916. Others including the King's Own Royal (Lancaster), the East Surrey, the North Lancashire and the Worcestershire Regiments spent varying lengths of time there. Other troops were based in Essex on anti-invasion duties including the 8th Battalion Dorsetshire Regiment, sent to Danbury as garrison troops in 1917, and 17th Battalion of the Gloucestershire Regiment (TF) which spent 1917 and 1918 at Clacton, Walton-on-

57 Walton-on-the-Naze: this open-fronted emplacement overlooking the southern approaches to Harwich, and said to date from the First World War, may have housed a field gun. Its rear half was clearly remodelled in the Second World War.

the-Naze and St Osyth. There were also numbers of second-line yeomanry cavalry, converted into cyclist units, encamped at Tiptree, and then posted to Wivenhoe and Walton-on-the-Naze. These included the North Somerset, Worcestershire and Wiltshire Yeomanries. The 2/7th (Cyclist) Battalion of the Devonshire Regiment was based in Southminster and Maldon in 1918.

The Land Defences

The preparations for the London Defence Position were activated once the first winter of the war had passed. The planned trenches of the more northerly sector were dug eastwards from Chelmsford beyond Danbury Hill to Maldon. The southerly position, based on the original plans formulated in the 1880s, ran from Epping to the redoubt at North Weald and on to Vange, passing north-east of Ongar and east of Brentwood. Labour was provided from both civilian and military sources. A battalion of the Herefordshire Regiment (TF) was based at Billericay, for instance, in May and June 1915, for the express purpose of working on the defences. There is no evidence that North Weald Redoubt was ever armed, merely fulfilling its intended function as a storehouse for tools, weapons and munitions.

Air Defence

At the beginning of the First World War the offensive potential offered by aircraft had barely been imagined so the notion that a need might evolve to develop defences against them was entirely alien. Britain might have been anticipating some form of assault but nobody could have predicted that it would come from above. In 1910 the RE Balloon School had tried dropping bombs from a tethered balloon, and the 1911 Hendon Air Show had showcased the capability of aircraft in a bomb-dropping role. Apparently ignoring all this, the 1913 annual army exercises in Northamptonshire had employed aircraft in only the reconnaissance role, and even then the military staff thought that airships could perform that role more effectively as they were capable of carrying the cumbersome radio equipment of the time. So when bombs rained down from the Zeppelins onto civilian targets both the military establishment and the populace at large were shocked.

Anti-Aircraft Defences

On the eve of war just twenty-six anti-aircraft guns defended the whole of Britain. Waltham Abbey, Thames Haven and Purfleet had two 3in AA guns and five 1-pounder pom-poms between them, manned by Royal Marines. By the time of the first bombing raids early in 1915 the total had increased somewhat, but much of the effort went into the defence of London by the RNAS. By May 1915 further fixed AA guns had been emplaced at Waltham Abbey and Purfleet, and in the Thames and Medway defences (including Tilbury Fort), and mobile guns had been assigned to defend Kynochtown and Pitsea. The Harwich defences received two ex-Naval Hotchkiss 6-pounder QF guns and two 1-pounder pom-poms mounted at Beacon Hill in an early recognition of the advantage to be gained by hitting the Zeppelins before they had got too far inland. By early 1916, Tilbury, Thames Haven and Purfleet had one 3in 20cwt gun, four 6-pounders and four pom-poms between them. Shoeburyness mounted one 3in 20cwt gun, two Nordenfeldt 6-pounders and a pom-pom. Out of this armoury, only the 3in 20cwt guns had been designed specifically as anti-aircraft guns, the rest being adapted naval guns. The two different types of 6-pounders were anti-boarding guns from the decks of pre-Dreadnoughts, and the pom-poms were intended to be used against small craft or as an anti-personnel automatic. Another adapted weapon, this time from RA sources, was the 18-pounder field gun, re-sleeved to take a 13-pounder shell and fire it to higher altitudes. Eventually, purpose-built 75mm French guns were made available. All sorts of ideas were attempted to point these weapons skywards – some of which, fortunately, were successful. On 1 April 1916, pom-pom guns at Purfleet Powder Works, including one mounted on the submarine-spotting tower by the riverbank, along with guns at Tilbury Fort, all manned by men of the Essex and Suffolk RGA (TF), shot down Zeppelin L15, the first such success of the war. It had taken the combined efforts of fourteen AA guns firing almost 300 rounds, and two RFC fighters, but it was a morale-boosting victory. More AA weapons gradually came on stream and the Thames AA defences consequently gained in strength, a cluster of five 12-pounder naval guns defending the port facilities of the Tilbury area, centred on Bowers Gifford. Shoeburyness, no doubt pleading a special case as the School of Artillery, had collected a full set of two 3in, 12- and 18-pounders, and a 75mm gun in mid-1917. Zeppelin losses mounted and their operation was abandoned, switching to assault by the giant Gotha bombers.

By 1916, great effort had been put into establishing the London Gun Barrier, initially comprising only fourteen AA guns but developing so that, by early 1918, it extended right around London, and was ultimately equipped with 116 of the 3in guns and thirty-three of the adapted 18-pounders. This system, its north-eastern sector centred on Epping, covered all the approaches to London, supporting the RNVR-manned batteries in the centre. General Ashmore, at the War Office, developed the ad hoc system of observation posts into the Metropolitan Observation Service, the forerunner of the ROC, as part of the London Air Defence Area (LADA). This was an integrated system combining a gun-belt 20 miles (32km) east of London, the observers, searchlights, a balloon barrage or 'apron', and the Home Defence fighter squadrons of the RFC and RNAS, all held together by reporting through a central control point at Horse Guards. The balloon apron began north of Tottenham and ran to the east of Wanstead, Ilford and Barking. Here fighter aircraft needed to keep above 10,000ft (3,050m) to avoid being caught by this barrier of taut steel cables which would rip their wings off. Forest Farm at Fairlop served as a balloon station, operating and maintaining the barrage. The experience of LADA, with the addition of RADAR, would provide the basis for the nation's air defence system through to the end of the Second World War.

Airfields

Early in the war the purpose of the few military airfields which existed was to train pilots who would then operate in the skies over the Western Front. Only when the Zeppelin raids had begun in 1915 was any thought given to countering them with fighter-aircraft based in airfields around the target areas. Essex lay directly in the path of the German bombing attacks on London and so was home to two Home Defence squadrons of the RFC. Within 50 Wing, No. 39 Squadron, with its HQ at Woodford, was spread across Suttons Farm (later reborn as Hornchurch), North Weald Bassett and Hainault Farm. The three flights of No. 37 Squadron, with its HQ at The Grange, Woodham Mortimer, were based at Flambirds Farm, Stow Maries, at Gardeners Farm, Goldhanger, and at Rochford near Southend. While the navy had responsibility for London's AA defences, the RNAS airfield at Chingford fulfilled a Home-Defence role, through No. 44 Squadron, but once the army took overall control the RFC supplied the main fighter response and Chingford largely reverted to its training commitments. At Rochford, a new No. 61 (Home Defence) Squadron, was formed in August 1917, operating alongside two depot squadrons training pilots.

It has to be said that although the fighters enjoyed more success than the AA guns, many casualties amongst the enemy airships and bombers were caused by accident, mechanical failure and navigational errors. The aircraft did have their successes, however, with 39 Squadron shooting down three Zeppelins, more falling to aircraft from Suttons Farm, and another being downed by an aircraft from Goldhanger. Sometimes direct hits were unnecessary, one Zeppelin, for instance, being forced to land virtually intact, outside Colchester. An improvement in fighting techniques, especially at night, and a five-fold increase in the number of fighter squadrons, together with a more effective integration of all the other elements of LADA, greatly enhanced the kill-rate. By late 1917 the airships had generally stopped even attempting to get through, and the incoming bombers were suffering up to 50 per cent casualties.

Initially the airfields themselves were rudimentary affairs. All that was needed was a flat, firm grass field with an airstrip about 500 yards long, a couple of aircraft sheds like those surviving at Hainault Farm or, more likely, some canvas Bessoneau hangars on timber frames, and some workshops for carrying out repairs and maintenance. Test-pits at North Weald Bassett have revealed what may be the remains of a timber-framed hangar, and a shed at nearby Moreton, conforming to the contemporary specifications, is thought to have been one of those hangars, recycled as a barn in 1919. The typical Home Defence airfield held a flight of around a dozen pilots and their twenty or so aircraft, Stow Maries holding sixteen Sopwith Camels on the strength at the end of the war. To keep these machines in the air required large numbers of ground-crew which, along with support staff of cooks and drivers and so on, could add up to a complement of between 200 and 300 men and women. The technical and administrative buildings might be quite substantial, but much of the accommodation was in huts. A photograph of Chingford shows lines of huts, apparently of timber, mounted on brick dwarf-walls, and archaeological investigation of the area between two of the Lea Valley reservoirs would appear to confirm this. The sergeants' mess from Goldhanger, now re-erected as St George's church at Heybridge Basin, is a timber hut, and there are a number of other examples nearby, in use as dwellings, which may also represent post-war recycling.

Towards the end of the war airfields became more permanent and more sophisticated. Chingford had permanent hangars with gables over front-opening doors, probably an adaptation of the Admiralty design for use by sea-planes, the F-shed. Suttons Farm had a nucleus of offices, workshops, two aircraft sheds and messes, surrounded by rows of barrack-huts and officers' quarters, with a women's hostel outside

58 Heybridge Basin: this timber hut, now re-erected to serve as a church, was originally the sergeants' mess of the RFC airfield at nearby Goldhanger.

the main perimeter. The entire site was cleared in 1919. At Stow Maries, however, there is a remarkably complete collection of airfield structures dating from early 1917, when the airfield commenced operations, and mainly brick-built. At one end of the complex are the aircraft workshops and dope shop along with a blacksmith's shop and technical stores. These were all to the rear of the two aircraft sheds, which have gone. Close to the former entrance are the MT sheds, which also housed vehicles for Goldhanger. Another group, around the water tower and facing onto the flying-field, include a squadron office and a duty pilots' room with verandah. The next group consists of the Institute or men's canteen and the sites of eight, presumably timber, barrack-huts. One hut and the sergeants' mess, both brick-built, survive. Next door is the officers' mess with three parallel blocks of officers' quarters nearby. On the south-west edge of the site are three, of the projected six, women's hostels, and at some distance across the parade ground is the building which housed the diesel generator. Finally, on the west side of the parade ground stands another substantial building identified by the present owners as the Squadron HQ, but described on the 1918 RAF plan as the Reception Centre. This is possibly the last building completed on site, since, although usage of the airfield continued into 1919, it is thought that the planned completion date of December 1918 for the building programme was not achieved.

One of the problems faced by the fighters tasked with intercepting the Zeppelins was that of staying in the air long enough to make contact on the basis of sketchy information. Consequently a network of landing grounds was established in addition to the recognised aerodromes. These enabled pilots, who were of course not equipped with radios, to judge the moment when their fuel would run out, and head for the nearest convenient landing field. Examples include Sible Hedingham, Thaxted and

59 Stow Maries' workshops, on the technical site of the RFC airfield.

60 Stow Maries: marked on the plan as the Reception Centre, this is now regarded as the HQ building of this RFC airfield.

Wormingford, this latter becoming a fully developed airfield in the Second World War. Facilities at these landing grounds were minimal, little more than a hut to shelter the ground-crew, a fuel tank and, for those fields used at night, a brazier for use as a beacon. Signalling stations were established to communicate with aircraft, one being located on top of the keep at Hedingham, and possibly responsible for the disastrous fire of 1918. Improvement in acoustic techniques, the development of the observer network, and increasing numbers of searchlights, all enabled pilots to adopt less of a hit-and-miss approach to interception.

Although Essex might have been regarded as being in the front line, some training was nonetheless located there, Chingford training pilots for the RNAS from 1916.

Towards the end of the war there was a need for pilots, especially those newly arrived from the USA, to be trained to fly the new de Havilland 0/400 long-range bomber, intended to return the compliment of the Gotha attacks. Chingford became No. 207 Training Depot Station (TDS) with Hainault Farm as a satellite, and Fairlop became No. 54 TDS but was soon transferred to London Colney (Hertfordshire).

The Royal Navy

Britain's major naval bases had always been located to focus on the French, but the emergence of a threat from Germany forced a re-orientation, with Harwich being developed as an important base for submarines and destroyers. In July 1914, the 8th Submarine Flotilla, with its depot ship, HMS *Adamant,* sailed into port, to be followed at various times through the war by the 3rd, 6th and 9th Flotillas with their respective

61 Osea Island: the generator house of the Royal Navy motor-boat base. (Photograph by Ivor Crowson)

depot ships HMS *Maidstone, Forth* and *Pandora*, most staying throughout the war. Also in 1914 the 1st Destroyer Flotilla arrived with HMS *Woolwich* as its depot ship. The Senior Naval Officer Harwich flew his flag in HMS *Hercules*, a Reserve Fleet battle-ship launched in 1910, until 1919. In 1917 a government research station was set up at Parkeston Quay under the direction of Sir Ernest Rutherford to explore the use of electro-magnetism in the detection of submarines. His experiments would ultimately result in the development of Asdic, of vital importance in the next war.

Off the coast the old Gunfleet anchorage was abolished, and in 1915 Brightlingsea became a naval base in its own right. A drifter, HMS *City of Perth*, acted as nominal base ship from 1916 to 1921, and HMS *Wallaroo*, a cruiser launched in 1890, became the depot ship for units of the Royal Naval Auxiliary Patrol from 1915 to 1916. Late in the war, Osea Island, in the Blackwater Estuary, was established as a coastal motor-boat base (from 1918 to 1921). Besides the Charringtons' mansion of around 1906, which served as offic-ers' quarters and ward-room, a number of buildings remain on the island. These include a chapel, a generator house, the torpedo store and a water tower. Some of the many huts which once housed up to 2,000 ratings have also survived.

The Army in Essex

The Deployment of Local Units

In August 1914 the 11th Infantry Brigade of four regular infantry battalions formed the Colchester Garrison and immediately went to France, with the BEF, as part of the 4th Infantry Division, becoming the 'Old Contemptibles' after the retreat from Mons.

Also on the way to France from Colchester in August 1914 were the 20th Hussars as part of the 5th Cavalry Brigade, and XIV Brigade, Royal Field Artillery, with three batteries of horse-drawn 18-pounder guns.

The Essex Regiment

During the war some thirty battalions of the Essex Regiment served along with three regiments of Essex Yeomanry, many of them on the Western Front or further afield. The 1st Battalion arrived back in England from Mauritius in December 1914; they then went to Gallipoli via Alexandria, ending up in France in March 1916. The 2nd Battalion went straight to France from Chatham in August 1914 and spent the entire war there. The four territorial battalions also served at Gallipoli but then went on to Palestine. The 9th (K1), 10th (K2), and 11th (K3) Battalions formed at Warley, with the 12th (K4) Battalion forming at Harwich, all serving in France. The 13th Battalion was raised by the mayor of West Ham, in the way of Pals battalions across the country, assembled at Brentwood, then accepted by the War Department and despatched to France in August 1915. The 14th Battalion formed at Brentwood in September 1915 as a local reserve and the 15th Battalion was an amalgam of TF units and went to Belgium in 1918 on garrison duties. Two dedicated Garrison Battalions were formed, with one serving in Gallipoli, Egypt and Palestine, and the other in India. The 3rd (Reserve) Battalion formed part of Harwich Garrison throughout the war. The 8th (Cyclist) Battalion was stationed at Wivenhoe and Southminster on anti-invasion duties, prior to being posted to Ireland in 1918. The remaining thirteen second- and third-line territorial or reserve battalions all had home postings, mainly on defence duties in East Anglia.

62 Belchamp Walter, Belchamp Hall: on the outbreak of war, this was the HQ of the Eastern Mounted Brigade, to which the Essex Yeomanry and the Essex Royal Horse Artillery belonged.

The Yeomanry in Essex

The Essex Yeomanry began the war as part of the Eastern Mounted Brigade (TF) with its HQ at Belchamp Hall, near the Suffolk border outside Sudbury. They were transferred out of the brigade and went to France with the 3rd Cavalry Division. By early 1918, it was clear that massed cavalry had little part to play in the static warfare of the Western Front and, along with many other yeomanry regiments, they lost their horses and joined with the Bedfordshire Yeomanry to form a battalion of the newly raised Machine Gun Corps, only regaining their horses near the end of the war. The 2/1st Essex Yeomanry had been formed in Colchester in 1914, losing its horses to become a cyclist unit in autumn 1917. Other such units went through the same process, units of the Warwickshire, Montgomeryshire and Nottinghamshire (Sherwood Rangers) Yeomanries, constituting the 1st Mounted Brigade, being converted to cyclists at Thorndon Park, Brentwood in July 1916, with other yeomanry units going through the same process at Great Bentley. Most of these new cyclist units were either based as an anti-invasion force on the Norfolk–Suffolk border at Somerleyton, Beccles or Thetford, or put to patrolling the more vulnerable stretches of the East Coast. At the same time a new 1st Mounted Division was forming at Stansted in November 1916.

Essex Artillery Units

The Essex RHA (TF) spent time at home, brigaded with the Hampshire and West Riding of Yorkshire RHAs, before proceeding to Egypt and Palestine with the 7th Mounted Brigade, serving under Allenby. The second-line Essex RHA served in France from 1916 to 1918. The 2nd East Anglian Brigade RFA, based at Stratford Green, went to France in 1915 and thence to Egypt and Palestine until the end of the war. Its second-line unit served in the UK, using West Ham Park for gun-drill, and was billeted in Water Lane School. Two regular companies of the Royal Garrison Artillery were based in Essex: No. 14 at Shoeburyness, and No. 13 at Landguard Fort (supported by the territorials of the Essex and Suffolk RGA based in Dovercourt and Felixstowe). The East Anglian (Essex) Heavy Battery RGA, also based at Stratford Green, served in France from 1916 to 1918.

Assembling the New Armies

Once the regular units had left for their destinations abroad, the first tranche of territorial divisions was brought together from their local drill halls and county camps. Following the formation of Kitchener's New Armies in 1914 and 1915, a second tranche of territorial divisions was raised in 1915. Chelmsford was chosen as the assembly area for elements of both the 48th and the 61st South Midland Divisions with battalions of the Warwickshire, Worcestershire and the Gloucestershire Regiments all camping in the area in autumn 1914 and their second-line units in August 1915. The 3rd South Midland Brigade RFA (TF), for instance, concentrated around Galleywood.

The second-line 66th East Lancashire and the 67th Home Counties Divisions were both assembled in Colchester, with several battalions of the Lancashire Fusiliers occupying Meeanee and Hyderabad Barracks prior to embarking for France. The 67th Division's Horse Transport Units of the Army Service Corps were also assembled, alongside the infantry, and a Reserve Park was set up to service these ASC units.

Colchester had also provided a base for New Army units such as 36th Infantry Brigade of 12th Division (K1) and the 53rd Infantry Brigade of 18th Division (K2), which included the 10th Battalion of the Essex Regiment. Many of these units must have been in tented camps but 7th Battalion, the Sussex Regiment, in 12th Division (K1) occupied Sobraon Barracks. The facilities were clearly stretched, and even Layer Road football ground had to be used for drill and parades, whilst the Severalls County Lunatic Asylum on Boxted Road became a recruit camp. Colchester also provided a base for the 5th and 6th Reserve Brigades in 1916, but dispersed some units to infantry camps at Dovercourt and Harwich. Belhus Park and Purfleet Camp were also involved in accommodating units of the New Armies, including the 37th Infantry Brigade of the 12th Division (K1), and the 55th Infantry Brigade of the 18th Division (K2).

Warley Barracks remained the Essex Regiment depot throughout the war but retained its links with the Guards, being the location for the formation of a 3rd Reserve Battalion of the Irish Guards, from whose ranks was formed an official 2nd Battalion in 1915 (which was sent to France, the 3rd Battalion staying at Warley for the duration).

Other camps were set up for specific units. Grey Towers Camp at Hornchurch, centred on the mansion of that name, became the base for one of the occupation-based units which were recruited alongside Pals' battalions. The 23rd (1st Sportsman's) Battalion Royal Fusiliers was raised in 1914. Following their move to Clipstone Camp (Nottinghamshire) for training, the 26th Battalion Middlesex Regiment (3rd Public Works Pioneers Battalion) was recruited in 1915. After that, in 1916, Grey Towers became the Command Depot for the NZEF and the principal New Zealand camp and hospital until 1919. In June 1915, the 18th (Service) Battalion (Arts and Crafts) Kings Royal Rifle Corps was raised at Gidea Park and accepted by the War Office in the September. At least one unit destined for K4, the 10th Battalion of the Border Regiment, was raised in Southend. It then moved to camp at Billericay prior to joining a reserve brigade.

The manpower shortages in all theatres of the war had become so acute that every fit man had been drafted to the Western Front at the expense of, amongst other formations, the forces committed to home defence. Over the winter of 1916-1917, the final batch of three new divisions, specifically for home service, was assembled. Once again, in early 1917 Colchester was called on to provide space for the 212th Infantry Brigade of the 71st Division. The Chelmsford area became the base for elements of the 73rd Division with 220th Brigade at Chelmsford and the 218th Brigade at Witham, Coggeshall and Kelvedon, and supporting ASC transport and supply units at Witham, Braintree and Maldon with their HQ at Chelmsford. About this time two battalions of Cameronians were at Billericay and Terling near Witham prior to service in Ireland.

Cadet Units

The war saw an expansion of the number of cadet units based on schools, the Boys' Brigade, the Church Lads' Brigade and volunteer battalions of the Essex Regiment. Schools such as Felsted, Bancrofts, Chigwell and Forest continued to run companies of the Junior (Officer) Training Corps. Many other schools including Colchester RGS, King Edward VI's Chelmsford, Sir Anthony Browne's Brentwood and Maldon GS had cadet units affiliated to particular battalions of the Essex Regiment.

The Volunteer Training Corps

With all eligible men apparently in the forces, those left behind in reserved occupations or in the lowest medical categories wanted to be seen to be 'doing their bit' for the country, and at the same time to avoid the accusations of cowardice that were beginning to be levelled at any man not in uniform. Eventually the government issued munitions workers with lapel badges, but that would not meet every situation. The Volunteer Training Corps was raised to take on duties which would release troops for other deployments. Membership included veterans who were too old to rejoin the colours, men of military age who were needed in their normal jobs and youngsters who were yet too young to get past even the most myopic of recruiting sergeants. A week's training was given, along with a 'GR' armband. At first the government refused both weapons and uniforms, but eventually saw the sense of encouraging a means of maximising manpower. The young lads would also have a more than rudimentary knowledge of drill, military ways and shooting when they did finally get called up. In Colchester, the VTC were armed with carbines and old Japanese rifles. Units would later man AA Lewis Guns and searchlights. The Chelmsford Company numbered 150 men and boys.

Another avenue available for lads involving participation in the work of the military was membership of the Scouts. Until the First World War the Coastguard service formed part of the Royal Naval Reserve, so most were called up to serve on ships of the Reserve Fleet in 1914. Many coastguards' wives kept the observation role going, especially on coasts liable to be invaded, their work often being aided by Boy Scouts whose semaphore skills proved useful. Scouts also served as orderlies and messengers in army camps, gaining badges for working three hours per day, for twenty-eight days. Scouts also guarded telegraph wires and generally kept their eyes open for anything suspicious.

Training

Whilst infantry recruits commenced basic training as soon as they had joined their unit in whatever camp was their initial base, there were many other specialist needs. In 1915 the War Department purchased the whole of Foulness Island, building a bridge, a road and cottages for permanent instructors. This enabled the School of Instruction for Royal Horse and Royal Field Artillery to expand its activities without encroaching on the land already heavily used for testing artillery and projectiles. As the New Armies formed, went into action, and lost large numbers of junior officers as casualties, so demand for new officers, already acute at the start of the war, became steadily more critical. The task of producing this new officer corps was entrusted to a number of territorial units. The 28th Battalion of the London Regiment (Artists Rifles) was converted into an Officer Cadet Training Unit (OCTU), and operated in the base depots in France. Its second-line battalion was given the same role in England, operating as No. 15 Officer Cadet Battalion at Hare Hall, Romford (now the Royal Liberty School). Prior to being deployed on the Western Front, infantry units were initiated into the mysteries of the new warfare, mainly by digging trenches, and lengths of practice trench survive outside Colchester running south from near Rowhedge to the Roman river (along with a possibly contemporary earthwork redoubt just to the south of the Middlewick rifle ranges).

Logistics

Barracks and Camps

Throughout the war, accommodation was to prove a permanent logistical problem. The sheer numbers of troops involved completely overwhelmed any existing provision and rendered billeting impossible as a complete solution simply on grounds of numbers. A battalion could number 1,000 men, a brigade 4,000 and a division up to 20,000, with attendant artillery, engineers, medical and service corps personnel. A very few TF units remained based in their home areas so their personnel could stay at home, but for the majority there were only two options: barracks or camps.

One way to get this space was to expand existing barracks, which was done at Colchester, Purfleet and Warley, rotating units in the barrack-blocks and filling every available space with tents. Shoeburyness was more difficult as it was both a School of Artillery and a front-line position for Coast Artillery and AA guns, but nevertheless set up a tented camp on the sports field. Purfleet already had an established hutted Musketry Camp which was capable of extension within its existing infrastructure.

The other alternative was to requisition country houses with their surrounding parks. This was what happened at Belhus Park, Aveley; at Grey Towers, Hornchurch; at Hare Hall, Romford; at Terling Place, Witham; and at Galleywood Hall, Chelmsford. The central mansion would provide HQ, offices, mess and quarters for the officers, and there would generally be stables and other outbuildings for use as an armoury and quartermaster's stores. The troops would then be accommodated in tents or huts. In this way it was possible to absorb 10,000 men in the Belhus–Purfleet complex. At Purfleet, 160 'Knuts of Purfleet' huts were built on part of the Rainham rifle-ranges to house recruits, but they would not all be so lucky. At South Ockendon, the West Ham Farm Colony became a tented recruit camp. At Colchester the War Office had acquired Reed Hall before the war and here an initially tented camp evolved into a semi-permanent hutted one. It may have been the huts at Grey Towers which commended it to the New Zealanders as a permanent camp and hospital. One would have to be content with what shelter one had been allotted. Recruits housed in Colchester's Severalls County Lunatic Asylum no doubt grew to appreciate the advantages they enjoyed over their colleagues in tents. However, even the requisition of lunatic asylums and country houses could not meet demand, and billeting on private houses was still a resort as late in the war as 1917, when householders were being prosecuted for obstructing the authorities by refusing to take in military lodgers.

Depots

Tilbury Fort had been designated a Mobilisation Centre under the old London Defence Positions scheme, holding guns and ammunition for two RHA units. On the outbreak of war all this equipment was issued, and in 1915 the fort was designated an Ordnance Store, supplying everything from tentage to weaponry to the new units assembling in the nearby infantry camps, initially at Belhus and Purfleet in particular, and then to the new divisions forming across the county. The stores operation was run by seventy-five men of the Army Service Corps and the Army Ordnance Corps. As the war progressed, so great a quantity of stores needed accommodation that neigh-bouring Coalhouse Fort and Cliffe Fort, on the Kent side, were pressed into use, and in 1918, the Northfleet chalk tunnels, the other side of the river, were kitted out as bomb-proof explosives storage. Next to the 'Worlds End' public house near Tilbury Fort was a depot for remounts to be shipped over to France. Much of the ordnance stores coming into Tilbury Fort were brought in by truck; the gateway next to the Water Gate was cut through the fort wall to improve access.

Munitions

At the beginning of the war there was an already well-established explosives indus-try in Essex, centred on updated facilities at Kynochtown, Waltham Abbey, Pitsea and Purfleet, supplying the Armed Forces. As cordite established itself as the military explo-sive of choice, a new plant within the Royal Gunpowder Works at Waltham Abbey came into operation for this new process, in converted obsolete buildings, along with a new nitroglycerine plant. The enormous volume of explosives demanded by opera-tions on the Western Front, however, exposed the inability of this existing provision to meet such rapidly accelerating demand.

There were three main ways of making up the shortfall. Firms such as the High Explosives Company Ltd, of Bramble Island, Harwich, or the Miners' Safety Explosives Company Ltd, of Curry Marsh, Stanford-le-Hope – both of which normally produced explosives for commercial purposes – could be diverted into meeting military needs. Existing commercial concerns with the relevant expertise and plant might be put to explosives production – thus the Ajax Chemical Company in Barking manufactured shells, and C. Bertrand Field's Soap Works in Rainham converted to the production of explosives. New government-run factories were established, the Synthetic Products Company's chemical works in Rainham becoming one of HM Factories making TNT, and the Grays Chemical Works Ltd becoming HM Experimental Picric Acid Plant.

Additionally, alongside these three strands, both the Admiralty and the Trench Warfare Department of the War Office ran their own networks of government fac-tories producing explosives to meet their specific requirements. The Admiralty maintained a shell-filling station in Stratford, and Baird and Tatlock of Blackhorse Lane, Walthamstow, supplied the Trench Warfare Department with explosives, proba-bly mainly grenades and mortar-bombs. Throughout the war the Shoeburyness ranges continued to test projectiles.

Other firms were encouraged to devote their production to meeting the demands of war, often because their peacetime markets disappeared. At Barking Wharf, for instance, one factory produced cork lifebelts for the navy, and in Dagenham, the Sterling Telephone and Electrical Company geared their production to military sig-nalling. Hoffman's in Chelmsford, making precision steel bearings, was central to many of the technological developments of the war. Most significant of all were Crompton's and Marconi in Chelmsford, both firms already producing large quantities of their radio equipment, and fully aware of its potential for both the Armed Services and the Merchant Marine. As – if not more – important was their pursuit of an active experimental agenda through dedicated departments working on radio-valves, and

63 Chelmsford, Writtle Road: Crompton and Company's works, established in 1896, produced generators, transformers and electric motors. It later became part of Marconi's.

further development of radio telephony. Eventually, attached microphones and head-phones would facilitate voice telephony, in many situations largely replacing the use of Morse code. This led to the extensive use of wireless in aircraft, of particular use over the Western Front for artillery spotting, but also for Home Defence aircraft being directed to intercept incoming bombers. By 1918, the integrated systems made possible by reliable telephony had become the basis for the developing success of LADA. Marconi's ran a signal station, with a mast adjacent to their Hall Street site, which was still operational in 1919.

Military Hospitals

Alongside the established hospitals at Colchester, Warley and Shoeburyness, there was a need for numerous extra beds to accommodate servicemen who were sick, or who had been wounded in battle. A number of additional military hospitals were established, particularly based on camps such as Purfleet or Hornchurch. At Shoeburyness the garrison theatre became a second hospital, necessary to cope with the increased numbers in the tented camp, and Colchester added 200 convalescent beds at Summerdown. At Hornchurch the Grey Towers camp hospital, along with the hutted convalescent camp, became the primary New Zealand medical centre as part of the NZEF depot, receiving casualties from Gallipoli and elsewhere. Under the patronage of Queen Mary, the Royal Navy set up a hospital in Southend's Palace Hotel. The Red Cross, with a depot for medical supplies at St Osyth, ran hospitals in Clacton and elsewhere. The other main provider of medical and convalescent facilities was the Voluntary Aid Detachment (VAD) who tended to use big houses, usually referred to as auxiliary hospitals, and often provided by their patrons or members. In Essex, these included

Fryerning Hall at Ingatestone, and Aveley School at Thurrock and Upminster. Cottage hospitals such as Woodford and Romford were also pressed into service, and there were even seventy military beds alongside the 400+ inmates of Romford Workhouse, and more in the LCC's Claybury Mental Hospital – surely an incentive to get well enough for a return to duty.

Prisoners of War and Internees

Large numbers of internees produced more pressure on the available accommodation and one solution was the floating camp. Two liners, the *Royal Edward* and the *Ivernia*, were moored off Southend Pier to take 3,000 internees, processed through the clearing house in Stratford. Despite calls to use PoWs as human shields against bombing at places like Kynochtown, many of those captured in battle ended up not in camps but working on the land, the first such German PoWs in Essex being based at Fox Burrow Farm, Barkingside. Here, seventy-five prisoners, working in groups of five, were guarded by thirty-five troops, a ratio which, given the acute manpower shortages, would appear extravagant.

seven

The Inter-War Years

By the end of December 1918, a start had immediately been made on dismantling the machinery of war. Airfields were closed, defences demolished, and army huts auctioned off. The cordite presses at Kynochtown, meanwhile, went over to the production of macaroni.

The early 1920s saw little development beyond adjustments to the infrastructure. In 1920 the Royal Artillery Coast Artillery School was established at Shoeburyness where, by 1929, two 9.2in (Marks VII and X), two 6in BL, two 4.7in QF and two 12-pounder QF guns were mounted for training purposes. Later, a twin 6-pounder was added. In 1922, access to the ranges on the islands of Havengore and Foulness had been improved by the construction of a military road, crossing the channels on bascule bridges. The North Weald redoubt was acquired by Marconi in 1919 for use as a radio station. In 1916 a Train Ferry Berth with two 42ft-high (13m) steel towers and a gantry had been built for the War Office at Richborough Military Port in Kent. Those port facilities were dismantled at the end of the war and, in 1923, the Train Ferry Berth was moved lock, stock and barrel to Harwich Pier, where it can still be seen.

Air Defence

Given that the bombing of British towns and cities had left a deep impression on the nation, defence against aerial assault inevitably became a significant preoccupation of the defence establishment. In 1920 the Territorial Army was reconstituted with one of its several responsibilities being the nation's AA defences. Having learned from the experience of setting up LADA, now expanded into Air Defence of Great Britain (ADGB), the War Office realised that it was of critical importance that AA units should be adequately equipped and trained to operate against enemy bombers. However, in the context of a bankrupt economy, a general war-weariness, and an approaching slump, the government found it expedient to introduce the Ten Year Rule. This stipulated that any potential aggressor, particularly if that aggressor happened to be a disarmed Germany, would require at least ten years to prepare for war. Therefore, a rolling decade's-worth of defence savings could justifiably be made.

Only in 1932, in the light of rumours of German re-armament at a time when, incidentally, the defence budgets had hit rock-bottom, was the rule suspended. It was not therefore until well into the 1930s that anything was done to raise new AA units, to manufacture effective AA guns, or to establish the necessary network of AA defences. The TA in Essex contained several such newly raised AA units. In 1935, the 7th Battalion of the Essex Regiment was converted into the 59th HAA Regiment RA (TA), and the 82nd HAA Regiment RA (TA) was formed as a new unit in Barking in 1938. That same year the 17th LAA Regiment RA (TA) formed at Stanford-le-Hope, and at Brentwood the 28th Searchlight Regiment formed as a RE (TA) unit, transferring to the RA in 1940. These AA units were recruited largely from the technicians being trained by the new technology-based industries such as Ford's at Dagenham, opened in 1931 and, at the time, the largest car factory in Europe. Only very slowly did the equipment arrive, and not until the summer of 1939 was an attempt made to mobilise the entire AA force in an extended dress rehearsal known as the 'couverture', whereby each TA unit put in a month's full-time service on a rota basis, manning the guns and searchlights continuously.

By early 1939 there were 75,000 men and women serving in the TA's AA units country-wide. Although some units were still using the old 3in 20cwt gun and waiting for the new 3.7in and 40mm Bofors weapons to appear in quantity, there was a whole range of new equipment – predictors, height-finders and sound locators – to be mastered. The searchlight-operators trained in planetarium-like high-ceilinged classrooms, blacked out and with the night sky projected over their heads. In addition to the traditional gunners, clerks and store-keepers, units now needed to recruit drivers and armourers, mechanical and electrical engineers, and signallers. The AA equipment was stored in Mobilisation Centres such as that in Colliers Row Lane, Romford, for issue to local units. On the outbreak of war, however, guns were still in such short supply that even the old practice 3in gun from Whipps Cross drill hall was issued to RAF North Weald. The RAF retained responsibility for the barrage balloons which would still be used to protect particular sites and No. 4 Balloon Centre opened at Chigwell in May 1938.

Radar

Into the 1930s the projected construction of a girdle of concrete sound mirrors and of vertical acoustic discs was still seen as the future of an early-warning programme, and Dengie had been selected as a possible location on a proposed coastal chain stretching from Plymouth to Felixstowe at 10-mile (16km) intervals, some forty in all. By 1934 a new scheme covering just the Thames Estuary by using seven bowl-mirrors with a strip-mirror at each end was planned with bowls at Asplins Head, Tillingham and Clacton, and a 200ft (60m) strip at Frinton.

However, there was a great deal of doubt expressed regarding the operational efficacy of the principle of acoustic detection, and work was fortunately redirected toward the development of RDF (later changed to the US terminology of RADAR). Radar was to be of critical importance to the ADGB, and Essex was to be crucial to its development. The experimental work carried out by Watson-Watt and others at Orfordness and Bawdsey, over the border in Suffolk, produced the first screen of five Radio Direction Finding (RDF) stations, referred to as AMES (Air Ministry Experimental Stations) and codenamed Chain Home (CH). These would protect the

Thames Estuary, being able to detect incoming aircraft up to 40 miles (64km) away, and above a height of 3,000ft (915m). Along with Bawdsey (Suffolk) and Dunkirk and Swingate (both Kent), Great Bromley and Canewdon in Essex formed the initial shield. It was thought at first that a combination of alternating transmitter/receiver and transmitter-only sites would be needed. Canewdon was one of the first pair of the former, started in 1935 and entering service in 1937, and Great Bromley was intended as one of the latter. However, once it was established that the system could function without two different types of site, Great Bromley and Dunkirk were both upgraded, opening for business in 1938 and taking part in that year's air defence exercise. Before the outbreak of war there would be twenty such East Coast RDF sites.

Although the expansion of the RAF had made ADGB unwieldy and separate commands had been created, there was still an integrated command and control structure based at Bentley Priory, at Stanmore (Middlesex).

Each RDF station consisted of a standard layout of four timber 240ft (73m) high receiver towers grouped in a square around the brick-built receiver (Rx) block. Close by was a line of four steel 350ft (107m) high transmitter towers with their transmitter (Tx) block alongside. These blocks and the generator houses were protected by earth traverses and covered in a thick layer of gravel on the roof. For use in the event of damage being incurred there were buried reserves (Rx and

Tx), with a timber tower, and the whole site was surrounded by dacoit fencing with a distinctive guardhouse and defended by pillboxes. Remains of such layouts may still be seen at Canewdon and Great Bromley, the latter retaining one of its transmitter towers and both of its protected transmitter and receiver blocks, as well as some other huts and the guardhouse.

The Marconi Research Centre, in West Hanningfield Road, Great Baddow, was built in 1937-9 on a greenfield site. It consisted of a two-storey office block and seventeen bays of north-light sheds with painted camouflage. Among its functions was the further development of RDF. Learning from the East Coast experience, Marconi designed, built and, in some cases, erected the 325ft (99m) high transmitter towers of many of the West Coast CH stations. Next to the factory building are two fields which contained masts and huts for carrying out trials of the equipment in production.

64 Great Bromley: one of the four original 350ft (107m) high steel transmitter towers at this Chain Home radar site. It is one of only a handful of such towers surviving nationally.

65 Great Bromley: the distinctive guardhouse found at CH stations.

66 Great Baddow: Marconi's new research centre, begun in 1937 and opened in early 1939, a significant element of its work being the further development of radar.

Marconi's various radio stations were also used to monitor foreign radio broadcasts in the years leading up to the Second World War, and a School of Wireless and Communications was established in Arbour Lane sometime in the early 1930s. One of the transmitter towers from Canewdon CH station was moved to Great Baddow in the 1950s to be used in post-war radar research.

The Observer Corps

The ad hoc arrangements of the previous war were regularised by the creation of a voluntary uniformed corps of observers organised on a regional basis. In 1929 the responsibility had been transferred from the Home Office to the Air Ministry and great reliance was initially placed on a string of coastguard posts in the south-east, which included Walton-on-the-Naze. Gradually the network was filled in with local centres having controlling functions. The quality of these inevitably varied and that at Colchester came in for some criticism from the local police, who were once more integrated into the system, being responsible for mobilising the observers. By 1936 the coverage was virtually complete with 18 Group, within the Southern Area, and based in Colchester, reporting to HQ at Uxbridge which controlled the response from the fighter airfields at Duxford (Cambridgeshire), North Weald and Hornchurch. The Colchester Group HQ moved several times in this period, starting off in 1926 on the top floor of the High Street post office for a year and then moving to the Corn Exchange, with a further move in 1931 to the penthouse of the GPO Telephone Exchange, where it stayed until well into the war. In 1938, as a result of exercises revealing gaps in the coverage, some of Colchester's posts were combined with some from the Norwich group to form a new No. 14 Group at Bury-St-Edmunds. An initial tranche of eighteen aircraft posts had opened in Essex in 1929, followed by a further twenty-one between 1937-9. Most of these posts were out in open country, usually raised on high ground if possible, and consisting of a timber platform with a covered section. The rudimentary post instrument which allowed observers to plot an aircraft's position on a gridded map had been introduced in 1935 and was mounted on a table in the open part. The covered part afforded minimal shelter. In more built-up areas, some posts might be located on the tops of high buildings such as the telephone exchange at Holland-on-Sea or Southend's Palace Hotel.

Airfields

During this period the newly created independent RAF was reduced to a skeleton force, from which state it had to rebuild in order to be ready for the war that nobody wanted or had anticipated. Most of the 400 airfields which finished the First World War had quickly been returned to agriculture leaving the RAF with barely twenty-five sites country-wide. At home, Trenchard was fighting to keep the RAF alive at all, as defence thinking had reverted to the notion of home defence as the preserve of the Royal Navy (with no role for the RAF, whose role should be to police the Empire). With the Ten Year Rule preventing any real growth, the future was looking bleak. Hints of French belligerence, however, prompted the suggestion that maybe there should be parity between the two countries' air forces and new defence plans, the Steel-Bartholomew Plan of 1923 and the 52 Squadron, or Romer Plan, of 1925, were formulated. Both were extensions of the LADA of 1918 but with extensions to north and west. Still regarding France as the most likely enemy, bomber bases were to be concentrated in Wessex, with an arc of fighter airfields protecting both London and these bomber airfields.

The sites chosen for the fighter airfields included North Weald and Suttons Farm, both of which had served as such in the First World War. Both had been disman-tled and given back to their farmer tenants. The land was again purchased by the Air Ministry with work commencing in 1926. North Weald opened in 1927 and Suttons Farm the next year, being renamed RAF Hornchurch a few months later. These new permanent stations were given buildings drawn from a centrally designed suite of plans. They had A-type hangars (19a/24), two-storey Type C barrack blocks, and a watch office that was still basically a bungalow for the duty pilot (1072 and 2072/26) but at fighter stations with an upper storey containing a pilots' rest room. Often, existing buildings on site were requisitioned as at North Weald where Ad Astra House had become the Station HQ in 1916, and this was pressed into service once more. A new mess for forty officers (1524/25) was built on each site, but the pilots still had only grass fields from which to operate.

By the early 1930s it had become obvious that war was likely, and that it would be fought against Germany again. This necessitated both a re-orientation of the RAF in order to face the new enemy across the North Sea, and a major expansion to increase the squadrons and airfields available for home defence and the bombers' retaliation. The Air Ministry commissioned the architect A. Bullock RIBA to design a set of buildings which would gain the approval of the Royal Fine Arts Commission and the Council for the Preservation of Rural England. Under the watchful eye of Edwin Lutyens, he came up with a neo-Georgian look which was felt to fit well in the British countryside. The buildings were grouped in coherent and easily recognisable clusters according to their function. However these were not neat country estates and bomb-proof roofs, the use of camouflage, and the grouping of hangars in arcs to lessen the chance of their destruction by a single stick of bombs, all testified to their warlike intent. Debden is a typical example of an Expansion Period airfield. It had three concrete C-type hangars (2029/34), measuring 225ft by 150ft (68m by 46m). Behind these were the stores, workshops (4923/35), MT sheds (660/36) and armoury. There were messes for the officers and the sergeants and an Institute/canteen for the other ranks, who were accommodated in T-shaped P-, Q- and R- type two-storey barrack-blocks. A new design of H-block, introduced in 1939 (2230/39) incorporated an underground

67 Debden: the station HQ building built to the standard design (1723/36) and still in use as such by the present occupants of Carver Barracks.

68 Debden: the motor transport sheds (660/36).

69 Debden: the officers' mess (570/37).

70 Debden: overspill accommodation block for single sergeants, built adjacent to the sergeants' mess (which also included some quarters).

air-raid shelter. The watch office was the 'Fort' type (207/36) in concrete, but Debden was not to receive a concrete runway until 1940. At the same time that Debden was being built, some improvements were being made at Hornchurch which was provided with a new C-type hangar and a 'Fort' type watch office (2062/34) but lacking the usual distinctive tower.

The 1930s saw a surge in the popularity of flying as a recreational activity, facilitated by the foundation of a number of private flying clubs. Southend Flying Club was founded at Ashingdon in 1931, on the old Rochford pony track, lasting until 1935 (when Southend established a municipal aerodrome on the former First World War airfield at Rochford, into which the club moved). By this time the RAF was beginning to anticipate an increased need for trained pilots, setting up the RAFVR in 1937, and establishing a network of flying training schools. Rochford was established as No. 34 EandRFTS operated by Air Hire Ltd, using Tiger Moths, until the outbreak of war. Stapleford Tawney had begun life as a commercial operation in 1934 but was vacant in 1938 when Reid and Sigrist Ltd were contracted to set up No. 21 E & RFTS, training RAFVR pilots on de Havilland Tiger Moths and Hawker Harts, Hinds and Audaxes. On the outbreak of war the school moved to Booker (Buckinghamshire), allowing the airfield to be upgraded as a fighter satellite. From 1936, Dengie Flats was used as an air-to-ground firing range by aircraft of No. 11 Group, the newly created Fighter Command.

The Regular Army and the TA

After the Armistice, the army was speedily demobilised – not speedily enough for many, but nevertheless quickly reduced to a fraction of its war establishment, which had totalled over 1,600 battalions in the infantry alone. By 1934 there were just seventy battalions of regular infantry, thirteen regiments of cavalry, one of which was equipped with armoured cars, five battalions of the Royal Tank Corps, and 117 batteries of artillery, six of which were AA units for service in the field with the Expeditionary Force, rather than for home defence.

We have already seen the AA element of the TA, but there were two other distinct strands. One was Coast Artillery, but the largest element – representing, by 1939, some 65 per cent of the total – was committed to the Field Force, either reinforcing the Expeditionary Force on foreign adventures, or taking its place at home. In a new world of mechanised warfare, the regular cavalry needed to undergo a radical conversion, becoming either tank units, or using armoured cars in the reconnaissance role. Similarly, those yeomanry regiments still with horses were reorganised, the Essex Yeomanry in 1921 becoming 104th Field Regiment (RHA Essex Yeomanry) RA (TA) with their HQ at Chelmsford. Serving as Coast Artillery gunners was the Thames and Medway Heavy Regiment RA (TA), two of whose batteries, Nos 175 and 192 were based at Southend-on-Sea.

With war approaching, the government rushed through legislation requiring all fit young men to undergo six months training in a new militia. The 1st Infantry Training

Group was set up at Colchester early in 1939 and hutted militia camps were established at Reed Hall, Colchester, and at Hargrave Park, Stansted Mountfitchet. It would
appear likely that there was another such camp at South Ockendon, as 'Buckles Farm
Camp' was still in use by TA units in 1950, but rendered as 'Bricklers Farm' in a schedule of railway sidings serving military establishments in 1942.

In 1939 the HQ of Eastern Command, along with the HQ of 4th Infantry Division,
were in Colchester, with the 11th Infantry Brigade and accompanying artillery and
engineer units serving as the garrison. Colchester was also home, until 1939, to the
4th Cavalry Training Regiment, preparing troops for service in the Royal Armoured
Corps. At Chelmsford, No. 108 (Essex) Electrical and Mechanical Company RE
(Supplementary Reserve) was based at Market Street. As war approached, all TA units
were required to clone themselves by splitting off cadres of experienced officers and
NCOs as the nucleus of new units. Thus 104 Field Regiment (RHA Essex Yeomanry)
begat 147 Field Regiment (RHA Essex Yeomanry) with its HQ in Chelmsford. Each
TA battalion of the Essex Regiment similarly divided, producing the 1/4th and 2/4th
and the 1/5th and the 2/5th Battalions (and so on). All these four units remained
as infantry, but the two battalions formed out of the 6th Battalion converted to
become the 64th and 65th Searchlight Regiments, based respectively in West Ham and
Southend-on-Sea.

Barracks and Camps

In view of the coming expansion of the army very little building seems to have gone
on during the run-up to hostilities, apart from the hutments hurriedly thrown up for
the militia. At Colchester the new Kirkee and McMunn Barracks were opened in
1938, and a new sergeants' mess and Institute had been added to the Cavalry Barracks
sometime in the 1930s. At Warley Depot a new officers' mess was built in 1939, still
standing as the Marillac hospital, along with mobilisation sheds to hold vehicles and
equipment for use in the coming conflict.

71 Colchester: Cavalry Barracks, a new institute added to the earlier Victorian buildings.

72 Warley Barracks: the new officers' mess, built in 1939 to an Air Ministry design (7035/30).

73 Warley Barracks' mobilisation sheds, storing equipment for the future war.

Drill Halls

The volunteers did slightly better than the professionals in gaining new buildings. New drill halls were opened in Great Dunmow in 1927, in Prittlewell, Southend in 1930, both still in use, and in Halstead, now Kingdom Hall. In line with a revised recruiting policy many of the new drill halls were in the expanding suburbs of West Ham, Dagenham, Ilford, Woodford Green and Romford. The 134th Field Regiment, cloned from the 85th, was based in a new drill hall on London Road, Romford. Brand new drill halls, both now demolished, were built in 1935 at Brentwood and at Chipping Ongar, but not all of those planned reached fruition. At Braintree, in 1939, a site was earmarked on Coggeshall Road for a new drill hall, but it was never built, the site being used for a temporary hutted transit camp. Existing buildings were also still being converted for TA use. Forest Lodge at Whipps Cross, a former coaching inn and house built in 1840 at 900 Lea Bridge Road, became a TAC in 1938. The OTC at Felsted School was given a new single-storey armoury in around 1931.

A Land Fit for Heroes

When the servicemen returned from the war one of their expectations was for decent housing. Romford Garden Suburb, at Gidea Park, was started before the war but remained unfulfilled, and was in any case aimed at a different market. After the war, the parklands of Hare Hall, Romford, and Grey Towers, Hornchurch, were given over to housing, but again remained outside the price-range of returning servicemen. However, there were a number of attempts to meet their needs. The Unit Construction Company built concrete-block houses in Cressing Road and Clockhouse Way, Braintree, in 1918-20, costing some 25 per cent less than similar brick-built houses. The client was the Crittall Manufacturing Company, whose works in Coggeshall Road were nearby. In 1926 Crittalls began the construction of 470 houses plus shops, churches, and a village hall at Silver End, along with a factory employing ex-servicemen. The vast Becontree Estate was built by the LCC in the early 1920s as part of a programme to ease the living conditions in London's East End.

74 Southend, Prittlewell: the new drill hall built opposite an earlier one, for a newly raised AA unit.

eight

Essex in the Second World War

Essex was in the front line of the air war, initially characterised by what has come to be known as the Battle of Britain of autumn 1940 but, in reality, lasting throughout the war, culminating in the assault of the V-weapons. Military activity in the county in the first half of the war centred on defending against invasion, whose likelihood only dissipated towards the end of 1941; on disrupting the onslaught of the bombers; and on maintaining lines of communication and supply-chains around the coast and into the Thames Estuary. Only towards the end of 1942 could the accent perceptibly shift onto the offensive, with the establishment of bomber airfields for the USAAF, and a range of preparations for the Normandy landings.

Defences Against Invasion

In May 1940 a German invasion of the British Isles was seen as inevitable. The BEF had been defeated, to be evacuated from Dunkirk minus most of its equipment and much of its confidence. Against all the prevailing military thought of the time, General Ironside, Commander in Chief of the Home Forces, was forced to plan defensively. He first put all the resources he could muster into what he called the 'Coastal Crust'. This was a belt of fixed fortifications running round the entire invasion coast, from John O'Groats down the East Coast and along the south, turning into the Bristol Channel as far as Weston-super-Mare, with additional stretches in Wales and above Liverpool, its purpose being to delay the consolidation of any invading force. As early as June 1940, GHQ Operation Instruction No. 3 stressed the need to hold any intact armoured or mechanised formations in reserve for counter-attacking enemy bridge-heads, IV Corps being formed in July to cover the whole area north of the Thames. Located in the south Midlands, on being given the codeword 'William', it would respond to an attack in Essex with the 2nd Armoured and the 43rd Infantry Divisions.

Behind the coast a continuous anti-tank barrier based on rivers, canals and newly dug AT ditches, and known as the GHQ Line, ran from Weston to Reading and thence to the Medway. One arm then ran down to Newhaven (East Sussex), whilst the other ran north through Hoo (Kent) across the Thames to Canvey Island, and then beyond Chelmsford and Cambridge to the river Welland, continuing northwards via the Trent into Yorkshire, notionally terminating at Richmond, but with extensions as far as the river Tay. London was given three concentric rings of defences, and shorter defensive

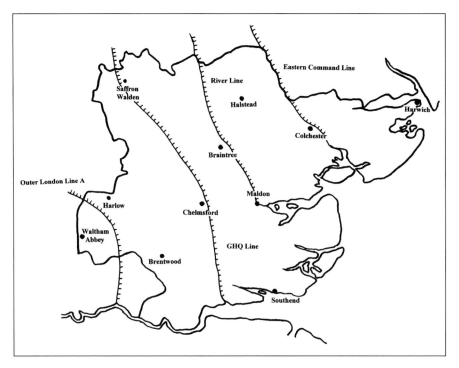

Figure 5 Map showing Second World War defence lines in Essex.

lines carved up the areas between coast and GHQ Line to form fresh barriers and boxes which would contain the enemy's advance. Examples of all these elements may be seen in Essex, many in good states of preservation.

The Coastal Crust

Coast defences were designed to perform three prime tasks. Counter-bombardment batteries of heavy guns were sited to protect ports against attack by enemy capital ships; batteries of medium guns were tasked with destroying the ships of an invasion fleet before they could land their troops; and lighter guns, supported by infantry strong-points and a wide variety of obstacles, were located to resist actual enemy landings on vulnerable beaches. An enormous minefield stretched right down the East Coast creating a 'safe' corridor for coastal convoys, with a gap level with Harwich for access. Smaller electrically-operated minefields, controlled from defensible EXDO Posts, restricted access to rivermouths. Minefields protecting Harwich Haven were controlled from two blockhouses at Landguard Fort and at the landward end of the breakwater at Beacon hill fort.

Further minefields blocking the Crouch and the Colne were controlled from blockhouses at Holliwell Point and Martello Tower 'A' at Point Clear, respectively. The free-standing blockhouses were of two storeys modelled on the bridge of a ship, with an observation cupola on top. An additional anti-invasion barrier was provided by 200 civilian yachts moored across the rivers Crouch and Roach. Ryder searchlights were emplaced to provide nocturnal illumination of many of these obstacles. Beaches

75 Beacon Hill Fort: EXDO Post at the landward end of the breakwater (TM263316) controlling the minefield. The RCHM(E) recorders suggest that it was superimposed on an existing pillbox.

76 Holliwell Point: another EXDO Post at TR017958.

77 Point Clear: Martello Tower 'A' with an EXDO Post, built on top for controlling the minefields in the rivermouth.

78 Shoeburyness: one of the two searchlight positions (the second can just be seen beyond it) serving the emergency 6in battery, installed in 1940 (TQ936841).

themselves were blocked by scaffolding, often festooned with anti-personnel mines, and steel stakes embedded in concrete to impale enemy landing craft, at the low-water mark, with AT blocks and barbed-wire entanglements higher up the beach. All these would be overlooked by pillboxes, field guns dug into pits, slit-trenches for infantry with rifles and light machine guns, and the exotic and terrifying barrages laid down by the Flame Warfare Department. Existing sea-walls were ready-made AT walls, preventing tanks exiting the beach, and new ones were added. Essex, with its 300 miles of coastline, the longest of any county, and lying opposite an expected invasion route from the Netherlands, could identify any number of suitably vulnerable beaches. The most likely landfall for an invading armada was the stretch from Walton-on-the-Naze southwards to Lee-over-Sands: in fact Clacton and Frinton appeared in the country's top-ten list of seaside towns most likely to be invaded. Very few traces of these waterline defences survive, but Fred Nash has located lengths of flattened scaffolding on Foulness Island.

The Thames defences relied on an ability to prevent attacking forces penetrating the outer line from Shoeburyness to Sheppey, secured by the three 9.2in guns of Fletcher Battery (Sheppey, Kent) alerted by a chain of OPs – visual to begin with but by 1941 using radar – taking bearings on approaching ships and feeding them to a central Fortress Control. In 1939 the Shoeburyness Coast Artillery School moved to the Great Orme at Llandudno, North Wales, taking all its modern practice guns with it. Of the two 9.2in guns left behind, the Mark V was dismounted and presumably scrapped, while the Mark VII gun was redeployed to Dover. A spare 6in gun may have been despatched to Nigg on the Cromarty Firth in northern Scotland. However, this key position was not to be left undefended and a battery of two 6in guns along with two CASLs was installed on the cliff between the Heavy QF battery and the officers' mess (TQ936841), one gun possibly being mounted in a vacated 9.2in gun-pit.

In the absence of any trace of a dedicated structure, the BOP may have been on the top of the experimental casemates tower. The Heavy QF Battery served as a magazine and BHQ, and had two Bren Guns mounted on the roof for local defence. This new battery at Shoeburyness was typical of many of the emergency batteries installed in 1940, with guns removed from scrapped First World War cruisers. A pair of 5.5in guns was emplaced on the roof of Coalhouse Fort, and two 6in guns were mounted at Deadman's Battery, also sometimes referred to as Shellness, on Canvey Island, with nearby Scars Elbow battery being equipped in 1940 with two twin 6-pounder rapid-fire guns to counter fast motor-boats, and to cover the adjacent boom. A further battery of two 6in guns was built on Foulness Point but moved to Bawdsey in 1942. All this provision was mirrored on the South Bank of the Thames. As well as the guns, there were minefields at Coalhouse, controlled from an EXDO Post, and at Holehaven, as well as a variety of other obstructions. South from Shoeburyness ran a boom, with another stretching nearly 2 miles (3km) across the river from Canvey to St Mary's Bay. This latter boom consisted of solid sections on piles, and others of A/S nets, with a removable section in mid-stream for ships to pass through. Mounted on shore at the Canvey end, and on the boom itself on the Kent side, were searchlights, supporting the boats of the examination service, and also providing illumination for

79 Coalhouse Fort: one of the two gun-houses for naval 5.5in guns built on the roof of the fort. The brick structure beside it is a degaussing station for protecting shipping against magnetic mines.

80 Scars Elbow, Canvey Island: the engine-house of the Twin 6-pounder battery (TQ788819).

81 Coalhouse Fort: the EXDO Post at TQ691770.

the two shore batteries. The defences at Holehaven included six torpedo-tubes, and all along the riverbank were pillboxes and long chains of AT blocks, nearly 2,000 along the seafront at Southend-on-Sea alone. At Coalhouse Point is a brick-built hexagonal tower, constructed by the navy and originally equipped with the aerial array of Type 287 radar. Its specific purpose was to detect submarines on the surface, but it was also useful for monitoring river traffic generally, and was guarded by a detachment of Royal Marines.

Harwich was defended on the Essex side by Beacon Hill Battery. Here, the two emplacements for 6in Mk VII BL guns, with overhead cover, were created from earlier 10in and 6in positions, the two covered gun-pits flanking underground magazines.

82 Coalhouse Point: the radar tower
at TQ689761.

In 1941 one of the guns was
moved to another earlier 6in gun
position in order to free up a pit
to receive either a newer Mark
XXIV gun or else a dual-purpose
5.25in gun. Neither of these alternatives was followed through,
but the new Cornwallis Battery,
consisting of Twin 6-pounder
equipment, was built with its
own BOP/Director Tower, magazine, crew shelter and CASLs. A
BOP for the 6in guns had also
been built in 1941 over a redundant 4.7in gun-pit, along with a
radar tower for tracking targets
and registering the fall of shot.
The overhead canopy for one of
the gun-houses incorporated the
mounting for a 40mm Bofors
LAA gun. Although many of the existing structures of the fort were re-used, new ones
were added. These included gun stores and RE depot, air-raid shelters and assorted
huts. The fort was contained within a defensible perimeter defended by hexagonal
pillboxes and at least four spigot mortars. On the seaward side by the breakwater, under
naval control, there was a pillbox with a hexagonal LAA gun position on its roof, a
smaller semi-circular pillbox and, below them, the defensible EXDO Post. A boom,
anchored halfway across the haven mouth by a boat, ran from here to Landguard
Fort. Closer to the old Navy Yard was Angel Gate Battery, opened in 1941, with two
12-pounder QF guns and two CASLs. The surviving 12-pounder emplacement shows
that the gun was mounted on a raised platform within a five-sided casemate, whose
gun-floor was accessed by a covered stairway. The gun was apparently mounted on a
concrete cylinder extending from ground-level. A square CASL survives, also of unusual design, now used by the yacht club.

There were four emergency batteries on the Essex coast between Harwich and the
mouth of the river Blackwater. Frinton and Clacton each had a pair of ex-naval 6in
guns whilst East and West Mersea were both equipped with two 4.7in guns, also ex-
naval, issued from Priddys Hard RN Ordnance Depot in Gosport (Hampshire) in July
1940, those at West Mersea being numbered 1402 and 1578, and manufactured in Japan
in 1918 (!). These guns were all emplaced in brick and concrete gun-houses with thick
reinforced concrete roofs as protection against shell-fire or dive-bombing. Each battery
had CASLs, magazines, crew-shelters and generator-houses. Some way back was the

83 Beacon Hill, Fort Cornwallis: Twin 6-pounder battery on the left with its distinctive director tower; on the right, the Victorian 10in gun emplacement, later converted for a more modern 6in gun. It was given overhead cover in 1940.

84 Beacon Hill Fort: the 1941 battery observation post built on top of an earlier 4.7in gun emplacement.

85 Harwich, Angel Gate Battery: one of the two gun-houses for 12-pounder QF guns.

camp with living huts, canteen, offices, workshops and vehicle sheds, many of these in Nissen huts. The whole was contained within a defensible perimeter with pillboxes, barbed wire and slit trenches, entered past a guardroom. One of the gun-houses at East Mersea survives along with a CASL, and a close-defence pillbox. Other short-lived temporary batteries may have existed at Canewdon and later at Creeksea.

Much of the coastline was guarded by pillboxes apparently built under the direction of relatively independent RE officers as different designs can be found on different stretches of coast, there being examples of several types of hexagonal pillbox along the coast between the Naze and Lee-over-Sands for instance. One type, originally sited along the cliffs of the Naze but now stranded below the high-water mark, had open annexes for LAA weapons attached to the landward, entrance face. Dotted around the area there are pillboxes with thickened skirts built up to loophole level and entered through tunnels. A third type is an almost standard type DFW3/22, built to War Office plans, but with a protected entry, either a low dog-legged tunnel with a loophole over the top, or an almost full-height porch containing a pistol-loop. One example of the skirted type at Holland Haven is raised up on a plinth in order to straddle the sea-wall. Many of these pillboxes retain steel plates set into their loopholes and one also has a steel door.

On Mersea Island the prevailing type changes again. Here are regularly hexagonal shell-proof pillboxes, some with solid roofs and large stepped embrasures for heavy machine guns, whilst others have an open central platform for a LAA gun. Another type, this time unique to Essex, is a double-ended pillbox with ten loopholes in the shape of an elongated octagon and designed to straddle the sea-wall facing both out to sea and inland. Some are built as two separate back-to-back hexagons, each with its own entrance. Two examples of these may be seen near the landward end of the

86 East Mersea Battery: the surviving searchlight position at this emergency battery for two naval 4.7in guns (TM020124).

87 Lee-over-Sands: a pillbox with long lines of AT blocks at TM110124.

88 Holland-on-Sea: a skirted pillbox straddling the sea-wall at TM224177.

89   Mersea Island: this hexagonal pillbox has six armoured ports and a tunnel entrance.

90   Osea Island: one of the double-ended sea-wall pillboxes, once described as sardine-tins, at TL924061. (Photograph by Ivor Crowson.)

Mersea Island causeway, two at the east end of Osea Island, eight at Fingringhoe, two at Bradwell and more at Holliwell Point. More unusual designs may be seen, including a two-storey pillbox reported at Havengore, a triple-chambered shell-proof pillbox near Southminster, as well as isolated square and rectangular designs. A rear line appears to have run a mile or two (2-3km) inland and parallel to the coast, consisting of type DFW3/22 pillboxes guarding road junctions. Such pillboxes survive at

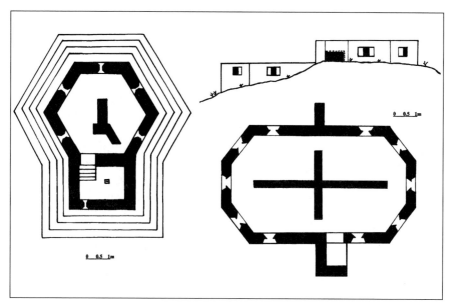

Figure 6 Designs of pillboxes found in the Coastal Crust defences: (left) Walton-on-the-Naze (TM267237), hexagonal, bullet-proof pillbox with open annexe for LAA mounting and integral thickened skirt up to loophole height; (right) Mersea, Osea Island, Bradwell, Holliwell Point etc. The pillbox/section post was designed for use on embankments and sea-walls, and sometimes built in separate sections back-to-back at different levels, and with separate entrances.

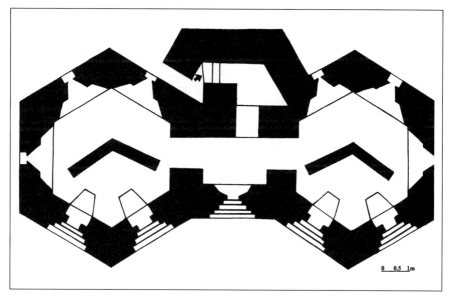

Figure 7 Plan of a unique pillbox near Southminster (TQ995983) apparently made up of two DFW3/22 shell-proof, hexagonal pillboxes joined by a gallery, with an open platform at the rear; there are five embrasures for Vickers heavy machine guns, four of them with concrete tables, and a further six loopholes for Bren light machine guns.

St Osyth and Thorrington and others have been reported elsewhere (including to the south of Great Holland). These may mark former Searchlight Sites, as within 2–3,000 yards of the coast these were considered part of the coast defences and furnished with fixed defences, long after such requirements at inland sites had been dropped.

At the beginning of the war the Harwich guns were manned by the Suffolk Heavy Regiment RA, TA, formerly the Essex and Suffolk RGA. In 1940 the regiment was reorganised into the 514th and 515th Coast Regiments RA, the latter unit taking over responsibility for Harwich and most of the neighbouring Essex emergency batteries.

Armoured Trains

After their successful use in previous wars, armoured trains were again used in East Anglia as a way of providing mobility. Countrywide, twelve trains were assembled, six of which were intended for patrolling the East Anglian coast. These trains were made up of two modified steel coal wagons, one at each end, each mounting a 6-pounder QF Hotchkiss gun, a Vickers heavy machine gun, a Boys AT rifle, and twin Bren LMGS on AA mountings. The truck was armoured by pouring 4in (100mm) of concrete between the two steel skins, and sheet-steel shields were added for extra protection at head-height. Two modified drop-side wagons carried supplies, and a Class F4 ex-Great Eastern 2-4-2 locomotive was coupled in the middle of the train. From 28 June 1940 the 1st Armoured Train Group, consisted of trains 'C', 'D' and 'G', was centred on Bury-St-Edmunds. Patrolling commenced on 3 July, with train 'D' based at Manningtree and operating along the Colchester, Clacton, Walton-on-the-Naze, Brightlingsea and Harwich lines. Train 'A' was retained at Shoeburyness for training purposes. Early patrols in south-east Essex appear to have been the responsibility of the 2nd Armoured Train Group, based south of the river, but when two trains from the West Country became available in 1942, one went to Tilbury. Its regular 40 mile-long patrol route took in Pitsea, Romford, Upminster, Hornchurch, West Thurrock junction, Purfleet and thence back to Tilbury, apparently planned to avoid trespassing on London District's territory.

It had been proposed in June 1940 that London District should run an armoured train along the Barking to Tilbury line, with all its vulnerable targets, but nothing was implemented before a moratorium on further such trains was introduced in early July. Colchester Garrison had also produced their own plans and had gone as far as obtaining and modifying two wagons. These ultimately became static pillboxes manned by the Home Guard at North Station. As the regular army units were redeployed to overseas duties, the contribution of the armoured trains in supporting the Home Guard grew in importance. Many of the armoured train units developed their reconnaissance role by acquiring light armoured vehicles. Trains 'C' and 'D' each had three armoured 30cwt Bedford trucks at their respective bases in 1942, armoured with steel plate, and loopholed for use by AT rifles and light automatic weapons. They were also equipped with four Bren-gun carriers, further increasing their flexibility. From 1941, many of the trains had been crewed by Polish troops, but the passive nature of the patrolling, and the diminishing threat of invasion, proved frustrating to these enthusiastic troops who sought action by transferring to the Polish Armoured Division. Only after D-Day were the armoured trains taken out of service.

The GHQ Line

The GHQ Line was the longest and most important of the Stop Lines which were part of Ironside's strategy for delaying the progress of an invading force. It comprised an AT ditch, as far as possible based on existing waterways, backed up by fixed fortifications, pillboxes for infantry armed with rifles and light automatic weapons, and gun-houses for AT guns. All these components were meshed together by fieldworks, minefields, bridges prepared for demolition and AT obstacles. Along the length of the GHQ Line, large towns were given all-round defences and treated as Defended Places, with the ability to hold out independently with their own garrisons. In the case of Essex, Chelmsford enjoyed this status. Other smaller towns and villages might be included in the three categories of Nodal Points which were considered worthy of an enhanced level of defence. Saffron Walden, for instance, was a Category 'B' Nodal Point, taking in the defences at Audley End, flanked by Category 'C' Nodal Points at Wendens Ambo and Littlebury.

The GHQ Line enters Essex at Pitsea Marsh with a concentration of a dozen pillboxes, of which at least nine survive, centred on Bowers Gifford. There being no natural water obstacle, AT ditches were dug from Vange Creek northwards as far as the river Crouch near Battlesbridge, a distance of some 6 miles (9.5km), supported by pillboxes at Nevendon, North Benfleet and elsewhere. From Battlesbridge to just north of Sandon, where the line met the river Chelmer, a distance of around 12 miles (19km), the AT ditch criss-crossed the (old) A130 road.

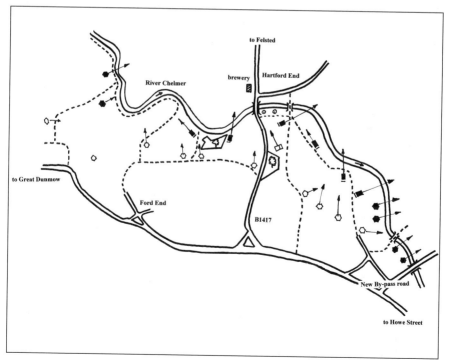

Figure 8 Sketch-map of a section of GHQ Line at Hartford End, which includes the four main designs of pillbox utilised in this line, and their orientation.

A continuous belt of pillboxes was therefore formed with a heavy density of shell-proof type DFW3/24 pillboxes and DFW3/28a AT emplacements, fronting or enfilading the ditch, and a rear line of bullet-proof type DFW3/22 and twenty-four pillboxes. Particularly vulnerable points such as the Hanningfield crossroads were defended by heavier concentrations of pillboxes (a total of eleven in that particular case). The line then followed the Chelmer for a short way before an AT ditch carved its way across the north of the city from Cuton Hall to regain the river at Broomfield. The next section of line, running north from Broomfield to Hartford End, follows the river with the same pattern of forward shell-proof pillboxes and a rear line of bullet-proof ones. Hartford End retains a heavy density of pillboxes with spigot mortars as well. From Hartford End the line continues to follow the river, recorded in 1940 as being 12ft (3.5m) wide with banks 10ft (3m) high, past Great Dunmow up to Duton Hill where it leaves the main channel to follow a stream as far as Cherry Green, then crossing the high ground as far as Debden Water in order to gain the valley of the Cam at Newport. From here the river and railway mark the course of the line northwards, with mainly shell-proof pillboxes along the riverside, and bullet-proof ones in a back line. Passing Audley End House the line exits the county at Great Chesterford, where an AT emplacement near the railway station has been removed.

Reflecting the compacted timescale of its construction in the months from May–November 1940, the designs of the component fortifications on the GHQ Line through Essex are drawn from the limited suite of drawings issued by Department 3 of the Fortifications and Works Directorate (DFW3) at the War Office. In fact only four basic designs were used for the 200-odd pillboxes and gun-houses of the GHQ Line in Essex. This will have made it easier for the contractors to assemble the reusable form-work on site, and also to source the prefabricated concrete loopholes which could be inserted after the relevant pour. The standard AT emplacement was the DFW3/28a which consisted of two elements. One was a chamber for the 2-pounder AT gun, accommodating the gun's forward-facing spade-foot in sockets under the wide embrasure, and its pivot in a further socket in the middle of the floor of the gun-house. The other was a separate chamber alongside with three loopholes for Bren Guns. The gun could be introduced through a wide opening in the rear wall which would then be blocked with sandbags.

Owing to the scarcity of the 2-pounder gun, however, some of these emplacements were built with a narrower forward embrasure and a concrete plinth with nine fixing bolts to take the 6-pounder QF Hotchkiss gun which had first been designed for use on Edwardian battleships as an anti-boarding gun, and then recycled as the armament for the First World War male tank. Numbers of these guns were issued from Woolwich Arsenal but solid AT shot was in short supply. By July a dozen or so of these weapons had been issued in Essex to be manned by 5th RHA Regiment, but at the end of August most of these guns had been redeployed to the coast for beach defence, with the rest following before Christmas, and the RHA handing over to the 6th Defence Regiment RA. Both models of these AT emplacements could be built without the second Bren chamber. In at least one case, possibly because its situation's limited visibility, the pedestal for the Hotchkiss

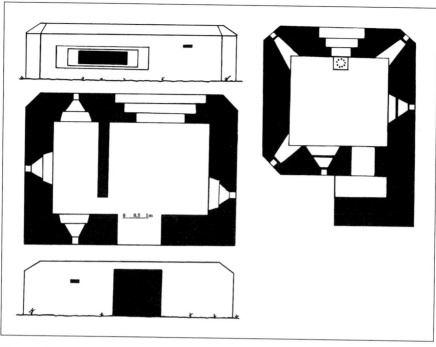

Figure 9 Designs of anti-tank gun emplacements: (left) standard DFW3/28a for 2-pounder AT gun, at Hanningfield crossroads, Duton Hill, Dunmow, Hartford End, Little Waltham, Sandon, Battlesbridge etc. (Plan and elevations after Colin Alexander); (right) modified DFW3/28 for 6-pounder QF Hotchkiss gun at Chappel Viaduct, Wakes Colne (TL897285).

91 Pitsea, Bowers Hall: DFW3/28a emplacement for 2-pounder AT gun, one of around a dozen on the GHQ line in Essex (TR751875).

gun was installed outside the emplacement. In 1941 the spigot mortar, or Blacker Bombard, was made available as a short-range (and high risk) AT weapon, and their pre-installed pedestals, with or without pits, can be seen. One at Wendens Ambo has been excavated; another, outside the Victory public house in Saffron Walden, has only the domed top and stainless steel pintle showing.

The next most common pillbox type was the shell-proof DFW3/24 which can be seen all along the line. Hexagonal with the rear face, containing the doorway flanked by rifle-loops, longer than the others, this had five loopholes for Bren Guns, housing a section of eight to ten men. The walls were 42in (105cm) thick. Another version of the DFW3/24 had thinner walls but was otherwise identical. The other common type in the GHQ Line in Essex was a shell-proof rectangular pillbox with three loopholes for Bren Guns. The entrance was protected by a loopholed blast-wall. One example at Sparrows End, north of Newport, has a concrete roof linking the triple-looped blast-wall to the main structure, forming an extension. The pillbox generally seen as the archetype was the DFW3/22, a bullet-proof regular hexagon with rifle-loops in five faces and an entrance flanked by one or two pistol-loops in the sixth. Examples of a local variation of this type, with a dog-legged tunnel entrance and six, often armoured, loopholes, can be found in Essex.

Many of the pillboxes were camouflaged, some at Hanningfield and Sandon having their sharp outlines broken up by upturned buckets of concrete on their roofs and dollops of concrete spread on their brick form-work to soften the colour. One at Tilty is hidden in a barn with loopholes cut through the weatherboarding, and another at Chickney has an overhanging roof extension to disguise its tell-tale hexagonal shape from above. Most would have been hidden under camouflage netting or foliage.

92 Broomfield: a shell-proof pillbox to DFW3/24 design for five Bren Guns firing through the narrowed loopholes, and rifles through the stepped embrasures either side of the entrance (TL714095).

93 Sandon: a rectangular shell-proof pillbox for three Bren Guns, with a blast-wall containing a fourth loophole offset from the entrance; another design common on the GHQ Line (TL740039).

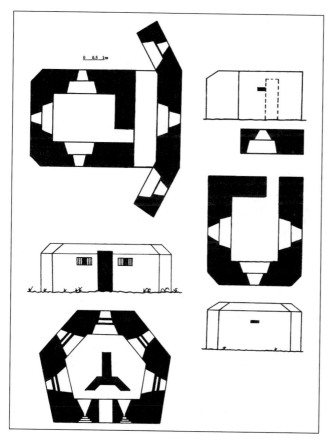

Figure 10 Designs of pillboxes on the GHQ Line: (upper left) Sparrows End (TL520361) shell-proof rectangular pillbox with blast-wall extended as a porch with three loopholes; (lower left) Howe Street (TL695126) DFW3/24 standard shell-proof pillbox; (right) shell-proof rectangular pillbox with blast-wall at Pitsea, Hartford End, Rettendon, Broomfield, Littlebury, etc. (Plan and elevations after Colin Alexander)

94 Little Waltham: a local Eastern Command design, basically an adaptation of the DFW3/22 with a tunnel entrance (TL701135).

95 Hanningfield Crossroads Downhouse: a standard DFW3/22 pillbox with camouflage added to break up the silhouette (TL745015).

One defence work peculiar to the line east of Chelmsford was a low open triangular section-post accessed via a trench. It must be remembered that the entire line was intended as a series of prepared positions not permanently garrisoned fortifications. The generals hated the defensive ideology that went with the notion of the line, and did all they could to avoid manning, or even completing, it. Nevertheless, it represents a remarkable achievement, and many of its most interesting and complete stretches survive in the Essex countryside. As a prepared fall-back position it was not manned permanently, but local units of 15 Division were allocated to garrison particular sectors. As Home Guard units became better-trained and better-armed then they too assumed responsibility for manning the line and its associated Nodal Points.

The Eastern Command Line

What had originally been conceived as a purely local Stop Line protecting Colchester by defending the line of the river Colne soon assumed a far greater importance as Ironside's strategy called for further barriers between the Coastal Crust and the GHQ Line.

Here it was Eastern Command's responsibility to plan a Command Line, to be implemented by XI Corps in the south and, after the Dunkirk evacuation, II Corps in the northern half of East Anglia. From Wivenhoe the river Colne provided an adequate AT barrier as far as the Chappel railway viaduct at Wakes Colne. The line then headed north following the railway line to Bures, which was established as a Nodal Point. From here the river Stour, with pillboxes on the Essex bank, acted as the AT obstacle up to Sudbury where the line entered Suffolk temporarily, re-entering Essex above Brundon as far as a point west of Long Melford, whence the line runs up through Suffolk, into Norfolk and on to the Wash.

Essex was defended by the 15th Infantry Division, made up of second-line Scottish territorial units. The two divisional RE Field Companies (279th and 280th) carried out much of the initial work, supervising civilian contractors based in Birch. Pillbox designs were originated in the offices of the Eastern Command CRE in Colchester and included an AT emplacement virtually indistinguishable from the DFW3/28 and

96 River Stour: Eastern Command Line south of Sudbury, the large shell-proof version of the CRE Colchester design with its central LAA platform (TM882402).

97 River Stour: south of Sudbury, the central LAA position in one of the CRE
Colchester-designed pillboxes on the Eastern Command Line.

Figure 11 Pillbox designs
from the office of the
Commander Royal
Engineers, Eastern Command,
Colchester: (upper left)
hexagonal bullet-proof
pillbox, possibly to CRE1094
design, used on the GHQ
and Eastern Command Lines
and elsewhere in Essex and
Suffolk;(upper right) version
of CRE1094 design with
covered gallery and open
LAA pit, used particularly on
the Eastern Command Line
in Essex and Suffolk; (lower
left) hexagonal shell-proof
pillbox possibly to CRE1113
design, used particularly
on the Eastern Command
Line in Essex and Suffolk;
(lower right) Mersea Island
(TM073154) variation of
CRE1113 shell-proof pillbox
with two embrasures for
heavy machine guns and four,
instead of the normal six, for
Bren light machine guns.

28a, but tending to incorporate more adaptations to suit the site, and pillboxes in the shape of regular hexagons. One of these was similar to the DFW3/22 with a tunnel entrance; another was a shell-proof version of this, plus variations of both with central open platforms for LAA weapons. All these may be seen along the line but there are interesting concentrations of examples around the Chappel Viaduct, with more at Henny Street and Rodbridge Corner. Standard DFW3/22 pillboxes, some with almost full-height loopholed porches, may also be found, a good example surviving at Fordham (TL929270).

The River Line

Inserted between the Eastern Command Line and the GHQ Line was another barrier, sometimes known as the River Line. Starting in Maldon, it followed the Blackwater as far as Witham where a string of three spigot mortar positions along the old Maldon railway, now a footpath, facing Little Braxted, would suggest that the line swung north-west to follow the river Brain as far as Braintree. A pillbox at White Notley, destroyed by British Rail despite the pleas of the villagers, must mark its route, and the report of an Allan-Williams turret on the eastern side of Braintree points to the line rejoining the Blackwater briefly, prior to swinging north-west up the river Pant.

River crossings at Shalford and Walthams Cross are defended by pillboxes, as were others at Church End and Great Bardfield, where there were also road-blocks, spigot mortars and a camouflaged defensive position built around the base of a tree. There is another Allan-Williams turret at Finchingfield but from there it is difficult to follow the line, there being no obvious linear obstacle, before picking it up again with a pillbox at Stambourne. From here the railway may have provided the necessary link to the Stour at Wixoe. The River Line then ran north into Suffolk, passing Kedington,

98 Walthams Cross: a pillbox to a CRE Colchester design, guarding a crossing of the river Pant on the River Line (TL694310).

with surviving pillboxes at Little Thurlow and Little Bradley, where the line appears to terminate. A pillbox at Steeple Bumpstead and Home Guard explosives and inflammables stores at the Bulls Bridge Farm crossroads and at Cowlinge, for instance, suggest that most villages and minor road junctions were also defended.

The Stanier Line

The Harwich defences were begun in late May 1940, and inspected by Major General Taylor, Inspector of Fortifications, at the end of June. He found beach defences along the coast and landward defences consisting of an inner ring of pillboxes, road-blocks, AT blocks and barbed wire from Parkeston Quay, across the golfcourse to Ramsey Creek, then past All Saints' church in Upper Dovercourt and thence to the sea. This was known as the Stanier Line and a line of AT blocks, now heavily overgrown, is just discernible north of the church. The line ran along what is now Laurel Avenue. Where the public footpath meets the corner of the schoolfield stands a pillbox, one of the usual Essex types of DFW3/22 with a tunnel entrance. Just inside the gate to the Sixth Form College is a hard-standing on a rise which dominates the southern part of the line, and this could mark the spot in the general area where a gun-house is known to have stood. Farther out from the line more defended localities were constructed.

The Back Line

The Back Line was adapted from an earlier plan by XI Corps to seal off the Colne-Stour peninsular by continuing the Colchester defences up the railway line to Manningtree, where a pillbox survives (TM099327). Using mainly fieldworks, this line was being consolidated, along the whole length of the East Anglian coast, by October 1940. The intent was to link up all the eastward-flowing rivers to create boxes from which an enemy force would be unable to break out. To the south the line ran from Colchester down to Maldon, on to the Crouch and then turned inland, stopping just short of the GHQ Line at Rettendon. From Manningtree the line ran northwards across the neck of the Shotley Peninsular to Ipswich, itself a Nodal Point on the river Orwell, and thence on through Suffolk into Norfolk.

The Outer London Line

There were three concentric rings of fortifications defending London, the outermost of which, Line A, ran through boroughs which formerly belonged to Essex. It began at the Beam, at the time the eastern boundary of the Ford works. At Dagenham East station (TQ504851) a long line of AT blocks runs alongside the railway, continuing through to the Pumping Station at Dagenham Beam Bridge with a pillbox, now partially buried, on the angle at TQ512850. Another long line of AT blocks runs along the south side of the Chadwell Heath to Romford railway line at Crow Lane (TQ487877). The line follows the river Rom toward Debden station, crossing the river Roding some way to the north-east, a stream probably marking the course of Line A as far as Centenary Walk in Epping Forest. Near Jacks Hill the AT ditch can be seen as it heads off past Ripley Grange, to cross the Epping road (TL432001 and

99 Parvills: north of Cobbins Brook, an octagonal shell-proof pillbox with eight loopholes for Bren Guns, a loopholed, covered porch, and a central platform for a LAA mounting, one of a type seen only on the Outer London Line 'A' (TL427037).

431006), south of Amresbury Banks, thence following the stream east of Copped Hall. From here on the line is marked by large, octagonal DFW3/27-type pillboxes, spaced every 0.5 miles or so, with crossing points on the ditch consisting of AT blocks and hedgehogs of AT rails set in concrete. Line A then curves around through farmland to Nazeing Marsh and the river Lea at Kings Weir (TL373053) where it enters Hertfordshire. Between Copped Hall and Kings Weir, there survive around a dozen of these octagonal pillboxes.

Nodal Points

By June 1940 a number of towns had been identified as important communications hubs, meriting their own all-round defences. Although the river Colne had been chosen as a Stop Line it covered only Colchester's northern and eastern perimeter so a more complete ring of AT ditches, AT blocks, pillboxes and roadblocks was constructed around the rest of the town, taking in both railway stations and the barracks. South of the town, nearly 4.5 miles (7km) of AT ditch, 20ft (6m) wide and 10ft (3m) deep, was dug. Some 120 pillboxes were erected as part of the town defences with more as outliers, and hundreds of AT blocks. Only a handful of these pillboxes have survived, as well as a few AT blocks, some of which can be seen on the riverbank near the castle. These fortifications constituted one of the earliest such AT islands in the country.

As the flow of new tanks and artillery from the factories began to speed up, and Alanbrooke had been tasked with being Home Forces' new broom, the emphasis on linear fixed defences was shifted to a defence in depth based on defended localities, often little more than elaborate road-blocks, and the AT islands which were now to be redesignated Nodal Points. Chelmsford was a Category 'A' Nodal Point astride the GHQ Line, defended by eleven major road-blocks, some of which were developed into defended localities designed for all-round defence, straddling the main routes into the town – Broomfield Road, Writtle Road, Moulsham Street etc. – whilst others controlled river-bridges nearer the centre. The most impressive was that at the Army and Navy Junction where large numbers of pyramidal AT pimples funnelled attackers into the killing grounds, watched over by eight spigot mortars. These weapons had an optimum range of around 100 yards and could fire a 14lb (6.5kg) anti-personnel bomb, or a 20lb (9kg) anti-tank projectile. It could be fired from a concrete pedestal or from a field mounting of a tubular steel tripod with spade grips. Several of the pedestal mountings, or 'thimbles', can still be traced. The east of the town, the most likely direction of attack, was defended by the GHQ Line itself, and the rest of the circuit was made up of fieldworks. A token cluster of AT pimples survives on Broomfield Road.

Audley End was part of the Saffron Walden Category 'B' Nodal Point, ensuring that the bridges over the river Cam were denied to the enemy. Chambers were excavated in them so that they could be mined, and they were further protected by AT blocks and pillboxes. Five bridges, including the Adam and Stable bridges, were treated in this way. The local defences were further strengthened by the Home Guard's introduction of musketry loopholes into some of the garden walls.

Chappel Viaduct at Wakes Colne on the Eastern Command Line was another Category 'C' Nodal Point marking the point where the Colne meets the railway line, representing the Eastern Command Line's linking of the rivers Colne and Stour. Under the viaduct are an AT emplacement, a DFW 3/22 pillbox, lines of AT blocks sealing the gap between the river and the railway embankment, and two spigot mortars, with other related structures nearby.

Airfield Defences

Airfields were seen as being particularly welcoming to enemy airborne troops from the start of the invasion scare, and directions went out to fortify them against enemy landings. A measure of the Air Ministry's anxiety was their invitation to the army's Director General of Fortifications and Works, Major General Taylor, to produce a plan maximising the resources available. His solution was to focus largely on location, giving those airfields near ports and other likely targets the maximum provision of fixed defences. His recommendation for these Class I airfields, which included Rochford, Hornchurch and Fairlop, was the provision of twenty-four to thirty-two pillboxes, a trio of Pickett-Hamilton forts, and a garrison of 274 regular troops. Some of these pillboxes would face outwards against enemy attacks from outside the perimeter, and others inwards opposing enemy landings on the flying field.

North Weald, Debden and Stapleford Tawney, as Class IIa airfields, were nevertheless subsequently brought into the Pickett-Hamilton programme but had not been given projected dates for the installation of their forts by early 1941, and Fairlop, whilst listed as Class I, appears to have missed out altogether in the end. Rochford was scheduled, as 'Southend', to receive its forts in February 1941, in the second tranche of installations along with Hornchurch. These front-line airfields had garri-

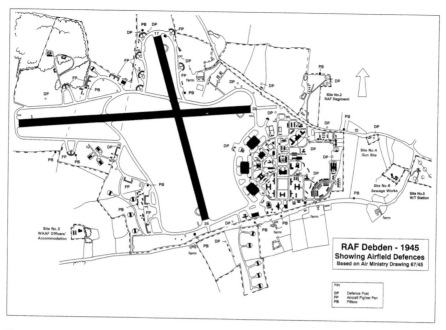

Figure 12 The defences of RAF Debden in 1945, where several of the pillboxes still remain. (Drawing courtesy of Paul Francis and ARG/AiX)

sons of regular troops: nine officers and 300 men of the 13th Battalion Royal Fusiliers at Fairlop, for instance. At Hornchurch were 258 men of the 70th Battalion Essex Regiment, probably a depot unit assembled for home defence duties, with the entire 10th Battalion encamped a mile away at Hacton House. Details of RAF ground-crew, cooks and administrative personnel were also organised as ground-defence troops under the command of their own officers.

Acting on Taylor's recommendations large numbers of pillboxes were constructed on airfields and radar stations, mainly of the thin-walled DFW3/22 type still to be seen at Hornchurch, Debden, Rochford and North Weald. These were generally laid out in two concentric lines giving linear protection against overland assault and also covering the flying field. By early 1941, most of the projected Pickett-Hamilton forts had been installed. Each consisted of a concrete, loopholed cylinder with the facility to be raised and lowered inside a slightly larger cylinder dug into the ground. When in the down position the roof was at ground level, and contained an entrance hatch. Action stations saw the crew of two sprint across the grass, entering through the hatch and raising the fort by means of pneumatic pressure from a compressed air bottle (or, failing that, manually). In a raised position, the trio of forts installed at the junctions of runway could command the landing area with automatic fire. The idea was that while friendly aircraft were landing the forts were sunken, and as the enemy attempted to land were raised. Captivated by such gimmicks, Churchill was greatly impressed, but although 335 were constructed by the New Kent Company of Ashford (Kent) and installed on over 100 airfields, they were considered to be of dubious reliability and of little practical use. A Pickett-Hamilton fort in the up-position survives at North Weald.

Figure 13 Plans of pillboxes found on airfields: (upper left) standard DFW3/22 pillbox found at Canewdon (CH radar site), Debden, Hornchurch, North Weald, Rochford and Stapleford Tawney; (upper right) FC Construction or 'Mushroom' pillbox found at Fairlop, North Weald and Rochford; (lower) unique octagonal variant at Debden (TL573344) of the thickened hexagonal pillboxes found at Debden, North Weald, Great Sampford and Stapleford Tawney.

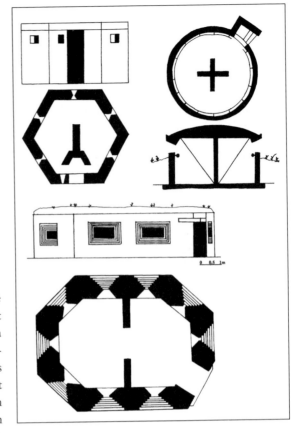

By mid-1941, then, those airfields considered the most vulnerable had been given a fair measure of concrete protection, Rochford having as many as fifty pillboxes, but airborne attacks by German paratroopers, culminating in those on Crete, fuelled the Air Ministry's anxieties. The RAF Regiment was formed with airfield defence among its roles, and new instructions were issued to inform the planning and construction of fixed defences, the only context in which such defences were still considered viable. Pillboxes were to be shell-proof, with walls at least 42in (1.07m) in thickness, and to have fewer loopholes, with better-defined fields of fire.

Some of the earlier pillboxes at North Weald have had their walls thickened to meet this new specification. Examples of these shell-proof pillboxes can be seen at Great Sampford, Debden, North Weald and Stapleford Tawney. The majority of their loopholes were fitted with Turnbull Mounts for machine guns. The linear layout was to be modified by the establishment of defended localities dominating the airfield's approaches. The various groups of defenders, by now comprising RAF personnel, regular troops, Home Guard detachments, AA gunners and even troops of light tanks, were now allocated specific sectors.

This is clearly demonstrated by the layout of the defences of Hornchurch in autumn 1941. Here there are fourteen distinct defence areas controlled from a new BHQ located between some of the fighter-pens which ringed the airfield. Whilst some of the earlier pillboxes were relegated to use as dummies or decoys, new structures appeared. This BHQ (11008/41) was a purpose-built bunker with underground telephone exchange and messengers' room, with a concrete cupola at ground-level

100 Great Sampford: this airfield-defence pillbox appears to have been thickened sometime after its original construction, with the result that the embrasures have become dangerously splayed (TL615360).

101 Debden: the inside of a loophole showing a Turnbull mount fitted. Designed to be shell-proof from the start, the loophole avoids the excessive splay of later modifications.

with a 360-degree horizontal observation slit, enabling the garrison commander to control the ground defence. Examples were built at Stapleford Tawney, Hornchurch and Rochford but have all been demolished.

Prior to this design a number of improvised BHQs had been built, one surviving at Hornchurch consisting of a hexagonal, loopholed turret over a sunken bunker. As well as the more substantial pillboxes, a radically-new design of cantilevered pillbox appeared. Built by FC Construction, it was known variously as the 'Oakington', 'Fairlop' or, referencing its appearance, the 'Mushroom' pillbox. A domed roof canopy was raised on central fan-shaped supports over a circular pit. This allowed two machine guns, clamped to a circular rail which ran round the lip of the pit, to enjoy 360-degree fields of fire. Examples of this design survive at Fairlop, North Weald and Rochford. Even after successive reductions in pillbox numbers, Debden finished the war with twenty defence posts, presumably fieldworks, and eleven pillboxes including several hexagonal and one octagonal shell-proof type. Hornchurch was furnished with Tett Turrets, cylindrical two-man tubes buried in the ground with a revolving concrete collar for a light machine gun. Two can still be seen and more are reported buried in hedgerows. In June 1941 it was decided to deploy eighty-seven light tanks, from re-equipped armoured formations, in troops of three with RAC crews, to fighter airfields. Great Sampford, Debden, Stapleford Tawney, Fairlop, North Weald and Hornchurch were amongst the twenty-nine airfields which benefited. These real tanks supplemented improvised armoured vehicles which had been cobbled together in the early part of the war. These included Beaverettes, lightly-armoured, open-topped cars based on the Standard 14hp automobile, and named for Lord Beaverbrook, Minister of Aircraft Production and a friend of Churchill. Armadillos were flatbed trucks with

102 Rochford: an FC Construction cantilevered pillbox giving all-round uninterrupted fields of fire (TQ865895).

a superstructure of wooden boxes filled with pebbles surrounding a central open LAA mounting. Neither offered much protection against aerial attack.

Radar Site Defences

RDF or radar was one of the great secrets of the early years of the war, and sites were seen as being particularly vulnerable, especially after it was anticipated that the removal by commandos of German radar equipment from the Bruneval site would provoke tit-for-tat raids. Marconi's factories were well-guarded but the working CH radar sites were remote and exposed. Canewdon, spread over 1 square mile (256ha) was ringed by over twenty pillboxes. These are mainly DFW3/22 type, one with a Hazzard 20mm LAA cannon mount on its roof.

Defence of Other Vulnerable Points (VPS)

These could be anything from road junctions to munitions factories and were often guarded by dedicated detachments of troops or Home Guardsmen, and might be given fixed defences. For close-defence and general security, Hoffmann's ball-bearing factory was provided with two brick guardposts with loopholes and concrete roofs, manned by the company's own Home Guard unit. North Weald Redoubt was used as a test-bed for communications equipment, and was provided with two 'Allan-Williams' turrets. These were domed, two-man, revolving turrets with lmgs on ground and air mountings. There are other examples of these at Nazeing and at Finchingfield. Very often points on the transport network were given protection, examples being the pillboxes at both Colchester railway stations and at Frinton. In the centre of Great

103 Canewdon: a DFW3/22 pillbox with an open upper platform with a Hazzard mount for an Oerlikon LAA gun (TQ903943).

104 North Weald Redoubt: an Allan-Williams turret, one of a pair added on the rampart of this Victorian London mobilisation centre. Each turret could be revolved through 360 degrees on a racer, had a crew of two and was armed with a Lewis Gun firing through the lower hatch, and a Bren Gun on an LAA mount through the upper (TL505039 and 506039).

Saling (TL703254) a small, square semi-sunken pillbox straddles the underside of a garden wall, commanding the road junction but also possibly protecting the approach to Saling Grove which may have housed a HQ of some sort.

Local Units and Their Deployment

The two regular battalions of the Essex Regiment both fought overseas, the 1st Battalion in North Africa and Syria before being posted to India, the 5th Battalion with the 5th Infantry Division in North Africa, Palestine, Italy and north-west Europe from July 1944. The other three territorial battalions were stationed in the United Kingdom for the duration, as were the newly raised 9th and 10th Battalions. Another new battalion, the 19th, served as part of the Sudan Defence Force between 1943 and 1945. The 8th Battalion was converted into the 153rd Armoured Regiment (RAC) in 1941 and served in the 34th Tank Brigade with the 21st Army Group in north-west Europe from 1944 to 1945, along with the 2nd Battalion, Essex Regiment and two former Essex Yeomanry artillery units, the 147th and 191st Field Regiments RA. The 191st Field Regiment had been formed in 1942 with cadres from both the Essex and the Hertfordshire former yeomanry field regiments. The original former Essex Yeomanry field regiment, the 104th, fought in Palestine, North Africa at El Alamein, and in Italy. One of its batteries was detached as the nucleus of a new 14th Field Regiment, RHA, serving in Burma. Some of the county's AA units also served overseas, the 17th LAA and the 59th HAA Regiment in North Africa and Italy, the 82nd HAA Regiment in Norway and Gibraltar, and the 64th and 65th Searchlight Regiments in north-west Europe after D-Day, for instance.

The Essex Home Guard

In May 1940 the Local Defence Volunteers were raised from the civilian population, and by mid-July King George VI was paying visits to Essex LDV units (who had apparently received uniforms but not weapons). Their title was soon changed to the Home Guard, and twenty-six battalions were raised in Essex (ESX), affiliated to the Essex Regiment and wearing the regimental cap-badge. Seven of those battalions were in boroughs now part of Greater London. Over the next six months weapons, uniforms and equipment were issued and a regular programme of training was instigated. Gradually, 12-bore shotguns gave way to rifles and machine guns, and Home Guardsmen took their place manning fixed defences, guarding vulnerable points and monitoring movement through road-blocks and check-points.

In the larger towns significant numbers could be recruited, often at their workplaces, with training based on company-sized units, maximising the available expertise of instructors. The whole of 'J' Company, 6th Battalion, for instance, was recruited from Marconi in Chelmsford, with a HQ in Mildmay Road, now the St John Ambulance base. The 8th Battalion in Colchester numbered 2,000 men. Towns were also more likely to raise specialist units, both Colchester and Chelmsford having AA units (see below); a Home Guard Transport Column with HQ at Chipping Ongar had troops in Romford, Chelmsford and Colchester (Nos 2005, 2009 and 2017 respectively), and even No. 22 Home Guard Bomb Disposal Company had been formed in Chelmsford from 1941, for example. In rural areas a battalion would be much more widely scattered, with its companies based on small towns, and its platoons distributed across a wide scatter of villages, making larger formation training extremely difficult to manage.

Each area drew up a Defence Plan which laid out the forces available and their deployment, the emergency measures to be taken in the event of an invasion, and the logistical organisation necessary to feed and supply military and civilian populations alike. Regulars, Home Guard, civilian police, medical services, council officers, ARP and voluntary organisations all had their prescribed roles and responsibilities, were drilled in the effective execution of those functions and were represented on every local Invasion Committee. Home Guard units in the west of the county trained in Hainault Forest and Weald Park, Brentwood. Units also ran their own local training facilities such as the leadership school at Crown Hall, Rayleigh. In the east, Bradwell offered camping facilities alongside the RAF ranges, with another site at Hockley being used by units in the Southend/Rayleigh area. In the less populous areas, training was carried out in smaller pockets in convenient woods and creeks. As new skills were gained and the regular units were shipped out to fight overseas, then the Home Guard assumed responsibility for manning Coast Artillery batteries and all types of AA batteries. From the static force of 1940, they were trained as mobile troops equipped with a wide range of weaponry. As well as the spigot mortar, or Blacker Bombard, there were Smith Guns and Northover Projectors as well as a whole range of AT mines and anti-personnel grenades.

105 Wendens Ambo: the spigot mortar pit excavated in his front garden by Robert Alsos, fitted with a replica Blacker Bombard loaded with a 20lb practice bomb. When in action, these bombs would have been stored in the lockers built into the sides of the pit. Normally both mortar and ammunition would have been kept nearby in a purpose-built explosives and inflammables store. (Photograph by David Bygraves)

The Smith Gun was a 3in (75mm) gun which could be towed into action by an Austin Seven car. On coming into action, the gun was unhitched and turned on its side, one wheel becoming a traversing platform and the other, overhead cover. This gun, incidentally, was issued to the RAF Regiment whose ammunition depots felt it advisable to segregate its shells as they were found to be so unstable.

In 1940 the Home Guard was encouraged to stockpile Molotov Cocktails as AT weapons. Very soon glass self-igniting phosphorous (SIP) grenades, fired from a drainpipe-like tube called a Northover Projector, had been substituted as a more easily-handled alternative, with an impressive range of 200 yards.

Training on all these weapons, known collectively as 'sub-artillery', had to be carried out regularly. It has to be remembered that many of these men, and from 1943 women as well, had already worked a long day in field or factory prior to turning out for drill-nights or night-time guard duties. If the larger towns enjoyed better facilities then smaller communities marshalled their resources as well as they could. At Burnham-on-Crouch the drill hall provided a HQ, but in many villages the CO's house had to do, as at Wendens Ambo, for instance, where the 'Beeches', with a spigot mortar pit in its front garden, served. In Newport the HQ of No. 2 Platoon, 'C' Company, 12th Battalion, was an old railway carriage in the garden of the CO's house, 'Willmary'.

The Essex Auxiliary Units

One aspect of Home Guard activity which remained secret for decades after the war was the work of the Auxiliary Units, also referred to as the British Resistance

Organisation. At the height of the invasion crisis small groups of men were recruited in the front-line areas to be trained as guerrilla fighters. The former Polar explorer Captain Andrew Croft, returning from the Norway campaign, was soon recruited by Colonel Gubbins, a promoter of irregular warfare at the War Office. Croft was sent home to his father's vicarage at Kelvedon to organise a network of Auxiliary Units in East Anglia. He immediately set about organising patrols in Essex, at least twenty of which are definitely known, and stockpiling arms and explosives at the vicarage. He tried to recruit men such as gamekeepers and poachers who could live off the land, but butchers also figure prominently in the roll-call. Captain Smith in Danbury was given a co-ordinating role, operating over a wide area as an Intelligence Officer. In the event of an invasion the patrols' role would have been to go to ground, to let the invading troops roll over the top of them, and then to harass the enemy by killing sentries and despatch-riders, by sabotaging supplies and reinforcements, and by generally creating opportunist mayhem. Each cell or patrol of seven or eight men was unknown to its neighbours and essentially independent, only intermittently receiving orders from an area organiser or by radio from a transmitter whose whereabouts was unknown.

Patrols would operate from specially prepared underground hides or Operational Bases (OBs). Each OB was equipped with beds, weapons and explosives, sanitation facilities and stocks of food and water intended to last around a fortnight. There was a standard design for these hides which resembled a buried Nissen hut, accessed by a disguised hatch, with a further emergency exit, but some examples adapted this model to local conditions. One OB, in Weeley Woods, was more substantial than the norm, being an artificial cave of brick and concrete dug into the side of a hill in a thicket of brambles. Others, perhaps in more built-up areas, might be underneath existing buildings. The Maldon patrol had been formed by the local butcher who closed his business to take on other catering work. While the shop became a munitions store, the patrol's OB was excavated under Beeleigh Mill. Here the usual corrugated-iron sheets were used to arch over the hide but the customary brick end-walls were apparently missing, and the escape tunnel was at high level, possibly to access the mill-race. This OB was excavated by the ECC Archaeology Unit in 2007.

At Little Leighs the OB was entered by trapdoor, but successive attempts to construct underground hides in the marshes of the Blackwater Estuary failed due to flooding. Despite the intense secrecy surrounding the location of the hides, wandering schoolboys inevitably made exciting discoveries but could usually be sufficiently intimidated into keeping their mouths shut. Not so a courting couple who chanced across a trapdoor entry at Great Leighs, forcing the OB to be abandoned. An OB at Trinity Woods, Hockley, near Rochford (TQ856937) is recorded in the DOB Project database. Patrols were usually expected to have fashioned two or three hides in their area of operation in order to prolong their resistance if one were to be discovered.

Some local organisers, such as one on Canvey Island, were school-masters who often recruited likely lads with Boy Scout experience, who knew their local area, but were as yet too young to join the forces. Many of these boys learned skills which later took them into the commandos. Other patrols in Essex included three around

Colchester, Chelmsford, Southminster, Rayleigh and Brightlingsea. Units north of the Thames were notionally attached to 202 Battalion, Home Guard, with HQ at Earls Colne, and later at Witham, mainly to establish their military credentials in the event of capture and the charge of being *francs-tireurs* (free shooters) which would entail automatic execution. It is doubtful, especially considering the later fate of captured commandos, if this would have made a scrap of difference – nor did anyone appear to have thought about the likely reprisals which would have been carried out against local civilians.

Official thinking was that patrols might survive for a few weeks before being tracked down and eliminated. Patrols were sometimes invited to test the Regulars' efficiency. One such exercise involved a group of auxiliaries from the Harwich area testing the defences of the Stanier Line by infiltrating it at night and securing souvenirs from supposedly secure areas. The Regulars were duly embarrassed as the auxiliaries turned in their trophies the next morning. Patrol leaders were sent on courses at Coleshill House in Berkshire, the national training centre, returning to share their new experience with their colleagues. One of the unfortunate side-effects of the secrecy surrounding the Auxiliary Units was that the sites of the OBs were forgotten. Only when houses were being built over an OB in a wood in Tendring, for instance, did a former auxiliary fortunately recall the large amounts of explosives he had buried there. Secrecy remained in force until the publication, in 1976, of a book about the Auxiliary Units' work, but even as late as 2000 many auxiliaries had still not broken cover.

Air Operations and Airfields

At the outbreak of war there were just three active RAF airfields in Essex: Debden, Hornchurch and North Weald. By 1940, Fairlop (Hainault Farm), Rochford and Stapleford Abbotts/Tawney had been added to these. Despite some improvements to Stapleford's perimeter track, for instance, these were all grass fields, used for fighter operations. Only after the outbreak of war was North Weald provided with two paved runways, the first to be laid at a fighter airfield. In 1940 Debden underwent a major refurbishment by W. and C. French, who put down two concrete runways, 4,800 and 3,950ft (1,460 and 1,200m) in length, and added a Bellman hangar, eleven Blister hangars, fourteen twin blast-pens and sixty-four PSP/steel-mat hard-standings, in order to be able to disperse aircraft around the edges of the airfield.

Debden, Hornchurch and North Weald were all bombed heavily during the Battle of Britain, and the centralised grouping of their pre-war hangars and technical areas was to maximise the resultant damage. Hornchurch was forced to move its operations room off-site to the half-timbered Lambourne Hall between Abridge and Romford. RAF squadrons were rotated during the heavy fighting of autumn 1940, but then settled down to a new organisation based on Fighter Wings. The three 'Eagle' squadrons made up of US volunteers operated out of Debden, and when the USA entered the war they were transferred to the US 4th Fighter Wing of the VIIIth USAAF in September 1942.

106 Debden: a Blister hangar, one of three survivors of the six installed early in the war.

Bradwell Bay had operated from the 1930s as a landing ground servicing the air-to-ground firing ranges of Dengie Flats. Work started early in 1941 to build a new fighter airfield with three concrete runways but very few permanent buildings. Apart from the watch office – which, according to the Air Ministry plan, was built to a design intended for night-fighter stations (12096/41) – there were only a Bellman hangar, twelve dispersed Blister hangars and pens and hard-standings for the aircraft. Many of the larger local houses were requisitioned to provide instant messes, living quarters and HQ buildings. Bradwell Bay was the only fighter station to be provided with FIDO, a system for burning off low-lying mist enabling aircraft to land in relative safety. Perforated pipes were run along the side of the runway to carry petrol whose fumes could be ignited to raise the air temperature.

Great Sampford was added as a satellite of Debden in 1942, but proved unsuitable for operations and underwent only intermittent use. Its buildings were mainly temporary brick, Laing or Handcraft huts; aircraft were stored in four Blister hangars and six twin fighter-pens; and the watch office was a single-storey type (17658/40) designed for fighter-satellite fields. In 1942 Somerfield track was laid down in an attempt to improve the flying surface but the airfield never really worked.

The US Bases in Essex

From August 1942, the VIIIth USAAF had been established as a strategic bombing force mainly operating out of airfields in Norfolk and Suffolk. One year later, the IXth USAAF redeployed to Britain to constitute a tactical air force in support of the Normandy landings and the subsequent campaign in north-west Europe, and Essex became home to 700+ medium bombers, mainly B26-Marauders.

107 Rivenhall: one of the two T2 hangars, both of which survive.

108 Matching: the watch office (12779/41).

109 Boxted: a pair of Romney huts with a temporary brick (tb) hut alongside, together accommodating the airfield's main workshop.

Whilst the VIII had generally been given ready-made former-RAF airfields, the IX required wholly new airfields over and above existing provision. Although some would be on sites previously earmarked by the Air Ministry for development, and where, as at Wethersfield, work might already have begun, eight of their Essex fields would need to be built from scratch. Of the fourteen airfields in Britain built by the US Army Engineer Corps, eight were in Essex, the first being Andrewsfield (Great Saling), and the last being Birch. Others were built by British contractors such as W. and C. French at Boxted and Earls Colne, Costains at Wormingford, and Bovis at Rivenhall. Little Walden had been started earlier for use by the VIII but completion was delayed and it was assigned to the IX in early 1944. Wethersfield, initially assigned to 3 Group RAF Bomber Command, also suffered delays, caused not by the weather in this case but by lack of materials.

All these airfields, begun in 1942 and completed in 1943-4, were basically laid out and built in a style one could label as 'utilitarian'; as was to be expected at that stage in the war, they were completely lacking any aesthetic dimension. Each had three concrete runways with two T2 hangars and a general purpose watch office, mainly 12779/41 or 343/43. Hard-standings, of either the frying-pan or the spectacle type, for the seventy-odd bombers, were spread around the airfield perimeter. The technical site contained stores and workshops, crew-briefing and locker rooms, for the most part in combinations of Nissen and Romney huts. Some buildings might be built with the single-thickness brick walls reinforced by brick buttresses and then stuccoed, officially known as temporary brick or 'tb'.

Synthetic, or simulated, training took place in more huts, with the Free Gunnery Trainer often occupying a Blister hangar as at Boxted and Chipping Ongar. The administrative offices occupied a further group of Nissens. In the same way that

110 Ridgewell Communal Site No. 4, which consisted of a group of Nissen huts for sleeping, with a water tower adjoining the ablutions block.

111 Boxted: the operations block (228/43), one of the only solidly built structures on the site.

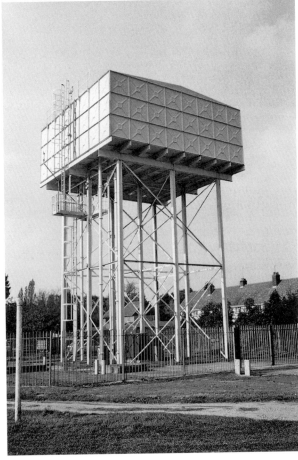

112 Andrewsfield: the Braithwaite water tank.

113 Little Walden: the parachute store (11187/41).

114 Wethersfield: the only known surviving Ctesiphon hut anywhere. (Photograph by Paul Francis, ARG/AIX)

115 Blake Hall: the location for Chipping Ongar's remote operations room.

aircraft storage was based on the dispersal principle, communal sites and sick quarters were scattered across the hinterland of the airfield for reasons of safety. Little enclaves of living huts would cluster around ablution blocks and a mess hall. The officers might be quartered in an adjacent grand house, but very often survived in similar circumstances to their men.

Three other distinctive structures graced most such airfields. One was a solidly built operations block, often with its own Nissen briefing-huts for company. Another was the Braithwaite tank containing 80,000 gallons (365,000 litres) of water perched on a 50ft (15m) high Meccano-like tower. The third was the parachute store (11137/41), with a signature clerestory roof. Although there is no complete surviving example of these airfields, which were once large communities of 2,000–3,000 souls, there are plenty of remains to be seen. There are watch offices at Little Walden, Gosfield, Boreham and Matching; T2 hangars at Rivenhall, Andrewsfield and Little Walden; the operations blocks at Boxted and Chipping Ongar and the administrative site at Great Dunmow.

Plenty of huts, however, survive, mainly Nissen and Romney, but a possibly unique Ctesiphon hut, at Wethersfield, is a 1930s design inspired by ancient structures in Iraq. The parachute store and dinghy shed can be seen at Little Walden. Blake Hall, now a wedding venue, was occupied by the RAMC early in the war. It was then requisitioned by the Air Ministry as the operations room for Chipping Ongar. One of the two T2 hangars from Matching can now be seen; it has been relocated at North Weald.

Command and Control

During the early part of the war both Debden and Hornchurch were Sector HQs and operations rooms for 11 Group, RAF Fighter Command. After the US Air Forces arrived, off-base HQs were established. Marks Hall served as HQ for the 4th Bomber Wing. The 65th Fighter Wing, VIIIth USAAF, turned away from the grammar school at Newport, used the gymnasium, now a theatre, at Dame Bradbury's School, Saffron Walden. The IXth USAAF, arriving on the scene when their airfields were in less danger of attack, located their HQs on working airfields with Bomber Wing HQs at

116 Saffron Walden, Dame Bradbury's School: HQ for the 65th Fighter Wing, VIIIth USAAF from 1942.

Chipping Ongar, Earls Colne and Great Dunmow, and a Fighter Wing HQ at Boxted, initially accommodated in Langham Lodge prior to the completion of a purpose-built HQ block, with Wormingford, Gosfield and Rivenhall under command. After the departure of the IX, Marks Hall became HQ for RAF 38 Group, which delivered airborne forces to their battlefields using both transport aircraft and gliders.

The XIIth USAAF in England

The XIIth USAAF had spent a short period of time in England, from 12 September to 22 October 1942, centred on RAF Wattisham (Suffolk), en route between the USA and its new bases in Algeria and French Morocco, in support of the Torch landings of November 1942. It was almost immediately broken up into its constituent wings as part of Mediterranean and North African Commands. From September 1944 the XIIth Fighter Command, by now redesignated the XIIth Tactical Air Command, came under the operational command of SHAEF, for deployment in northern France. For six weeks it was attached to the IXth USAAF, with its notional HQ planned for Beaumont (actually designated as USAAF Station 148), one of those airfields which were never built.

Training

Dengie Flats had been a ground-to-air firing range before the war, continuing as such throughout the war, being used by No. 2 Armament Practice Station, located at Bradwell Bay until 1944. North Weald and Rochford were home to No. 17 Armament Practice Camp until it moved to Warmwell (Dorset) in 1944. Tollesbury was a bombing range used by the VIIIth USAAF.

Air Defence

Anti-Aircraft Defences

Fully aware of the official line that the bomber would always get through, the inhabitants of Essex must have taken some comfort from the presence of the local AA forces, within what appeared to be a well-established infrastructure. The seventeenth-century chapel at Tilbury Fort housed the AAOR of the northern sector of the Thames and Medway Gun Zone, moving to a purpose-built bunker at Vange in mid-1940. RAF Debden was a Sector Operations Room within 11 Group Fighter Command, and to underline the joined-up nature of the system, the HQ of 41st AA Brigade was co-located there in September 1940.

However good it might all have appeared, the resources were spread dangerously thinly on the ground. Debden itself was defended by 118 Battery of 30th LAA Regiment with just thirteen Lewis Guns, later supplemented by, initially, two 40mm Bofors guns delivered straight from the factory and, by October 1940, a further four, with four old 3in 20cwt guns being provided by 245 Battery of the 78th HAA Regiment, a territorial unit based in Norwich.

The vital airfields of North Weald and Hornchurch went through a period of having no HAA guns of their own at all, relying on their proximity to London's Eastern

AA Zone, which would eventually consist of a screen of over twenty sites extending from Breaches Farm (ZE6) by Waltham Abbey down to Creekmouth (ZE15) near Dagenham. By May 1940, Rochford and North Weald each had four 3in 20cwt guns. These meagre defences were often padded out with extemporised weapons such as the parachute-and-cable (PAC). This consisted of a line of eight or so rocket launchers firing steel cables up to 600ft (185m) into the air, then being held in the vertical by small parachutes, to provide a barrier against low-flying enemy aircraft, by threatening to slice off their wings. The idea, as with their larger relatives, the barrage balloons, was that such disruption would make accurate bomb-aiming more difficult.

HAA Batteries

The war diaries of AA units at this time read like the schedules of removals firms as guns are shunted around the country in attempts to plug gaps and to give protection to the hundreds of competing sites likely to be the targets of aerial bombardment. On occasion defences were stripped from those apparently most in need. In February 1940, elements of the 51st HAA Regiment assembled at Great Easton. Their guns had been taken from six batteries of London's Inner Artillery Zone, and they were expecting to be on their way to join the BEF in France. In fact, they were diverted to Norway and from there on to the Middle East. Such conflicting demands were commonplace. Even as late as June 1942, of Harwich's six HAA sites, only one was armed with the most useful 3.7in mobile guns, two with static 3.7in guns, two more with old 3in guns, the sixth being unarmed. The gunners of 121st HAA Regiment thus had three different weapons to operate and had to be supplied with two different calibres of shell.

The other major concentration of HAA defences was the Thames and Medway GDA, split by the Thames into North and South sectors. From early 1940, all but two of the twenty-four HAA gun sites, spread along the north bank of the Thames, were in place, from the farthest east at Crouchmans (TN21), north of Shoeburyness, back to Dagenham (TN20). In 1942, ten of these sites were armed with 5.25in, 4.5in or either static or mobile 3.7in HAA guns, half these sites also being furnished with GL radar. Through the war provision on individual sites fluctuated. Buckland (TN13) at Bowaters Farm near East Tilbury, was initially armed with two, then three 3.7in mobile HAA guns, but by February 1941, four 4.5in guns had been emplaced. Then in November 1944 these were replaced by four of the new state-of-the-art dual-purpose 5.25in guns.

Provision was steadily increased and by mid-1942, three sites had been built on Foulness Island with an extra site added at Shoeburyness (N25), although this was unarmed. Completing the HAA provision were four sites in the Clacton area, two at Colchester and six around Chelmsford, although not all were armed, and of those that were, several still lacked GL radar. These HAA sites were quite substantial constructions. The guns were mounted in octagonal concrete pits with low walls incorporating ready-use ammunition lockers. In the centre of each of these pits was the holdfast for the gun, which could be traversed and would also eventually be powered through cables running from the remote generator-house. Behind the guns was the command post with covered sections and open platforms for predictors and height-finders, often crewed by women of the ATS. Nearby were crew shelters and sunken concrete magazines. Further back still was the camp with hutted offices, workshops, garages, gun stores and living quarters.

The introduction of gun-laying radar brought further structures to the site. Depending on its location, the whole site might be surrounded by wire and pillboxes, and entered through a gate with a guardroom. A number of these sites survive in reasonable condition including Buckland (TN13), Hadleigh (TN9) and Butlers Farm (TN2).

LAA Guns

Whilst the heavy guns were sited so as to be able to disrupt concentrations of enemy bombers over a wide area, LAA guns were meant to protect individual sites, listed as 'Vulnerable Points', against hit-and-run raiders generally, but especially from low-flying aircraft. The ideal weapon was the Swedish-made 40mm Bofors LAA gun, early in the war being in great demand but short supply. This meant that until a regular and sufficient delivery of this weapon might be secured, all sorts of automatic weapons were pressed into service in LAA roles, many of them remaining in use for the duration. Tilbury (VP112), for instance, was defended by sixteen Lewis Guns in 1939, soon to be supplemented by seven sites each with a Quadruple Vickers mounting. By 1943 four Bofors had been emplaced, increased to eight by 1945 – by which time the seven Quads had been upgraded to single, but deadlier, 0.5in Browning machine guns.

Close parallels can be seen at Shellhaven (VP113), the RN Mines Depot at Wrabness (VP115) and Rainham (VP116). Each site eventually received Bofors guns, two at Shellhaven being mounted on barges. The airfields finally received their Bofors guns: eight more at Debden, eleven at North Weald, ten at Hornchurch, eight at Bradwell, seven at Rochford and just three at Stapleford Tawney. The vital radar sites were given LAA cover from early on, and even some coast batteries had been given Bofors guns by mid-1943, two at Beacon Hill and one at East Mersea. All these sites retained their Quads and Lewis Guns, some places such as Southend Pier, important as an assembly point for convoys of merchant ships, mounting Vickers guns throughout the war. Purfleet was the main AA ammunition store so needed its own AA protection of four Quads. These sites fortunately all appear to have missed out on the more exotic guns, such as the Hispano-Suiza, forced into the LAA role, but the Americans made up for it by utilising both 0.5in Browning machine guns and 20mm cannon from aircraft, mounted on jeeps or trailers, sometimes in their hydraulically-operated turrets, against enemy aircraft.

AA Guardships

As well as land-based AA guns a number of floating AA gun-platforms were used, both at Harwich and in the Thames. Between 1941-3, HMS *Bournemouth Queen*, of 350 tons and armed with two 2-pounders and two quadruple 0.303in machine guns, in Boulton and Paul aircraft turrets served as the Harwich guardship. Throughout 1942 and 1943, HMS *Thames Queen*, an auxiliary AA ship, was anchored off Landguard Point as another guardship. Prior to conversion in 1939 as a minesweeper, she had had a number of previous lives as the *Queen of Southend* and the *Yarmouth Belle*. This 500-ton paddle-steamer, completed in 1898 by Denny Bros of Clydeside, was then armed with a range of AA guns and rockets, including a 12-pounder naval gun, and two Boulton and Paul aircraft turrets. After service in Antwerp in 1944, she was returned to her previous owners in 1947. She had been preceded in this role by the HMS *Princess Elizabeth*, a paddle-steamer of 388 tons built in 1927, carrying a similar armament, and credited with shooting down a German bomber in May 1941, as was HMS *Thames Queen* herself a year later, and the Harwich/Felixstowe-based paddle-minesweeper HMS *Queen Empress* in May 1943.

In the Thames were several AA guardships, most originally commissioned as paddle-minesweepers. They included HMS *Aristocrat* (*née* LNER *Talisman*), of 544 tons and mounting two 2-pounders, five 20mm Oerlikon LAA guns, two quadruple Boulton and Paul turrets and six Lewis Guns. HMS *Golden Eagle* had been a balloon-ship. Then, from 1941, it became an AA ship carrying a similar armament to her companions. The ancient HMS *Plinlimmon*, launched in 1895, also served as an AA ship from 1942 to 1946.

The Sea-Forts

By 1941 it was realised how much could be gained by advancing the AA defences out from the coast. The guns would be capable of engaging enemy aircraft sooner, and the GL radar would increase the low-level coverage over the estuary. The Admiralty had commissioned Guy Maunsell, a distinguished civil engineer, to come up with designs for AA towers and platforms to be sunk on the seabed providing permanent forward AA defence against enemy aircraft. His four forts for the waters off Harwich each consisted of a hollow concrete raft carrying two hollow cylindrical towers support-ing a rectangular gun-platform. The raft could be flooded so that it would sink to the seabed leaving the top two of the towers' seven storeys out of the water.

The platform held two 3.7in HAA guns with an upper level for two Bofors LAA guns, and a central control room with GL radar on top, similar, in both appearance and function, to the bridge of a ship. The towers carried living quarters on the upper floors, magazines and stores in the middle levels, and tanks for fresh water or fuel at the bottom. The forts Maunsell then designed for AA Command, originally intended for the Mersey Estuary and emplaced both there and in the Thames, were quite different. Each of the three consisted of a cluster of two-storey steel drums, mounted on four tubular concrete legs embedded in hollow concrete bases. Once again the bases could be sunk so as to bed themselves into the sand rather than sitting on top of it. A typical cluster consisted of seven towers, all linked by walkways, and replicating the layout of a HAA gun site on land, so that units manning them were already familiar with the inter-relationship of the components.

Four towers were grouped in an arc round a central control tower, each mounting a 3.7in gun. Two further towers held a 40mm Bofors LAA gun and a searchlight respec-tively. The drums contained living quarters, magazines and stores. Access was by fixed ladders suspended from a platform just below the bottom of the drum and reaching down to wave height. In 1942 these forts were installed, first in the Mersey, and then in the Thames.

ZAA Batteries

Despite the vast increase in the numbers of both heavy and light AA guns – from 1,650 and 950 in mid-1941 to 2,400 and around 2,000 respectively in 1944 – there was a need for a weapon which could produce something approaching a barrage. The 3in unrotated projectile (UP) was basically a rocket, equivalent in weight and explosive charge to a 3.7in HAA shell, launched from a projector mounted on a concrete plinth, and cheaply and simply produced. During 1940 several thousand were manufactured but lack of personnel and explosives meant they could not immediately be deployed. By 1941 they were entering service in groups of sixty-four projectors and referred to as Z-batteries. Many of these weapons were crewed by Home Guard personnel. In Essex, the 7th AA Regiment Home Guard, with HQ at West Bergholt, had two rocket batteries under its command: 196 (102 Essex Home Guard) Battery was based in Colchester, and 211 (101 Essex Home Guard) (Mixed) Battery in Central Park, Chelmsford. The sites left little in the way of a footprint with only its sixty-four 8ft square (2.4m), 5in thick (13cm) concrete pads for the projectors, and a few Nissen huts to accommodate the crews, standing where the bowling green now is. Chelmsford's AA defences were controlled from an Area Command in Sandon.

AA Personnel

The Home Guard manned many HAA and LAA guns, the latter by units often raised specifically for the defence of their own workplaces. Examples include E.K. Cole Ltd at Southend-on-Sea ('A' Troop, 16th Essex Battalion), Hoffman's and Marconi's works in Chelmsford ('A' and 'B' Troops, 6th Essex Battalion) and Hoffman's at Witham ('A' Troop, 4th Essex Battalion). Although nominally under the control of AA Command, it proved more practical on a day-to-day basis to leave these LAA Troops with their parent Home Guard battalions. Later on in the war the AA defences were bolstered by US Army units. There was an AAA depot and camp at Stansted airfield and another at Vange (where the 34th AAA Group occupied a camp in Brickfield Road, which later became a TA camp). As early as 1943 there had been help from the Americans in the London IAZ, with the 184th AA Battery, US Army, manning the guns at Lippitts Hill. Bois Hall, Halstead, was the HQ of a US Army Signals Air Warning Battalion. As the war progressed and the competing demands on manpower escalated, ATS units were trained to fill the technical roles on gun sites as well as being drivers and signallers. The Chelmsford ZAA battery, for instance, was a mixed unit containing ATS personnel from 1943. A US Army BD unit was based at Moor Hall Camp, Harlow.

Searchlights

Supporting the gun sites were searchlights, early on in the war spaced at regular intervals to fill their assigned sectors of sky laid down in the ADGB planning. Many of these sites were then designated as resistance points in the anti-invasion plans and given a pillbox, slit trenches and wire. Isolated pillboxes, with no other apparent rationale, at Wendens Ambo (TL498363), Clavering (TL476309) and Roos Farm, Debden (TL547360) probably mark examples of such sites which were all re-used in a later deployment. In January 1940, The Limes, Stansted Mountfitchet, was HQ of 33rd AA

Battalion, a searchlight unit with two companies centred on the White Hart Hotel, Great Yeldham (332 Company), and Hargrave Park, Stansted (333 Company).

The parent unit, 41st AA Brigade, also established a searchlight school at St Stephen's, Silver Street, in Stansted Mountfitchet. Policy then switched to clustering lights in groups of three, but by late 1941 the practice had reverted to belts containing single lights. A narrow but widely-spaced Indicator Belt picked up the incoming aircraft; the 'Killer Belt', of greater depth and with stronger lights and radar, aided night-fighter interception, and then lights in the GDAs illuminated targets for the guns. These last two zones formed grids of squares with sides of roughly 3 miles (5.5km) with searchlights placed at each intersection. By October 1941, 33rd Searchlight Regiment was manning forty-eight sites on the borders of Hertfordshire, Essex, Cambridgeshire and Suffolk, all part of that later deployment of single lights. It is possible to trace parallel lines of lights from Lodge Farm, Elmdon (TL475413), through Church End, Ashdon (TL576412), to Olmstead Hall (TL626407) and Cornish Hall End (TL675366); then further to the south from Wendens Ambo (TL498363) to Roos Farm, and from Clavering through Debden Green (TL575318) to Bardfield End (TL629312). Another triangle is formed by sites at Castle Hedingham (TL791365), Twinstead Green (TL852365) and Belchamp St Paul (TL775416). Searchlight sites had minimal buildings and hence have left few traces. Personnel were accommodated in tents or huts at best. The equipment occupied earthworks, a ring-ditch for the light itself, and sandbagged pits for a command post and an LAA machine-gun mounting.

An unusual device which appears to have been confined to Essex was the 'circle of light' reported in the *Essex Weekly News* of 15 January 2002. This was a 40ft (12m) diameter circular galvanised iron dish with reflective sides. A carbon arc light, powered by an on-site generator, was lit and the reflective surround threw up a powerful beam of light into the night sky – so powerful, in fact, that it blinded friend and foe alike and had only minimal use. Local information pinpointed its use to December 1939 and it was apparently built by Christie's of Chelmsford. Enquiries via the newspaper's readership elicited responses confirming the existence of at least eight of these installations in the Chelmsford, Danbury, Great Baddow, Southminster, North Fambridge and Rayleigh areas.

Operation Diver – Combating the V1 'Doodlebug'

The final effort demanded of AA Command was to contain the V-weapons in 1944 when the successful D-Day landings cruelly created expectations of an early end to the war. Between June 1944 and March 1945 over 400 V1 'Doodlebugs' launched from aircraft and from sites in Holland and north-west Germany, and fell on Essex. Over 250 more fell on parts of the county within the London Civil Defence Region. Of a total of over 9,000 launched, over 4,000 were destroyed by AA guns (1,900), fighters (1,900) and barrage balloons (300). From September 1944 to March 1945 over 1,100 V2 rockets were launched against south-east England. These travelled too fast for any sort of action to be taken against them and nearly 400 fell on Essex, with a further 200 falling on boroughs within the London CD Region, thirty-five on Ilford alone, and a further forty on Barking and Dagenham together.

117 V2 (A4) rocket, part of the combustion chamber found in the river Blackwater Estuary near Maldon. (Photograph by Ivor Crowson)

Whilst nothing could be done against the V2s, there was a robust defence set up against the V1s. This consisted of a concentration of firepower in the shape of every available AA gun, heavy and light, in formations along the stretches of coast which the V1s would cross. The Diver Box, whose northern boundary was marked by a line drawn from Thames Haven through Chelmsford to Clacton-on-Sea, straddled the Thames Estuary, with dozens of AA sites stretching from Southend-on-Sea to Bradwell-on-Sea, further reinforced by the sea-forts and barge-mounted LAA guns. Many of the sites in the Box, such as Butlers Farm (TN5 at TQ898889), or Crouchmans (TN21 at TQ940869), had been long part of the GDAs, but were now re-numbered as N2 and N21 respectively.

New sites, such as Churchend on Foulness Island (N27A at TR004934) or East Wick to the east of Burnham-on-Crouch (A8 at TR000961), built to supplement those existing sites, usually had eight HAA guns and GL radar, often the unfamiliar American SCR 584 sets, with instruction being provided at an AA school set up in Dovercourt. As launching sites were overrun and the axis of attack shifted north and east, then it became necessary to widen the defences, and the Diver Strip, stretching from Clacton (TM164139) to Great Yarmouth was established, later still extended even further right up past Hull into east Yorkshire. Local HQs for the Essex part of the Diver Strip were located at 'Four Views', Maldon Road, Burnham-on-Crouch, at St Audrey's School, 64, The Broadway, Thorpe Bay, and at Thorpe Lodge, Thorpe-le-Soken. The most southerly part of the Strip, stretching from Jaywick to Dovercourt, contained sixteen fresh HAA sites (K2-17) and two existing sites, H3 and H5, of the Harwich defences. There were also six fresh LAA sites (IM1-6) between Seawick and Little Oakley. These two dozen sites were manned by 40th AA Brigade. The Jaywick site (K17 at TM156134) was at a different location to its predecessor (C3 at TM149139). It would appear that of the other earlier sites in the area, Lee-over-Sands (C2 at TM108126) was never armed but Little Holland (C4 at TM215170) and Jaywick itself (C3 at TM149139), might have been retained for the Diver operation.

RDF and Radar

As the war began, there were the two CH stations at Canewdon and Great Bromley feeding information to the filter room at Bentley Priory. Although each of the CH stations was provided with a Buried Reserve which could continue to operate if the station had suffered damage, an additional back-up was afforded by mobile radio units with two 105ft (32m) towers, Canewdon's being at Loftmans (TQ919938), and Great Bromley's at Frating (TM083225). At this early stage in radar's development, it could only pick up activity above 3,000ft (915m), missing low-flying or surface targets completely. The army had developed CD radar intended to detect minelaying aircraft and surfacing U-boats, and Harwich and the Thames Estuary were identified as the most urgent recipients of this new equipment. Prototype emergency sets, later referred to as CHL, were therefore installed at Foreness Point near Margate (Kent) and 30 miles (48km) to its north, at Walton-on-the-Naze, up on the Trinity House Naze Tower of 1791.

Initially manned by naval crews and civilian technicians, these were soon replaced by RAF personnel. During the Battle of Britain in autumn 1940, the Walton CHL station was one of three trying – generally unsuccessfully, owing to the limitations of the equipment – to direct RAF night-fighters, themselves equipped with rudimentary A1 radar, onto intruder aircraft. Only in October 1941 (although apparently unreliable station logs may indicate an earlier date) were effective CHL sets installed at Walton and elsewhere. In April 1941 Walton's equipment was mounted on two gantries holding the transmitter and receiver aerial arrays. By 1942 a new CHL set was being developed and both Foreness and Walton received it in the form of a new paral-

118 Walton-on-the-Naze: the Trinity House Tower of 1791, used for experiments with radar; to the left of the tower is the engine-house.

lel installation, that at Foreness being very close by at North Foreland, but Walton's, further distant on Martello Tower CC at Slaughden, south of Aldeburgh (Suffolk). The intention was to alternate between each pair as new equipment became available.

In July 1942, Walton was equipped with a hand-turned 1941-type duplicate and an 80ft (24m) tower. There was still a problem with coverage of low levels at very low-lying sites. Dengie, occupying a virgin site below the sea-bank, was selected as a test site for a new centimetric radar NT271, operating as a CHEL station from late 1942, with a 200ft (60m) tower and permanent buildings. In the meantime work had proceeded to perfect a GCI system, and by the end of 1941 such a station was operational at Foulness, the link between Sandwich (Kent) and Trimley Heath (Suffolk). Types 7 and 8 radar sets were mounted on gantries at these Intermediate GCI sites, the only permanent building being a generator-house, operational functions being carried out in vehicles and the odd hut. By the time the Final GCI set-up had been adopted the situation had changed, and it would appear that Foulness was never upgraded. The final piece in the radar jigsaw in Essex was the installation of a Type 57 set at Walton in November 1944, which stayed there until the Diver operations were over. Some of the concrete bunkers which housed the radar equipment at Great Bromley and Canewdon can still be seen, along with guardrooms and other ancillary buildings.

Royal Observer Corps

Starting the war with a developed network of thirty-nine posts in the county, only minor changes were made subsequently. In November 1939, Colchester 18 Group HQ in the Telephone Exchange was connected to the Sector Operations Rooms at North Weald and Hornchurch, whilst Debden was connected to 17 Group HQ at Watford. In 1943, 18 Group HQ moved to Errington Lodge, 22 Lexden Road (TL985249) and a number of re-sites of posts also took place at different times. Brightlingsea (post D3) moved from the oyster beds to the 25ft (8m) high Batenicus Tower or Bateman's Folly, in use from October 1939; Walton-on-the-

119 Colchester: Errington Lodge, 22 Lexden Road (TL985249), from 1943 the HQ of 18 Group, Royal Observer Corps.

Naze (post D4) was re-sited to the roof of Walton Hall in July 1940; and the windmill at Great Dunmow (TL634225) was adopted (post B1) in 1944.

In September 1940, at the height of the Battle of Britain, the ROC came in the front line. For most observers their experience was of long periods of boredom interspersed with the odd moments of excitement or terror. The Colchester 18 Group logbook reveals that a train travelling between Kelvedon and Colchester was reported to the police for having no cover over the locomotive cabin and was thus guilty of show-ing a light which could easily guide enemy bombers along the line to their targets. Latchington (post A2) reported three unexploded parachute mines at Cold Norton, and an observer at Woodham Ferrers (post K2) was severely injured by bombing and his family killed. In 1941 the post on top of the telephone exchange at Chigwell (J1), belonging to Watford's 17 Group, was badly damaged when the public house oppo-site was hit by a large HE bomb. Four off-duty observers and three of their wives were killed in the pub, and the two duty observers severely injured in the blast, whilst attempting to assess the damage – it had at first appeared that the bomb had failed to explode. The observers worked assiduously at refining their aircraft recognition skills, even forming 'Hearkers' clubs and running competitions, as keeping on top of air-craft recognition became more and more important. One such club, the seventh to be formed across the country, was in Southend-on-Sea.

In May 1941 posts were equipped with flares to signal enemy landings, particularly of troop-carriers, gliders or parachutists (red flares), but also by sea (green flares). Posts were also involved in supporting RAF 80 Wing's beam-bending work with Meacon beacons, by plotting the progress of enemy pilots confused by falsified transmissions. In November 1942 a number of ROC posts, including Lexden (post C3), had been given GL radar sets in order to carry out IFF interrogations to eliminate unidentified aircraft from the night-fighter plots. ROC posts also made a contribution to helping returning aircraft, whether damaged, low on fuel or just plain lost, to find an airfield. Sandra was a cone of searchlight beams. Braintree (post B2) and Tendring (post D2) were equipped with Darky, a short-range radio set for talking aircraft down within a 10-mile (16km) radius. Granite was a pattern of flares to be used if aircraft were flying dangerously low, but used usually only in hilly country.

Balloons

Despite their many shortcomings barrage balloons, mostly crewed by WAAFs, con-tinued in use as protection for particularly vulnerable targets. Chigwell was HQ of 30 Group RAF Balloon Command, along with Hook, Surrey and Kidbrooke, South London, protecting the capital. In the docks, balloons were often tethered on barges and Tilbury had two motor-boats for servicing such floating barrage balloons. At Harwich the Haven was protected by a ring of balloons starting at Landguard Point and running clockwise via five balloons tethered to barges, stretching at intervals across the water to Dovercourt. From here a further ten balloons hovered over the peninsular as far as Parkeston and then over the water to Shotley (Suffolk). Half a dozen more protected the anchorage in Stour Bay, the area around HMS *Ganges*, and RAF Felixstowe, although there they seriously impeded flying-boat operations.

Bombing Decoys

Even if the bomber was always going to get through it might be induced to drop its bombs harmlessly in open countryside. Bombing decoys were developed to protect different targets in different ways. The earliest were for the benefit of military airfields, and could operate in daylight ('K') when dummy aircraft, many of which were built at Shepperton film studios, were deployed on simulated flying-fields. There would be a small RAF ground-crew to move things around and give an appearance of operational activity. Night-time ('Q') decoys displayed lights which would be doused just after the sounds of the approaching bombers had been heard. The crew operated these lights from a brick and concrete blockhouse with an attached generator.

After the Battle of Britain, there were fewer bombing raids directed at airfields and efforts were made to divert enemy bombers away from civilian or industrial targets. Special Fire, 'SF' or Starfish decoys were fires lit to suggest that the enemy pathfinders had located and bombed the target ready for the follow-up aircraft to home in on. Initially, both North Weald and Hornchurch had 'K' decoys, at Nazeing and Bulphan respectively, each provided with dummy Hurricanes, and operating from March 1940 until June 1941, when both had been identified as decoys by the Luftwaffe. North Weald had a second decoy near Blackmore, at Radley Green, which later also served Chipping Ongar. Debden had a 'Q' decoy at Stambourne, also later allocated to Ridgewell. These proximities, however, highlight the problem of site density. Once real airfields have been built close to decoys, then the whole system begins to look implausible. Decoys were designed to mimic the characteristics of their particular targets. The 'QF' oil programme, represented in Essex by decoy sites at Stanford-le-Hope and Fobbing, masking Thames Haven and Shell Haven respectively with a combination of lights and fires, was not a success. People knew how to extinguish oil fires but

120 Harwich: Spinnels Farm (TM162298), the control blockhouse of the naval 'QF' bombing decoy site.

no one knew how to start them effectively, the oil companies refused to construct or to staff the decoys. When experimentation took place it was found that unacceptable amounts of oil were consumed, rather defeating the object of protecting inadequate oil stocks.

The Civil Series Starfish decoys fared better. Both Chelmsford and Colchester were provided with decoys, reckoned 'temporary' in 1942 after the Baedecker raids had highlighted the vulnerability of towns whether legitimate targets or not. These decoys consisted of a network of baskets of flammable material, treated with creosote, which could be quickly and easily lit by the crew on receiving an order from the local CD control, Chelmsford's being based in County Hall's cellars. Various mechanisms, such as embedded flares, were included to produce realistic explosions and fireballs, simulating the effect of high-explosive and incendiary bombs on built-up areas with low-intensity industries. Both Chelmsford and Colchester received supplementary protection in the shape of 'Mobile QL' equipment. The Royal Navy also had its own network of decoys protecting naval bases, but using the same methods and materials that had been developed for the RAF and rolled out to cover civilian targets. Harwich had five decoy sites, one near Wrabness to impersonate the Mines Depot, two at East Mersea and Sandy Point, Brightlingsea, and a further two at Kirby-le-Soken and Walton-on-the-Naze. These sites appear to have been closed down sometime in 1942 – which was just as well, since the Kirby-le-Soken site was subsequently occupied by a Diver HAA Battery (K16). Colchester's Starfish site was at Great Bromley, only 2 miles (3km) west of the CH radar station, and Chelmsford's was midway between Great and Little Baddow.

Given what was known about the inaccuracy of bombing, some of these sites appear merely to have substituted one target for another. London was provided with five permanent Starfish sites, and given the direction of approach of the majority of the bombing raids on the capital, not surprisingly two of them were on the Essex side, at Rainham Marshes and at Lambourne End. With the exception of the oil decoys, most were lit in response to warnings of raids and many, those last two in particular, were actually bombed, suggesting that at least some of the time they were taking hits destined for real targets.

Camps and Barracks

It has been suggested that to be requisitioned by the Armed Forces in the Second World War, a house had to have electricity. Before the war, properties, especially stately homes or even more modest country houses with attached parks had been earmarked for use by the services and by government departments. Some like Belhus Park had been used in the previous war, for others it was a novel experience, and for several the experience was fatal. Rolls Park was occupied by thirteen different units and surrounded by HAA sites. The owner felt that so much damage had been caused that its demolition, in 1953, was his only option. Felix Hall, the centre of an army camp, was gutted by fire in 1940, and the main house at Easton Lodge, occupied by the army, was demolished in 1950. Weald Hall and park were used by the army, the house being damaged by fire and demolished in 1950. Whilst significant damage was undoubtedly caused by military occupation, some of it gratuitous, this sometimes provided an excuse for getting rid of a house which its owner could no longer afford to run. Hill Hall, Theydon Bois, was home to two battalions of Welsh Guards prior to their move to Holland in the spring of 1940. Orsett Hall survived its occupation by the RASC and is now a hotel. Shortgrove Park, Newport, was occupied by the Northamptonshire Regiment, the RASC, RAMC and REME, finally becoming the US 280th Station Hospital. Both Hill Hall and Shortgrove Park suffered disastrous fires in the 1960s but have since been rebuilt. Like most of his other camps, Billy Butlin leased his Clacton holiday camp to the army for the duration, and it became a training camp for the Pioneer Corps, inevitably suffering extensive damage in the process. Apart from the established camps at Colchester, Warley and Shoeburyness, there was a large transit camp at Dovercourt. D-Day marshalling areas are included in another section below.

Training

Despite being in the front line a number of training establishments remained in Essex, mainly because they were needed and there was nowhere else for them to go. Colchester was home to a Royal Engineers Training Battalion and the 4th Cavalry Training Regiment until 1940, when a change of name confirmed its role as a tank training unit serving the RAC. The Royal Artillery Coast Artillery School at Shoeburyness, which ran instructor training courses up to 1939, moved to Llandudno in North Wales for the duration, taking its guns with it. Beacon Hill Fort hosted a searchlight training camp, and Purfleet Range was the London District Machine Gun Training School. The Essex Regimental Depot at Warley housed No. 1 Infantry Training Centre, after a reorganisation in 1941, remaining one of twenty-five such centres carrying out basic recruit training.

In 1943 a mock-up of a length of Atlantic Wall was built on Foulness Island for pre-D-Day gunnery practice, intended to measure the weight of fire necessary for the destruction of its different components. A number of airfields were used for practising the glider-borne landings which would be key to the successful crossing of the Rhine. Great Sampford had proved to be most unsuitable for operation as a fighter airfield so had become a training-ground for the RAF Regiment throughout 1943-4. Along with the equally unsuccessful IXth USAAF airfield at Birch, which was barely used at all for flying, it could be used for glider landing practice. All sorts of facilities were pressed into service at a local level, particularly to meet the needs of Home Guard units. Gravel pits near Newport were used as an assault course until explosions began to threaten structural damage to the town's houses and activities ceased.

The Royal Navy

Covering the approaches to the busiest port in the world provided the RN presence in the lower Thames with an enormous task marshalling and protecting some of the thousands of merchant vessels which kept the country going. The East Coast harbours provided bases for the defensive activities of the early years of the war, preparing to resist an invasion and protecting convoys, and later for the offensive preparations for D-Day.

Harwich

After its important role in the previous war, its former status was quickly regained, as Harwich initially operated six fleet minesweepers and a dozen A/S trawlers. Soon the 1st Destroyer Flotilla, consisting of seven 'G' Class and three Polish boats, submarines and MTBs were added. Its vulnerable location, and the continuous stream of vital convoys, meant that it operated the largest group of minesweepers anywhere – over fifty of them by 1941. As well as the 4th (Auxiliary) M/S Flotilla of three boats, there were three paddle-minesweepers and eight groups each containing four requisitioned M/S trawlers.

The HQ of the naval officer in command was in the LNER Station Hotel in 1939, but then in 1940 it was moved to Hamilton House, the Customs House, where an underground bunker housing an operations room was opened in 1941. Harwich Command's HMS *Badger* remained centred on Parkeston Quay throughout the war, being paid off in 1946. HMS *Epping* was an LNER tender hired in 1939 as a minesweeper depot ship, giving its name to the whole base, with HMS *Hydrograaf* serving as

121 Parkeston Quay, Hamilton House: the Royal Navy HQ building.

accommodation ship for Dutch M/S personnel. The old Navy Yard was taken over for the rescue and salvage tugs, with HMS *Minona* acting as tug base-ship.

The 1st Destroyer Flotilla was soon replaced by the 16th, with a mixture of veteran 'V' and 'W' boats with the equally old HMS *Campbell* as leader. These destroyers' most notable operation was the attempt to intercept the German battle-cruisers on their Channel Dash, but they were involved, along with the eight escort vessels of the 1st Corvette Flotilla and four groups of A/S trawlers, in never-ending convoy protection and patrol work. As the naval presence gradually increased to a peak of 1,300 ashore and 4,000 afloat, then the facilities were improved. Michaelstowe Hall became an officers' club and the County School a club for other ranks. The Cliff Hotel at Dovercourt and many of its neighbours became billets for the close to 400 Wrens who carried out driving, maintenance, signalling and administrative tasks.

Harwich had quickly become one of the busiest naval ports in the country and ships were moored up to four-deep alongside the quay, as well as to buoys out in the Haven. An inventory of harbour craft shows that a fleet of over thirty small boats was required to keep the port functioning, and that did not include the AA guardships. In the last year of the war the 16th Flotilla had exchanged most of its old destroyers for seven newer Hunt Class destroyer escorts, and had been joined by 1st and 2nd A/S Striking Forces containing, between them, seven of the nine Kingfisher Class patrol sloops, as well as the 1st Minesweeper Flotilla with nine Halcyon Class sloops. Compared to the number of escort vessels stationed in the Western Approaches, this was a small force, but these boats nevertheless had a vast expanse of extremely dangerous waters to patrol against constant attacks on merchant convoys by U-boats, E-boats and aircraft.

122 Thorney Bay, Canvey Island: the degaussing station which de-magnetised merchant ships to protect them from magnetic mines.

Southend-on-Sea and the Coastal Convoys

The 1.25-mile long (2km) Southend Pier (served by the narrow-gauge railway which had thrilled pre-war day-trippers) was the main assembly point for East Coast and Channel convoys. The offices were in the Palace Hotel and three houses in Royal Terrace, centred on number seven. Here there was also a DEMS office. Masters were briefed by convoy commodores in the Solarium at the end of the pier, a procedure eventually replaced by messages delivered to the ships themselves by speedboats. By 1941 it had become obvious that the level of activity here justified a separate independent command, so Southend continued the war as HMS *Leigh*, ultimately handling nearly 85,000 sailings in over 3,000 convoys. Before ships passed the Shoeburyness boom, they needed to be protected against magnetic mines. There were degaussing stations on the roof of Coalhouse Fort, and at Thorney Bay, Canvey. The convoy system relied on reliable signalling reflected in the presence of RN Shore Signals Stations at Westcliff and at Shoeburyness, where there was also an Army Liaison Officer to brief the coast batteries, and the WRNS Signals Unit at Hampton, Beehive Lane, Great Baddow.

After the transfer of the RN College Dartmouth (Devon) to the US Navy in 1943, HMS *Westcliff I* took on the role of training base for Combined Operations, with a holding camp for personnel. Prior to Operation Overlord, the M/S depot ship HMS *Ambitious* was based at Southend for a while, joining a flotilla of small boats which constituted the Naval Control Service. After D-Day, HMS *Southern Prince*, the former HQ ship on Juno Beach in Normandy, returned to Southend as an accommodation ship.

Brightlingsea

HMS *Nemo*, on the north side of the creek, was primarily an Auxiliary Patrol base from 1940 onwards, and the NOIC had his HQ in the Anchor Hotel where there was an operations room. *The Duchess of Rothesay*, never actually commissioned into the navy, served as the base accommodation ship and later as Depot Ship for LCTs. The Manor House was the early HQ of the motor-launch force, but when this was subsumed by *Nemo* it became the ward-room. A sizeable fleet of up to seventy drifters, motor-boats and yachts, crewed by several hundred sailors, carried out a variety of duties including patrol, minesweeping, recovery and rescue. Motor-launches came to the boatyards to be equipped and armed. River patrols were transferred to the RASC in 1942, whose base on the Blackwater was at West Mersea. At St Osyth, on the south side of the creek, was HMS *Helder*, a combined operations training base, and on the roof of Martello Tower 'A' was the EXDO Post for the controlled minefield.

Burnham-on-Crouch

Early in the war the sole naval presence was an examination yacht in the Crouch, and an office in the Royal Burnham Yacht Club. Transferred to Harwich Sub-Command in 1940, another half-dozen patrol yachts were sent to the Crouch and an Auxiliary Patrol base was established ashore, also responsible for the moored yachts blocking the estuary. By 1943, HMS *Westcliff III* had been established as a Combined Operations base.

Tilbury

As part of the ongoing operation to arm merchant ships (DEMS), there was a gunnery training sub-centre at the Green and Silley Weir yard at Tilbury Docks. Tilbury was one of the bases of the Thames River Patrol with nine boats. The depot-ship, HMS *Worcester*, was berthed at Greenhithe on the Kent bank with a further fourteen boats, and there were six more at Dagenham, seven at Holehaven, and five more at Cliffe, opposite Coalhouse Fort. Tilbury Docks themselves were important for refitting RN vessels and, during the Overlord operation, despatching follow-up convoys carrying troop reinforcements and supplies.

The Secret War – Electronic, Irregular and Clandestine

After the existence of Bletchley Park and its production of the priceless intelligence known as Ultra, one of the best-kept long-term secrets of the war must have been the work of No. 80 (Signals) Wing RAF, the so-called 'Beam-benders'. This was the Radio Counter Measures operation with its Eastern Area HQ at Braintree. The Luftwaffe used directional radio beams such as Knickebein, known as 'Headache' in Britain, to direct its bombers onto British targets. Using such devices as 'Aspirin', which transmitted a signal masking the German one, the RAF countered enemy efforts by jamming or distorting their signals. The Germans, in turn, reciprocated by attempting the same against the RAF's GEE, for instance, a directional beam enabling Allied bombers to maintain direction flying over enemy targets, and transmitted from Canewdon CH radar station. From February 1942

123 Canewdon: one of the radar station's transmitter towers. It was re-erected at Great Baddow after the war for use in Marconi's ongoing experiments. Not only is it one of only a very few survivors, but it also retains its platforms.

at Holland Haven, Walton-on-the-Naze, there was an out-station of 80 Wing, one of three such sites, reporting to the Radlett (Hertfordshire) Operations Room, and engaging in anti-jamming operations by locating the enemy's own jamming sites so that they might be neutralised. With the introduction of GCI radar, effectively enabling fighters to be vectored by radio onto incoming targets, there was a need for the RAF to establish DF stations, like that at Wix, to boost the range of RAF Debden's VHF radio in its fighter control application.

The Polish branch of SOE based its cloak-and-dagger training in Essex at Audley End House (Station 14) which included wireless telegraphy in its curriculum, and at Briggens, Roydon, where operatives learned the art of forgery at No. 43 Training School. Waltham Abbey worked on explosives research and development for SOE. A number of units involved in commando-style operations were based in Essex at different stages of the war. No. 8 (Guards) Commando, recruited from the Household regiments, and numbering Randolph Churchill amongst its officers, formed at Burnham-on-Crouch in June 1940, prior to training at Largs (Ayrshire) and then a deployment to the Middle East. They were accommodated in Creeksea Commando Camp. Hylands Park, Chelmsford, hosted 1 SAS from November 1944 to October 1945, with their officers' mess in Hylands House, and Colchester provided a base for 2 SAS until October 1945. Brightlingsea was a Combined Operations base from November 1942, as HMS *Helder*, an off-shoot of HMS *Quebec* at Invereray (Strathclyde), serving as the parent ship for the Raiding Craft Flotilla of some twenty-odd craft. Accommodation was in the naval camp at St Osyth Stone and Martello Tower 'A', Point Clear, on the south side of the Creek. HMS *Westcliff III* at Burnham-on-Crouch was another Combined Operations base with HMS *St Matthew* as its training establishment. At Coalhouse Fort, HMS *St Clement(s)* also served as a Combined Operations base from 1943 to 1946. Some of the boats designed for clandestine missions, such as running SOE operatives into France, were built by Aldous Successors shipyard in Brightlingsea.

Preparations for Overlord

Mulberry Harbour

The success of the Normandy landings, or Operation Overlord, was predicated on one key part of the Royal Navy's Operation Neptune. This was the construction and conveyance across the English Channel of two artificial harbours codenamed Mulberry. These called for a bewildering array of specialist components of which the most fundamental was the caisson, an enormous floating concrete box, over 200 of which were needed in six different sizes. The A1 Caisson was the biggest, displacing over 6,000 tons and measuring broadly 200ft (60m) long by 60ft (18m) high and a bit less in breadth. All the caissons were of similar length but the Bs and Cs were lower and slimmer. The Ministry of Supply oversaw the operation to build these monsters using docks all over the country, particularly in London and Southampton. However, there were not sufficient spaces available there, so more had to be found.

In the Tilbury Graving Dock Balfour Beatty built nine A1 Caissons, and Holland, Hannon and Cubitt built nine C1 Caissons. At Grays, fresh basins had to be excavated behind the river embankment, Gee, Walker and Slater building four B1 caissons here. The Vospers Yard (formerly Husks) at Wivenhoe also built caissons, which were then floated to their assembly points in the Solent. One which failed to make it can be seen marooned on a sandbank off Southend.

Pluto

Another mammoth construction project was the network of pipelines which criss-crossed the country distributing fuel from mainly the Liverpool/Wirral area. Sandy (Bedfordshire) was one of the main terminals with a spur to a depot at Thames Haven.

In order to keep the invasion forces supplied with fuel after D-Day, this network was extended under the Channel and codenamed PLUTO (initially Pipeline Underwater Transport of Oil but then, more popularly, Pipe Line Under The Ocean). A number of engineering firms, the Stewart and Lloyds' factory at Tilbury amongst them, had contracts to supply the miles of pipe necessary to assemble the two pipelines which stretched from the Solent and from Kent into France. HMS *Abastor* at Tilbury was a PLUTO training establishment from 1943 to 1945.

Assembling the Forces for D-Day

Whilst we usually think of the south- and west-coast ports as the jumping-off points for the Normandy landings, a significant number of troop-ships, and particularly con-voys of merchant ships carrying supplies, left from the Thames ports and Harwich. Camps were established around Purfleet and Tilbury to accommodate troops awaiting embarkation. Some of these troops were from the US Army, the 987th Field Artillery Battalion, for instance, being based in Clacton and establishing an airstrip for their Aerial Observation Posts outside the town. Others were part of the British I Corps, whose 51st (Highland) Division, based in the Maldon area prior to shipping out for France, sailed from Tilbury and Harwich as Follow-up Force L. The 7th Armoured Division had been in the Ipswich area after its return from the Middle East but moved into Essex prior to D-Day, the Gloucestershire Hussars of 22nd Armoured Brigade, being encamped at Hatfield Peverel. There were at least eleven D-Day Marshalling Camps in the south Essex area with the HQ of camps 'S1–S8' in St Chad's School, Tilbury, and HQ of those camps with a 'T' designation at the Royal Wanstead School. Large concentrations of men and, especially, vehicles were assembled in any suitable space – Wanstead Flats, for instance, or West Ham Greyhound Stadium, which held 2,000 vehicles. Not all the formations officially recorded as being present in the area, however, would actually make it to France.

Operation Fortitude South

One of the most ambitious and successful deception operations of the Second World War was Fortitude South. This was designed to convince the German High Command that the Normandy Landings were merely a feint, intended as bait for the reserves' coun-ter-attack, and to be followed by the real invasion in the Pas de Calais. A wholly notional

1st US Army Group (FUSAG) was established under General Patton, a plausible leader, with his HQ at Chelmsford. Parts of the British Fourth Army were gradually fed in as reinforcements in Normandy, but the non-existent rump, along with completely fictitious units of the US Fourteenth Army, purported to remain in Essex for at least a month after D-Day. Soldiers wearing fake regimental insignia were to be seen around Essex and the south-east driving vehicles with spurious divisional badges. These would be 'spotted' by the Nazi spies turned by the XX organisation, 'corroborated' by their colleagues, reinforced by newspaper reports, and fed back to Germany as hot intelligence. Parks of dummy tanks and artillery with their associated supply dumps – bolstered by large volumes of meaningless radio-traffic – maintained the deception. It was planned to sustain this ruse for the few weeks it would take to establish and secure the Normandy bridgehead, but it lasted well into July, long past its expected shelf life. The very real 35th US Infantry and 7th US Armoured Divisions left for Normandy in July and August respectively. Another illusionary Army Group was 'present' in Scotland as part of Fortitude North, a similar deception simulating a projected invasion of Norway.

Logistics

Napoleon's armies may have marched on their stomachs, but by the 1940s fuel and ordnance had become just as important as food. It was not enough merely to organise the distribution of these commodities, but to sustain a continuous process of developing new weapons, essential for speeding up the resolution of this conflict.

Storage and Distribution Depots

The long-established Powder Magazine at Purfleet continued to function right up to 1952, with the addition of the London area AA ammunition magazine. White Colne was a RASC depot, and the US Army had an ordnance depot at Ashford Lodge, Halstead. After 1942, a REME depot was set up in Colchester. The Royal Navy's Principal Magazine at Purfleet served the Thames Estuary area, and another at Wrabness, which was also their main Mines Depot, served Harwich. The RAF ran an Advanced Ammunition Park sub-site at Warley Barracks from 1943 to 1946, in 1944 establishing No. 422 RAF Advanced Fuel and Ammunition Park at Copped Hall, Epping, which then moved to nearby Bury Lodge, before transferring to Arundel (West Sussex) in support of the 2nd Tactical Air Force operations in northern France. There was an Air Ministry petrol depot at Saffron Walden. Stansted was USAAF 30th Air Depot Group, 1942 to 1945, storing, maintaining and repairing aircraft. Bures, USAAF Station 526, began as the forward depot serving Andrewsfield, Boxted, Ridgewell and Parham (Suffolk), but later served only the IXth USAAF airfields, replacing Sudbury which was in use from 1942 to 1943.

Munitions Production

In Dagenham, Ford's manufactured large numbers of trucks and other vehicles for the military – as many as 360,000 in some accounts, though fewer in others. These were

124 Wrabness: the sheds of the Royal Naval Armaments Depot which stored all types of munitions but the majority of the navy's mines.

mainly trucks, but also included 13,000 tracked Universal Bren-carriers. The figure of a quarter of a million V8 engines is also recorded in the war-production tally.

The De Lisle carbine was designed by George Lanchester and George Patchett of the Sterling Armaments Company of Dagenham for use by Combined Operations, the commandos and the Parachute Regiment. Based on the SMLE rifle, it went into a large number of variants, seventeen being put into production at Ford's. Sterling won an order for 500 in 1944, and went on to produce the Sterling sub-machine gun which was to replace the Sten gun as the standard light automatic weapon of the British Army.

The Royal Gunpowder Factory and explosives works at Waltham Abbey was one of only four propellant factories in operation in 1939. Like many other industrial concerns the production of the Miners' Safety Explosives Co. Ltd at Curry Marsh, Stanford-le-Hope, was switched to meet military needs. At Tilbury, the British Bata Shoe Co. Ltd secured contracts from the Ministry of Supply for boots and shoes for the Armed Forces. Weapons trials continued at Shoeburyness, testing projectiles produced at Woolwich Arsenal and, at Walton-on-the-Naze, an operation codenamed Brakemine testing wire-guided rockets, operated from 1944 to 1946.

Shipbuilding

The Thames yards around Barking Creek and Deptford had a long history of building ships for the Royal Navy but both Green and Silley Weir and Harland and Wolff also maintained shipyards downriver at Tilbury, building, between them, nearly thirty LCT (4)s from 1942 onwards. Johnson and Jago, of Leigh-on-Sea, built thirty-three Fairmile 'B' Class MLs, and twelve MFVs (Nos 49-52, 125-128, 200-01 and 313-4).

Much of the small craft construction was carried out in the shipyards of the Essex coast river estuaries. Many of these yards had suffered from lack of orders through the 1930s, but were mobilised for the construction of a large number of small naval craft. On the Colne, Husk's of Wivenhoe was taken over by Vospers and built four 300-Series MTBs (Nos 351-4). The other two Wivenhoe yards merged under the existing names of Rowhedge Ironworks, with the Wivenhoe yard turning out twenty-one MM/S and ten MFVs (Nos 1537-1546), on the east bank, whilst Rowhedge Ironworks, on the west bank, built three MM/S, coasters, high-speed launches for the RAF, and six MFVs (Nos 1561-66). They had long been specialists in building small steam-powered vessels, producing some forty-odd steam pinnaces during the war. Aldous Successors, downriver at Brightlingsea, launched two MGBs (Nos 318 and 329), ten Fairmile 'B' Class MLs, and several LCM(1)s, as well as hundreds of smaller landing craft, pontoons for the army, and tenders for the RAF.

The two smaller yards, James's and Stone's, had been busy refitting and repairing small craft for Coastal Forces and, after merging in 1942, they went on to produce small boats, including landing craft. Sadd's of Maldon, on the Blackwater, built four Fairmile 'B' Class MLs and seven MFVs (Nos 1, 2, 45-8 and 282), and Cardnell Bros of Maylandsea, built four Fairmile 'B' Class MLs and four MFVs (Nos 657-60). William King of Burnham-on-Crouch built three Fairmile 'D' Type MTBs (Nos 609, 631 and 667), and four Fairmile 'B' Class MLs, whilst the neighbouring Wallesea Island Yacht Station built four Fairmile 'D' Type MTBs (Nos 606, 623, 640 and 656), and four Fairmile 'B' Class MLs.

Hospitals

Colchester Garrison Hospital catered for the immediate needs of troops based there, backed up by clinics and sick quarters in other camps and barracks, and a network of

Red Cross Convalescent Homes/ Auxiliary Hospitals. At the beginning of the war, Blake Hall was partly occupied by the RAMC, prior to its total requisition by the Air Ministry as a RAF operations room. The US forces established military hospitals at White Court, Braintree and Shortgrove Park, Newport.

125 High Garrett: the distinctive water tower of prisoner-of-war camp 78.

Prisoner-of-War Camps

Early in the war, there were few PoWs as a result of military action, but a large number of civilian aliens – including refugees from Nazi persecution – were interned.

Butlin's holiday camp at Clacton-on-Sea served as a temporary internment camp prior to its later use by the military. The militia camp at Lippitts Hill served as an Italian PoW camp from 1940. The former TA camp at Thornwood, Epping, was pressed into service, and a new camp, No. 78, was established at High Garrett, Braintree, where the characteristic water tower may still be seen by the entrance to the Three Counties Crematorium. For most of the war prisoners were dispersed throughout the Empire, but by autumn 1944 thousands of German PoWs were being brought to Britain and sorted into Nazi goats and non-committed sheep. Many of these prisoners were accommodated in camps, such as Ashford Lodge, Halstead (No. 129), vacated by troops deploying abroad. Berechurch Hall, Colchester (Nos 186 and 204), however, opened in October 1944 as a tented transit camp for German PoWs on a greenfield site. Only in November 1945 were the tents replaced by some 400 Nissen huts, housing a population which peaked at 10,000. There were also medical facilities, canteens, administrative offices in Berechurch Hall, and at least two theatres. Although prisoners travelled out on work parties and, particularly after the end of the war, were increasingly permitted to attend local churches and to visit local families, the camp was surrounded by barbed-wire fences with stilted watchtowers. Not until late in 1947 were the last of the prisoners moved to a smaller camp near Bury-St-Edmunds.

Late in the war, other PoW camps had been established at Langdon Hills, Laindon (No. 266), at Purfleet (Nos 654 and 655), and in Mill Lane Camp (No. 116) at Hatfield Heath, now an egg-packing plant. Other sites such as a former HAA camp in Whalebone Lane, Dagenham, and parts of Stansted airfield were temporarily used to accommodate PoWs. Shaftesbury Camp, Harwich, Dovercourt (Nos 670 and 680) and the transit camp (No. 740), were used for prisoners being repatriated, some as late as 1948.

126 and 127 Hatfield Heath, Mill Lane, prisoner-of-war camp 116. *Right:* The water tower and one of the huts built of hollow clay blocks and asbestos. *Below:* Two of the camp's more substantial structures.

nine

The Cold War and Beyond

The period from 1945 through to the Millennium and into the twenty-first century has been one of constant change. The very real risk of nuclear exchange which dominated the Cold War era, up to the late 1980s, has been supplanted by increased threats of terrorist action. This is perceived as more dangerous than the IRA bombing campaigns of the 1970s, and has generated an escalation in public security and surveillance activities. At the same time that such threats are increasing, each year, from around 1967, there has been an incremental reduction in the regular Armed Forces and, most recently, a projected expansion of the reserves and volunteers.

Air Defence

The replacement of Germany by Russia as the origin of aerial assault made little difference to air-defence strategy. Enemy aircraft approaching the capital from the east, admittedly flying faster, and carrying greatly more destructive ordnance, would still need to be detected, intercepted, and destroyed, by either fighters in the air or guns on the ground. Operation Diver, against the V1, had produced highly effective AA defences. New systems set out to sharpen this up even more against the Russian threat, integrating CH radar, fighter aircraft guided by GCI radar, the observers of the ROC, and the AA guns, now completely radar-directed and automated. Following the realisation that Russia had acquired the capability of producing and delivering atomic weapons, a system for the protection of the RAF's Sector Operations Centres (SOC) and AA Operations Rooms (AAOR) against nuclear attack in the early 1950s, codenamed ROTOR, was developed. Later in the Cold War optimistic preparations for surviving a nuclear attack and continuing the functions of government were made, utilising some of these earlier structures.

Sector Operations Centres

One of the six new SOCs was Kelvedon Hatch, controlling the Metropolitan Area. Here, a three-level underground R4 bunker was constructed in 1951, the only structures visible on the surface being the guardhouse and the remote power-house, disguised respectively as a bungalow and a church. The guardhouse, whose pitched roof contains the tell-tale porthole window in its gable-end, gave access via a long sloping ramp to the lowest level of the three floors built into the side of a hill.

128 Kelvedon Hatch: the characteristic guardhouse housing the access ramp to the underground control rooms of this ROTOR scheme radar station.

At the other new SOCs the ramp led to the uppermost of the underground levels. It was intended that, were sufficient personnel to be available, the SOC would operate continuously round the clock, with accommodation at RAF North Weald. The SOC is built of reinforced concrete 10ft (3m) thick in the walls and 14ft (4.25m) in the roof. The internal rooms were sealed by gas-proof blast doors, and there were water tanks and generators making it self-sufficient. Its function in an attack was to collate all available information and to transmit evaluations to Fighter Command at Stanmore (North London) and the nearest GCI stations at Bawdsey (Suffolk) and Chenies (Buckinghamshire) in order to co-ordinate their defensive response. On the bottom floor was the map-room where the control tables presented an up-to-the-minute appreciation of the situation. This was connected by open well to the two floors above which contained offices and domestic facilities.

With subsequent improvements in radar, particularly the Type 80 sets, initially known as 'Green Garlic', it was found that the GCI stations could quite adequately operate without the SOCs (which soon became redundant and were mothballed). In 1955 Marconi were instructed to research anti-ballistic missiles, and an early-warning system. In view of the prevailing state of the technology, the first was found to be premature, but the second became achievable thanks to some help from the USA, in whose interest it was to include northern Europe in its defence systems.

The GCI system relied on a network of VHF Fixers, with duplicate sites very close by, which allowed fighter aircraft to establish their own position in order to intercept the enemy on whom they were being vectored. Established by 1951, there were six such Fixer beacons in the Metropolitan Area, one of which was at Wix, and a further six in the Eastern Area, including locations at Halstead and Debden.

The AA Operations Rooms and the HAA Batteries

In 1945 there were over 1,000 active AA sites in Britain, but post-war economies quickly reduced this figure to 200, and then to eighty, as the decision was taken to confine AA defences to three key areas, one of which was London and the south-east. Notwithstanding this contraction, there were three AAORs in Essex: Lippitts Hill (controlling north London's nine HAA sites); Mistley Heath as control for the Harwich GDA; and Vange, with its six sites defending the north bank of the Thames. Within a very short while Russian nuclear capability pointed up the futility of point defence, the country's AA defence was transferred to the RAF who would girdle the coast with a screen of Bloodhound surface-to-air missiles, and AA Command was wound up in 1955 with Coast Artillery following the next year.

The AAORs, set up by the army to receive information from the SOCs and to pass orders on to individual gun sites, were accommodated in rectangular, reinforced concrete bunkers with one level above ground and one below. This enabled two tiers of balconies to overlook the plotting table in its central, double-height well, surrounded by offices and domestic facilities.

The HAA sites were of two types, permanent ones with four 5.25in guns, largely manned by the regular army, and prepared emplacements for 3.7in mobile guns, manned by the TA. Buckland (N13) at Bowaters Farm, East Tilbury, a site for four 4.5in guns in an arc of octagonal emplacements in the Second World War, received four 5.25in guns in a diamond of their characteristic igloo-shaped emplacements in 1944, remaining operational until 1955. A gun store, a modified command post and other ancillary buildings were also added. By the Cold War period the guns had developed to such a pitch that the crews' duties were merely to ensure that they were fed ammunition. Each gun was fully automatic, being directed by radar, laid by computer, and powered by its own individual generator, built into the emplacement. There are also a number of brick barrack-type buildings, MT garages and a guardroom adjacent to the site, built in 1951 and replacing earlier buildings, but the site-owner is of the opinion that these may have constituted a separate camp, unconnected to the HAA battery. They now house farm machinery, while the gun-pits are

129 Mistley Heath: the AA operations room built to control the AA guns of the Harwich Gun-Defended Area.

130 Bowaters Farm, East Tilbury: one of the 5.25in HAA emplacements of the Buckland HAA site (N13). To the left can be seen the circular pit in which the gun was mounted, surrounded by lockers; to the right is the underground room with its ventilator, housing the generator which powered the gun.

131 Bowaters Farm, Buckland: 5.25in HAA site and the gun store.

overgrown and stand within fenced paddocks. Halls Green, Roydon, is an example of a post-war HAA battery for four 3.7in mobile guns. It consists of four octagonal gun-pits in an arc, each with four built-in ammunition lockers and a generator-house, with openings through which the gun might be introduced to be connected to the holdfast with its electrics. The other two structures on the site are a command post and a stand-by generator building.

After 1955, apart from the SAM sites, all AA weapons were mobile, being deployed as and where necessary either with the field army or for home defence. LAA weapons, both Bofors guns and Rapier missiles, were towed, along with their accompanying Marconi Blindfire radar. These AA missile systems were the direct descendants of the Brakemine rockets being tested at Walton-on-the-Naze back in the mid-1940s.

132 Bowaters Farm, Buckland, HAA site: the camp guardroom.

133 Halls Green, Roydon (TL418087): HAA site for 3.7in (mobile) guns; this shows one half of an emplacement with protected access to ammunition storage.

Bloodhounds were deployed in a linear shield stretching from Yorkshire down to Suffolk, the most southerly of these sites being Rattlesden, with Bawdsey Manor being added when Mark II missiles became available in 1979, remaining operational until 1990.

The Royal Observer Corps and UKWMO

The established control centre in Colchester continued to operate in the ROC air-craft-spotting service which reformed in early 1947, by now more closely integrated into the RAF's fighter control system. The wartime 18 Group was part of the RAF's Metropolitan Sector, and in 1953 it became 4 Group, with thirteen clusters of posts under command, numbering forty-one in all, actually in Essex. By stand-down in 1991, this figure had been drastically reduced as twenty posts had been closed in the reorganisation of 1968, followed by Little Waltham in 1975. Reporting was to the Filter Plot at the RAF's local SOC at Kelvedon Hatch. One of the problems for the wartime observers had been the exposed nature of many of the spotting posts, so in 1951, Messrs Orlit, manufacturers of small concrete buildings, were commissioned to produce a ROC post which would become standard. In essence it was a concrete box with one roofed section, and one open to the sky for mounting the new graduated post chart on its removable pillar. The post could either stand on the ground (Orlit A) or on concrete legs, 6ft (1.9m) above the ground (Orlit B).

According to Nick Catford's survey in 1999, no Orlit A posts survive in Essex, but Orlit B posts may be found at Hatfield Peverel, Tendring and Rochford. It quickly became apparent that the human eye, even aided by primitive sighting instruments, was unequal to the task of identifying and tracking high-speed jet aircraft, and the ROC faced an uncertain future. However, a new role had been identified through the need for a network of warning posts to report on nuclear strikes and to track the movement of radiation or nuclear fall-out. The ROC, combined with the old ARP service, under the title of United Kingdom Warning and Monitoring Organisation (UKWMO), was assigned this task. To enable them to carry out this new role an underground post was designed and between 1957 and 1964 some 1,500 of these were constructed, if possible on existing sites, but around half the Essex posts needed to be re-sited to suitable underground locations above the water table. Chigwell was moved into the RAF complex, and Clacton/Holland-on-Sea, which had already been moved in 1950 onto the roof of the Alton Park Hotel, underwent a further move into the basement of Martello Tower 'D'. Orlit's underground post consisted of a concrete box, 19ft (5.8m) by 8ft 6in (2.6m) by 7ft 6in (2.3m), with access through a hatch and

134 Tendring: (TM144245) Royal Observer Corps Orlit Type B aircraft spotting-post; the roofed area is nearer the camera.

135 Fyfield: (TL560059) on west side of the B184, a Royal Observer Corps underground monitoring post.

down a ladder. Inside were a desk, a double-bunk and a chemical toilet. On the surface were the turret with hatch and the Ground Zero Indicator, a ventilator, and the Fixed Survey Meter Probe. Each post had a crew of four, was in a cluster of three or four, and in telephone contact with ROC Group HQ.

If the posts were to be protected, then so should the group HQs. A new, semi-sunken control centre was built to the rear of the existing house in Lexden Road, its superstructure, with ventilators, on the surface, and a buried, double-height operations room with central well overlooked by balconies. The plotting table was updated by information coming in from the scattered posts and recorded on Perspex panels by volunteers who became expert at mirror-writing. This bunker has been demolished and replaced by housing, although the house remains.

Government Nuclear Bunkers

Both national and local government made provision for carrying on after a nuclear attack by building underground bunkers as centres of administration. As it happened, the early demise of ROTOR brought two suitable and conveniently redundant bunkers, at Kelvedon Hatch and Mistley Heath, onto the market. That at Kelvedon Hatch, in 1961, barely ten years old, was converted into a sub-Regional Seat of Government, SR HQ 51, for the control of the London Region. It was furnished with dormitories and domestic facilities to enable a staff of 300 to be self-sufficient for up to three months. Once a state of emergency had been declared, these chosen ones would have proceeded with all despatch to the bunker. If necessary, they would have gone through the decontamination chambers after passing through the security measures taken to prevent the locals getting in. The imminence of an attack was indicated by colour codes. Whilst equipped to collate information relating to levels of nuclear fall-out, the establishment's prime purpose was to issue advice and instructions to any survivors on the outside. The communications centre therefore contained a BBC studio which could transmit the diktats of the Regional Commissioner who would have assumed absolute power under the prevailing state of martial law. The bunker's capability was maintained into the late 1980s.

Mistley AAOR, also built in 1951 and redundant by the early 1960s, first became the Essex Civil Defence Centre, and then served as the Essex County Council Emergency HQ from 1963 to 1993. The two-level central control room, with its underground lower level, would have co-ordinated public order, fire and rescue operations, public health, communications, action to aid refugees (but also to prevent them impeding military action), and food distribution. Whether anything of this activity would have had any meaning was fortunately never discovered, although Peter Watkins' film *The War Game*, suppressed at the time, probably came nearer than most to describing the futility of the 'Protect and Survive' injunction. Essex County Council maintained other sub-controls at Billericay, Harlow and in the basement of Chelmsford County Hall's extension. This latter provision became liable to flooding by the late 1970s and was replaced by a further extension, completed in 1985 when the Thatcher government was promoting the construction of municipal bunkers. Another example dating from this inexplicable paranoia was the Castle Point Borough Council's bunker at Thundersleigh near Southend, only completed in 1992 and modelled on a Water Authority bunker at Staverton, near Gloucester. At the other extreme, Basildon declared itself a nuclear-free zone, earmarking a pair of portacabins as its emergency centre. Sited in the middle of a council depot, they would have been protected by skips piled high with rubbish. Another recycled bunker was at RAF North Weald, where Epping Forest District Council took over and extensively refurbished the former Fighter Command Sector Operations Centre. Tendring District Council was allocated space in the Mistley bunker, whilst Thurrock constructed an emergency centre in the basement of its council offices.

136 North Weald: former RAF Fighter Sector's operations block, converted into Epping Forest District Council's nuclear bunker.

Military Aviation

After all the activity of the war, Essex saw a significant reduction in military aviation. Many of the operational airfields were quickly returned to agriculture by 1946, but some were retained in case they might be needed. Boxted and Earls Colne were kept under Care and Maintenance, and Great Dunmow and Ridgewell served as USAF stores depots into the 1960s. Debden accommodated the Empire Radio School (1949 to 1960), as well as a division of the RAF Technical College and the RAF Police Depot (1960 to 1975), after which it became Carver Barracks. Hornchurch hosted the Officers' Advanced Training School until 1948, when it moved to Bircham Newton (Norfolk), and the RAF Aircrew Selection Centre (from 1952 to 1962). The Ministry of Aviation Fire Training School was established at Stansted in 1960. Rochford, Stansted and Stapleford Tawney had all resumed civilian flying as soon as the war ended, and Rivenhall was taken over by Marconi for systems testing in 1956. That left the USAF base at Wethersfield and RAF North Weald as the only operational military airfields in the county. After runway extensions, Wethersfield became home to the 20th Fighter-Bomber Wing of the US 3rd Air Force in 1951, with its F100 Super Sabres, until its move to Upper Heyford (Oxfordshire) in 1955. Ultimately it hosted four fighter-bomber wings with a nuclear capability, as well as flying 'covert infiltration' missions involving special forces operations in Europe using 'Combat Talon' MC-130E Hercules transport aircraft. The U-2 spy-planes, part of the Precision Location Strike System for scanning the battlefield from 15 miles (24km) up in the sky, also used the base from May 1975 when five of these aircraft visited.

USAF support services, including heavy engineering runway-repair ('Red Horse') and search-and-rescue units, stayed at Wethersfield through to 1991, when the station

137 North Weald Control Tower (5223a/51): built in around 1952 as part of this RAF airfield's upgrade.

was taken over by the MOD Police. North Weald also received runway extensions and a new Type 5223a/51 control tower in around 1952, in order for its two squadrons of the RAAF to fly their de Havilland Vampires. By 1953 it was a sector station with a regular squadron of Hawker Hunters which provided the Black Arrows aerobatic team. However the RAAF was disbanded in 1957 and on the departure of 111 Squadron the station was reduced to Care and Maintenance. In recent years only civilian light aircraft have been flown.

The Army in the Later Twentieth Century

Colchester continued as a garrison town after the war, with Flagstaff House remaining HQ Eastern District (Army). By the late 1950s the 3rd Infantry Division, along with the 19th Independent Infantry Brigade, reformed in 1950, were based there, the latter occupying Le Cateau and Cherry Tree Barracks. In 1989, 19 Brigade was still in residence, its task being to join the 4th Armoured Division in Germany at forty-eight hours' notice. In more recent times Colchester has been home to 16th (Air Assault) Brigade, an independent formation comprising parachute battalions with supporting artillery, engineer, signals, medical and logistics units, all equipped and trained for their airborne role.

In 1975 the RAF handed over Debden to the army as Carver Barracks, referred to by the MOD as 'Wimbish'. It was occupied by a succession of armoured reconnaissance regiments, including the 13/18th Hussars, 9/12th Lancers and the 1st Queen's Dragoon Guards, until 1993, slated to join the 4th Armoured Division in Germany if necessary, along with 19 Brigade from Colchester at the same short notice. Since then Carver Barracks has been home to 33 and 101 Engineer Regiments, EOD units.

138 Wimbish: Carver Barracks (formerly RAF Debden), vehicle repair garage.

139 Wimbish: Carver Barracks (formerly RAF Debden), barrack block.

The Territorial Army Since 1947

Despite the many units being disbanded or amalgamated in the immediate aftermath of the war, a significant number of TA units still reformed in the county in 1947. The schedule of Essex TA units produced in 1950 shows AA Command alone accounting for eight AA regiments along with a further nine support units including RASC, RE, REME and WRAC. Eastern Command was responsible for field, coast and LAA artillery units; the 4th Battalion of the Essex Regiment; a company of 10th Battalion the Parachute Regiment; Light Aid Detachments of REME; companies of RE, RASC, RAOC and Royal Signals. In all, some seventeen units, plus ten assorted WRAC platoons, troops and squadrons, were in operation. The winding-up of Coast Artillery and AA Commands in 1955 to 1956, however, started a process of successive reductions. There are, in 2012, barely half a dozen active TACs in the county. One example will suffice to demonstrate the extent of the TA's contraction in recent years: Whipps Cross and Chelmsford TACs provide homes for 68 (Inns of Court and City and Essex Yeomanry) Signal Squadron (Volunteers) TA, representing the successor unit to five regiments of yeomanry cavalry, which have severally been horsed cavalry, armoured reconnaissance troops, tank regiments, armoured signallers and field artillery.

Barracks

In 1945 the army had decided to develop Berechurch PoW Camp as a replacement for Military Detention Centre 19 at neighbouring Reed Hall. Now known as the Military Corrective Training Centre, this opened in 1948, taking in 'Soldiers under Sentence' from other centres such as Fort Darland, Chatham. By the end of the war, the Colchester Barracks estate had essentially little changed since Edwardian times. Something had to be done to make army life attractive to volunteers. During the 1960s Meeanee and Hyderabad Barracks were modernised; Roman Barracks, the former Roman Way camp, was built in 1962; Goojerat was rebuilt in 1970; and Sobraon demolished in 1971. More recently Merville Barracks has been added. As the garrison has contracted, so many of the old buildings have been either demolished or redeveloped. The old Riding School has now been converted into a health centre serving the new houses and apartment blocks which have filled out the Cavalry and Le Cateau Barracks sites whilst retaining the officers' mess and the old cavalry barrack blocks. Meeanee and Hyderabad Barracks have been completely demolished but for the officers' quarters and mess. The senior officers' houses in the angle of Napier and Flagstaff Roads appear to be awaiting conversion to apartments, but the REME Command Workshops next to Le Cateau's officers' mess still functions. At Harwich the coastguard cottages at Angelgate, built in 1858, were used as army married quarters until 1972. Wimbish continues to develop twenty-first-century facilities on its 1930s site.

Drill Halls

The size of the TA in 1947 meant that finding sufficient premises still presented problems. In some places public halls were used, as at Brightlingsea, where the Foresters' and YMCA Halls served as drill halls in 1950 (as did the Women's Institute Hall at Thorpe-le-Soken). Old hutted camps at Buckles Farm, South Ockendon and at Coggeshall Road, Braintree, were also pressed into service; much later, another camp at Brickfield Road, Vange, was also added. There have been a very few new builds. The new TAC at Old Road, Harlow, opened in 1947. A three-storey building on Butt Road, Colchester, was built in the late 1960s as a TAC but functioned as such for only a very short while, being superseded in 1984 by the present buildings on Circular Road East. In 1994 an impressive new TAC at Springfield Lyons in Chelmsford opened, a blend of contemporary style with some traditional gravitas.

140 Chelmsford: Springfield Lyons, the new Territorial Army Centre, opened in 1994.

Logistics

Transportation Movements

The bunker under Hamilton House in Parkeston, the wartime RN HQ, was refurbished in the 1980s for use as the RN Auxiliary Service (RNXS) HQ and operations room. This had hitherto occupied Martello Tower 'P' in Felixstowe, and in 1972 the RNXS had also been using Martello Tower 'F' in Clacton. The role of the RNXS had been extended to the defence of Ports and Anchorages, so the bunker was equipped to enable the NOIC to control shipping movements in and around Harwich, Parkeston, Felixstowe, Ipswich Docks and the river Orwell. This would have been particularly important as Felixstowe and Harwich were both designated as Major Movement Centres, and their approaches via Colchester were designated Military Road Routes. Felixstowe operated in the Cold War period as a US Army Transportation Terminal, permanently manned by US staff handling personnel and 35,000 tons of military stores annually. These included explosives and nuclear warheads being brought in to supply the air bases in East Anglia, and the cruise missile bases of Molesworth (Cambridgeshire) and Greenham Common (Berkshire). The system of Military Road Routes, together with its accompanying, and often overlapping, network of Essential Service Routes (ESR) were intended for military use in an emergency and would have been kept clear of civilian traffic by TA troops under the supervision of the civil authorities controlled from the RSGs such as Kelvedon Hatch. The Military Road Routes in Essex included the A12, codenamed 'CAT', the eastern end of a through route originating in Cornwall, and the A45, now the A14, codenamed 'YAK' and linking with the routes north and west. The ESR network was much more extensive embracing most of the country's trunk roads including the A12, A127, A133, A218 and A604.

Emergency Food Stocks

As well as keeping the roads clear of refugees in order to be able to move troops and munitions freely, there was also a fear, voiced during the various exercises that were held, that attempts would be made by organised gangs coming out of the cities to loot food stores. The Ministry of Supply and the Ministry of Agriculture, Fisheries and Food maintained a network of depots which stored foodstuffs, water-purification equipment, mobile kitchens and bakeries, fuel and medical supplies, for controlled distribution and community use in designated centres such as schools. Essex being regarded as potentially being in the firing line, there were only two such depots provided within the county, at Elsenham Station (521G) and at Station Road, Marks Tey (521J). These therefore needed protection, and a general denial of access to the main roads was a start.

Communications

The introduction of early warning systems in the early 1960s only made sense if the information gained from the scanners could quickly be disseminated across the country, particularly if the vaunted 'four-minute warning' were to prove significant. The microwave tower network, most commonly exemplified by the Post Office Tower in

141 Elsenham Station: the emergency buffer depot (521g), one in a nationwide network, set up by the Ministry of Agriculture, Fisheries and Food by the early 1970s, to store food and cooking utensils.

Tottenham Court Road, built in 1961, was developed primarily for military use as part of the 'Backbone' system, but with an overt civil function in relaying TV transmissions. Whilst satellites have assumed the original military function, the two original towers in Essex, at Sibleys (TL562301) and at Kelvedon Hatch (TQ578990), still function in civil use. Kelvedon Hatch had been a key junction, linking the eastern and western spurs of 'Backbone'.

In order to safeguard internal security the Home Office maintained a network of 'Hilltop' radio stations. In Essex, one stands on top of the bunker at Kelvedon Hatch (TQ562995); another is at High Garrett outside Braintree (TL780273), and a third at Sewards End (TL572393). The US military also operated a radio transmitter and microwave relay system. A spur from the masts at Barkway (Hertfordshire) ran to the former Home Office mast at High Garrett, then on to the former radar station at Great Bromley (TM102261) and thence to the USAF bases in Suffolk (with a further link to NATO in Belgium and Holland).

Other Military Facilities

The RNAD at Wrabness closed in 1966 and the buildings are now occupied by a haulage firm. Defence Fuel Support Points at West Thurrock and Purfleet were maintained by the US Army and Air Force into the 1980s. At Braintree, HMS *Cicero* was the Royal Navy Orthopaedic Rehabilitation Centre, 1947 to 1948, and Colchester Military Hospital continued in use until 1977, its buildings having almost reached their centenary when they were demolished in the 1990s. Wethersfield airfield was designated an emergency mortuary as lately as 2000. Purfleet range remained in use by the regulars until 1961, but was used for at least a further ten years by cadets. It is now a RSPB reserve.

From 1947, under the auspices of the Atomic Weapons Research Establishment (AWRE), development activities continued on Foulness Island as an extension of the Shoeburyness ranges. Along with an administrative block housing the office of the director of the British atomic bomb project, a number of specialist structures were constructed including a blast tunnel, workshops and non-descript sheds. After curbs

142 Kelvedon Hatch: microwave tower for relaying warnings of a nuclear emergency to the military and the civil authorities.

on nuclear testing had been agreed, it became necessary to rely on small-scale simulations. Work at Foulness concerned aspects of the behaviour of nuclear weapons, involving tests to determine the effects of the heat and blast generated by atomic explosions. Scale models of buildings, vehicles and aircraft, and manikins, were therefore used to replicate, as closely as possible, the effects. There was also some preparation of explosives, supplied by the Royal Ordnance Factories, for use in nuclear weapons.

The Cold War-generated nuclear threat may be over but it has been replaced by a heightened awareness of a potential threat from terrorist action. This necessitated the mounting of a large-scale operation to safeguard the 2012 Olympics by placing AA missiles on apartment blocks around the Olympic Park in Stratford, and by holding jet fighters ready at a moment's notice to intercept and, if necessary, to shoot down unauthorised aircraft over-flying sensitive areas.

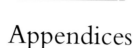

Appendices

Appendix One: Prehistoric Camps

Asheldham Camp, oval Iron Age fort
Billericay, Norsey Wood, Iron Age camp
Brentwood Camp
Colchester, oppidum of the Trinovantes; Gosbecks Archaeological Park
Danbury Camp
Epping, Ambresbury Banks, plateau camp
Great Hallingbury, Wallbury Camp
Great Totham, double-ditched Bronze Age enclosure
Highwood, Birch Spring, quadrilateral enclosure
Ilford, Uphall Camp
Littlebury, Ring Hill Camp, early Iron Age
Loughton Camp, oval, early Iron Age camp on spur
Mucking, North Ring, Bronze Age enclosure
Orsett, Neolithic causewayed enclosure
Pitchbury Ramparts, Great Horkesley, oval enclosure
Portingbury, Iron Age, ditched mound
Southend, Prittlewell Camp
South Weald Camp, fort
Springfield Lyons
Witham, Chipping Hill, Iron Age fort

Appendix Two: Medieval and Tudor Fortifications

Norman earthwork castles
Berden, Stocks Farm, The Crump, small ringwork   TL470289
Berden, The Rookery, failed ringwork   TL466292
Birch Castle   TL943198
Bocking, Mill Hill, low motte   TL764278
Canfield, large motte   TL594179
Chrishall, Park Wood, motte   TL452386

Clavering, large moated platform   TL471319

Elmdon, Castle Grove, ringwork   TL460400

Felsted, Quaker Mount, probably a mill-mount   TL695204

Great Easton, motte and bailey   TL608254

Great Ilford, Lavender Mount, possible motte and bailey   TQ437852

Great Wakering, earthworks   TQ948895

Hockley, Plumberow Mount, possible motte   TQ840938

Magdalen Laver, motte   TL516084

Mount Bures, motte   TL904326

Navestock, Slades, doubtful motte   TQ544988

Ongar, motte and bailey   TL554032

Orsett, Bishop Bonner's Palace, ringwork and rectangular bailey   TQ641823

Pleshey, motte and bailey   TL665145

Purleigh, motte   TL841017

Rayleigh, c. 1070, motte and two baileys   TQ805909

Rickling Hall, motte   TL499302

Stansted Mountfitchet, ringwork and bailey   TL516250

Stebbing, motte   TL657244

Willingale Doe, possible motte and bailey   TL600082

Stone castles

Colchester   TL999253

Hadleigh   TQ810861

Hedingham   TL787358

Newport   (possibly) TL520344

Pleshey   TL665145

Saffron Walden   TL540397

Writtle, King John's Hunting Lodge   TL676068

Later-medieval fortified manor houses

Boreham ('Walkfares', now Newall Convent,) licensed 1491 to Earl of Ormond;
　　(Henry VIII built quadrangular palace after 1518)   TL734103

Faulkbourne, licensed 1439, to John Montgomery   TL803164

Maldon, Moot Hall, fortified town-house of Darcy's, 1435   TL850070

Nether Hall, Roydon, built c. 1460s by London lawyer   TL397083

Rickling Hall, in bailey of Norman castle, brick house of 1490-1500   TL499302

Rochford Hall, rebuilt 1430 (and again in the sixteenth century by Lord Rich)   TQ870903

Saffron Walden, Humphrey de Bohun granted a licence, 1347 for house, possibly in the
　　castle bailey   TL541386

Southchurch Hall, late twelfth-century moat, with mid-fourteenth-century manor
house   TQ894855

South Ockendon Hall, moat and stone gatehouse; new house built 1862   TQ603832

Stanstead Hall, Halstead, licensed 1341   TL826288

West Horndon, Old Thorndon Hall, licensed 1414, reconstructed 1570   TQ618917

Tudor strong houses
Beckingham Hall, Tolleshunt Major, 1543, gatehouse   TL910113
Gosfield Hall, after 1539, quadrangular with gatehouse in west front   TL775297
Horham Hall, 1502-20 and later, tower of 1580, gatehouse and moat   TL588294
Ingatestone courtyard house with gatehouse licensed 1551, built 1539-66   TQ654985
Layer Marney Tower, only gatehouse built c. 1525   TL928174
Leez Priory, inner and outer gatehouses, by Lord Rich from 1536   TL701184
St Osyth's, Lord Darcy built house out of priory, by 1600   TM119156
Wickham Bishops, moated palace of bishops of London, then manor   TL831106

Appendix Three: Sea Fencible Units During the Napoleonic Wars

These were based at:
Bradwell-on-Sea
Brightlingsea
Burnham
Clacton
Colchester
Harwich
Holland and Walton
Maldon
Manningtree
Mersea Island
Paglesham
Southend-on-Sea
Tollesbury

Appendix Four: Camps and Barracks

Before the First World War
Colchester, Meeanee Barracks, 1898
Colchester, Hyderabad Barracks, 1904
Great Baddow, military camp, 1900-1950s
Lexden Heath Camp
Romford Cavalry Barracks 1795-1825
Shoeburyness, Horseshoe Barracks, 1860-9
Warley, East India Company Barracks, 1804, Chapel, 1857
Weeley Barracks, Napoleonic
Widford Barracks, Napoleonic
Writtle, Napoleonic camp at TL680065

First World War

Camps with some of the units known to have been accommodated in them:

Aveley, Belhus Park tented Infantry Camp: 11 Bn Glosters; 15 Bn KRRC

Billericay Infantry Camp: 2/5 and 2/6 Bns Cameronians; 6 Bn Warwicks; 10 Bn Border Regt

Braintree, Panfield Camp: No. 2 Coy (HT) ASC Train; 73 Division

Chelmsford No.1 (HQ); 3 and 4 Coys (HT) ASC Train; 73 Division

Chelmsford 220 Bde 73 Division, 1917

Chelmsford, Galleywood: concentration area for 3rd South Midland Bde. RFA, TF; assembly area for 61 South Midland Division, including 2/7 and 2/8 Worcesters, 2/4 and 2/5 Glosters, and eight battalions of the Warwickshire Regt, 1915

Clacton (between Little Clacton and Thorpe): Essex Territorial Force Camp, 1914

Coggeshall: 12 Bn King's Own Lancasters, 73 Division, summer 1917

Colchester Sobraon Barracks: 7 Bn Sussex, Regt 36 Bde, 12 Division, K1

Colchester Infantry Camp: 8 Bn Royal Fusiliers; 36 Bde, 12 Division, K1; 10 Bn Essex Regt; 53 Bde; 8 Bn Sussex Regt, 54 Bde, 18 Division K2

Colchester, Hyderabad Barracks: 2/7 Bn Lancashire Fusiliers, 3/16, to France 2/17

Colchester: 3/5th Bn Lancashire Fusiliers 3/1916, to France 3/1917

Colchester, Meeanee Barracks 2/6th Bn Lancashire Fusiliers 2/17, to France 1/18

Colchester: No. 1 (HQ); 2 and 4 (HT) Coys ASC Train; 67 (Home Counties) Division

Colchester: 51 Reserve Park (HT) ASC; 11 Auxiliary MT Coy ASC, 1915–20

Colchester: No. 1 (HQ) 2, 3 and 4 Coys; (HT) ASC Train 71 Division

Colchester Infantry Camp: 212, 213 and 214 Bdes, 71 Division, 1917; 51 and 52 Bns Sussex Regt to 71 Division, early 1918

Colchester: 5 and 6 Reserve Brigades 1916; also at Dovercourt and Harwich

Colchester, Boxted Road, Severalls County Lunatic Asylum: Recruit Camp

Colchester, Layer Road football ground: used for drill and parades

Colchester, Reed Hall Camp: tented then hutted

Dovercourt Infantry Camp: 10 (Reserve) Bn Bedfordshire Regt

Gidea Park: 18 (Service) Bn (Arts and Crafts) KRRC, June 1915

Hornchurch, Grey Towers Camp: (23rd (1st Sportsman's) Bn Royal Fusiliers 1914; 25 (Reserve) Bn Middlesex Regt, 1915 (recruited at Crystal Palace); 26th Bn Middlesex Regt (3 Public Works Pioneers Bn) 1915

Command Depot: NZEF 1916, NZ camp/hospital 1916–19

Kelvedon: 26th Bn Kings Liverpool Regt 218 Bde 73 Division, 1/1917

Maldon: No. 3 Coy (HT) ASC Train, 73 Division

Purfleet Barracks: tented camp for 10,000, plus 160 'Knuts of Purfleet' huts on part of Rainham ranges for recruits

Purfleet Camp: 37 Bde, 12 Division, K1; 55 Bde, 18 Division, K2

Romford, Hare Hall Infantry Camp: 28 Bn London Regt (Artists' Rifles), and 24 Bn (2 Sportsman's) Royal Fusiliers

Shoeburyness, School of Instruction for Royal Horse and Royal Field Artillery, 1915

Southend Local Auxiliary HT Coy. ASC, West Riding Reserve Bde, TF

South Ockendon, West Ham (Salvation Army) Farm Colony: tented recruit camp.
Terling, Witham Camp: 2/5 and 2/6 Bns Cameronians, 7/1916
Warley Barracks: Essex Regt Depot
Warley Barracks: 3 Reserve Bn Irish Guards; 2 Regular Bn, formed 1915
West Ham Water Lane School / West Ham Park billets: drill ground for TF artillery
Witham: No. 2 Coy (HT) ASC Train, 73 Division

Second World War

Camps with some of the units known to have been accommodated in them:

Aveley, Belhus Park: D-Day Marshalling Area Camp S4
Brentwood, Weald Park: D-Day Marshalling Area Camp S8
Bures: US Army 2108th Ordnance Ammunition Battalion (Aviation)
Burnham-on-Crouch, Creeksea Camp: 8 (Guards) Commando, 1940
Chadwell St Mary/Tilbury: D-Day Marshalling Area Camp S2
Chelmsford, Hylands Park: camp for 1st SAS, 1944
Clacton-on-Sea, Butlin's: No. 4 Pioneer Corps Training Centre
Coggeshall: US Army 136th Radio Security Section
Colchester, Cherry Tree Camp: base for 19 Infantry Bde
Colchester: Berechurch Hall, Reed Hall and Roman Way camps
Dovercourt: Beacon Hill, searchlight training camp
Dovercourt: army transit camp
Easton Lodge: army camp, assembly point for 51 HAA Regt, 1940
Grays, Orsett Heath golf club: D-Day Marshalling Area Camp S1
Halstead, Ashford Lodge: US Army Ordnance Depot
Harlow, Moor Hall Camp: US Army 25th and 34th Bomb Disposal Squadrons
Hatfield Peverel: army transit camp
Kelvedon, Felix Hall: army camp
Laindon: D-Day Embarkation Camp
Lippitts Hill: camp for 184th AAA Battery US Army, 1942-5
Mistley Heath: hutted camp behind AAOR
Newport, Shortgrove Park: Northants Regt, RASC, RAMC, REME, then US hospital
Orsett Hall: RASC camp
Purfleet Ranges: London District Machine Gun Training School
Purfleet Camp: D-Day Marshalling Area Camps E6, S3 and T6
Rolls Park: army camp
St Osyth: HMS *Helder* Combined Operations training camp
Shoeburyness: Horseshoe Barracks and overflow camp
Somers Heath, Ford Place: D-Day Embarkation Camp and HQ Area S
South Ockendon Mental Hospital: field bakery for D-Day Marshalling Area S
Stansted airfield: US Army AAA depot
Theydon Bois, Hill Hall: assembly area for Welsh Guards Bns 1940
Tilbury, St Chads School: HQ D-Day Marshalling Area S
Tilbury Docks: D-Day Embarkation Camp E5

Vange: camp for US Army 34th AAA Group
Wanstead Flats: concentration area for transport units pre-D-Day
Wanstead, Royal Wanstead School: HQ D-Day Marshalling Area T
Warley Barracks: Essex Regt Depot
Warley Barracks: No. 1 Infantry Training Centre
Warley Barracks: D-Day Marshalling Area Camp S7
West Ham Greyhound Stadium: D-Day Marshalling Area Camp T4
Wivenhoe Park: D-Day Embarkation Camp

Appendix Five: Air Defence

Radar sites in Essex

No.	Site name	NGR	Type
22	Canewdon	TQ905946	Chain Home/GEE
22M	Loftmans	TQ919938	Mobile Radio Unit
24	Great Bromley	TM102261	Chain Home
24M	Frating	TM083225	Mobile Radio Unit
M68	Wln-on-the-Naze	TM252213	Coast Defence/Chain Home Low (temp)
23A	Wln-on-the-Naze	TM254235	Chain Home Low
M138	Martello Tower	TM463553	Walton duplicate CD/CHL
M140	Dengie	TM000030	Coast Defence/Chain Home Low
30G	Foulness	TR006932	Ground Controlled Interception
K140	Dengie	TM000031	Chain Home Extra Low

Bombing decoy sites in Essex

Blackmore, RAF North Weald and Ongar, TL619043, airfield 'Q'
Brightlingsea, Harwich, TM091144, Naval QL/QF
Bulphan*, RAF Hornchurch, TQ656857, airfield 'K' and 'Q'
East Mersea, Harwich, TM052157, Naval QL/QF
Fobbing, Shell Haven, TQ731838, Oil QF
Great Bromley, Colchester, TM076257, civil temporary SF
Kirby-le-Soken, Harwich, TM222239, Naval SF/QL
Lambourne End, London, TQ493938, permanent Starfish
Little Baddow, Chelmsford, TL758064, civil temporary SF
Nazeing*, RAF North Weald, TL421055, airfield 'K' and 'Q'
Rainham Marshes, London, TQ529800, permanent Starfish
Spinnels Farm*, Harwich, TM162298, Naval 'QF'
Stanford-le-Hope*, Thames Haven, TQ700811, Oil QF
Stambourne, RAF Debden and Ridgewell, TL727394, airfield 'Q'
Walton-on-the-Naze, Harwich, TM262247, Naval SF/QL

N.B.: The control blockhouses of those marked * survive (2012)

AAORs and HAA sites in the Cold War period

Vange: AAOR for north Thames at TQ719864 with HAA on-site; controlled sites at Hadleigh at TQ799864; Rayleigh at TQ797923; Ramsden Hall at TQ701954

Bucklands (East Tilbury): at TQ678772; Ridgemarsh Farm at TR022943; and Stondon Massey at TQ574999

Halls Green, Roydon: TL418087, site for mobile HAA guns

Lippitts Hill: AAOR for North London at TQ396970

Mistley Heath: AAOR for Harwich GDA at TM123314

Royal Observer Corps posts (selected examples)

Colchester ROC, HQ 18/ 4 Group: Errington Lodge, 22 Lexden Road, at TL985249

Brightlingsea: Bateman's/Batenicus Tower at TM077162

Chipping Ongar/Fyfield: u/g post at TQ559057

Clacton/Holland-on-Sea: Martello Tower 'D' at TM162134.

Finchingfield u/g post: TL695328

Hatfield Peverel: ROC u/g post + Orlit B at TL801125

Tendring: ROC u/g post + Orlit B at TM144246

Appendix Six: Secret and Covert Operations, Second World War

Audley End House: Station 43 SOE Polish W/T training

Braintree: Eastern Area HQ for RCM out-stations of RAF No. 80 (Signals) Wing

Brentwood: HQ 35th US Infantry Division (real unit assigned to FUSAG)

Burnham-on-Crouch: 8 Commando training base

Canewdon: GEE station

Chelmsford: HQ US 3rd Army, XII and XX Corps (notional FUSAG units)

Chelmsford: HQ US 7th Armoured Division (real unit assigned to FUSAG)

Chelmsford, Hylands Park: 1 SAS base from November 1944-October 1945

Chelmsford, Hylands Park, Hylands House: 1 SAS officers' mess

Colchester: 2 SAS base until October 1945

Roydon, Briggens: Station XIV SOE Forgery and Polish Section

Saffron Walden, Audley End House: SOE Polish Section STS 43

Waltham Abbey: Ministry of Supply post 1945, SOE explosives R and D

Walton-on-the-Naze, Holland Haven: anti-jamming site run by RAF No. 80 (Signals) Wing reporting to Radlett Operations Room from February 1942

Wix: RAF DF station to boost VHF range from RAF Debden for fighter control

Appendix Seven: Munitions Production

Pre-First World War

Chelmsford: ordnance depot, 1815

Colchester: gunpowder works, Civil War

Dagenham: fitting-out yards for Dreadnoughts, 1906-14
Great Oakley, Bramble Island, Harwich: The High Explosives Co. Ltd, 1899
Harwich: Royal Naval Dockyard
Kynochtown: explosives factory, 1897-1920s
Pitsea Hall Farm: British Explosives Syndicate, explosives factory, 1891-1920s
Purfleet: Powder Stores, 1760s-1950s
Shoeburyness: rocket testing, nineteenth century
Stanford-le-Hope, Curry Marsh: Miners' Safety Explosives Co. Ltd, late nineteenth century
Tilbury Fort: cartridge filling station, 1892
Waltham Abbey: Royal Gunpowder Factory and explosives works, 1664-1945
Warley: cartridge filling station, 1892
West Ham, Abbey Marsh: Congreve's rocket works, early nineteenth century

First World War
Barking Wharf: cork lifebelt factory, destroyed by fire, 1915
Barking, Hertford Road: Ajax Chemical Co., shell production
Chelmsford: Hoffman Manufacturing Co., ball-bearings production
Chelmsford: Marconi, wireless-telegraphy, radio-valves, telephony
Dagenham: Nitrogen Products and Carbide Co., chemical works
Dagenham: Sterling Telephone and Electrical Co.
Great Oakley, Bramble Island, Harwich: The High Explosives Co. Ltd, 1899
Kynochtown: explosives factory, 1897-1920s
Pitsea Hall Farm: British Explosives Syndicate, explosives factory, 1891-1920s
Purfleet: Powder Stores, 1760s-1950s
Rainham: C Betrand Fields Soap Works, explosives factory
Rainham Chemical Works Synthetic Products Co., HM Factory, chemical works,
    explosives factory, TNT plant
Shoeburyness ranges: projectile testing
Stanford-le-Hope, Curry Marsh: Miners' Safety Explosives Co. Ltd
Stratford: Admiralty Filling Station, explosives factory
Waltham Abbey: Royal Gunpowder Factory and explosives works, 1664-1945
Waltham Abbey: new cordite and nitroglycerine plants in Royal Gunpowder Works
Walthamstow, Blackhorse Lane: Baird and Tatlock, HM Factory Trench Warfare Supply
    Department factories

Second World War
Bures: USAAF Forward Ammunition Storage Depot, 1943
Dagenham: Ford's, vehicles, engines, tracked carriers and De Lisle carbines
Dagenham: Sterling Armaments Co., De Lisle carbines, 1944
Epping, Copped Hall: No. 422 RAF Advanced Ammunition Park, 1944. Moved to:
Epping, Bury Lodge: No. 422 RAF Advanced Fuel and Ammunition Park
Leytonstone/Gants Hill: unopened Central Line tunnels, Plesseys factory
Purfleet: Powder Stores, 1760s-1950s
Purfleet: Principal Royal Naval magazine

Purfleet: AA ammunition store

Shoeburyness: projectile testing

Stanford-le-Hope, Curry Marsh: Miners' Safety Explosives Co Ltd

Stansted: USAAF 30th Air Depot Group, 1942-5

Tilbury: British Bata Shoe Co Ltd, boots and shoes for Ministry of Supply

Tilbury: Stewart and Lloyd's factory built pipes for PLUTO

Waltham Abbey: Royal Gunpowder Factory and explosives works, 1664-1945

Walton-on-the-Naze: rocket test facility, Brakemine, 1944-46

Wrabness, Harwich: Principal Royal Naval magazine and Mines Depot

Warley Barracks, Brentwood: RAF ammunition storage sub-site, 1943, 1945-2000

Dagenham: Sterling Armaments Coy smg Mark IV, and Armalite rifle, 1963-80; ceased production 1988

Ridgewell: airfield used as RAF chemical weapons storage site, No. 95 MU, with satellites at Riseley, Bedfordshire (FFD), Comberton Heath, Orwell and Lords Bridge, Cambridgeshire (FFD), 1946

Ridgewell: RAF munitions storage facility, No. 95 MU, 1953/4

Stansted: Airwork refurbishing Sabres for NATO air forces, 1958; Aviation Traders moved Carvair production from Southend, 1961

Waltham Abbey: Explosives Research and Development Establishment, until 1973

Appendix Eight: Military Hospitals

Pre-First World War

Colchester Military Hospital, 1893-8

Shoeburyness, Horseshoe Barracks hospital, 1856

First World War

Clacton, Holland Road, Middlesex Red Cross Convalescent Home

Claybury LCC mental hospital

Colchester, Sobraon Barracks military hospital

Colchester, Summerdown Camp Military Convalescent Hospital

Hornchurch, Grey Towers: a New Zealand Expeditionary Force hospital

Ingatestone, Fryerning Hall, a convalescent hospital

Purfleet Military Hospital

Romford Military Hospital (in the workhouse, seventy-plus beds)

Romford, Victoria Cottage Hospital

St Osyth, Red Cross depot

Shoeburyness, Horseshoe Barracks: the garrison theatre became a hospital

Southend, Queen Mary's Naval Hospital (in the Palace Hotel)

Thurrock, Aveley School, an auxiliary hospital

Upminster Auxiliary Military Hospital

Woodford Cottage Hospital

Second World War

Blake Hall, Ongar, RAMC depot 1939-42 (then RAF operations room)

Braintree, White Court, US Military hospital

Brentwood, Kelvedon Hall, a Red Cross convalescent home/auxiliary hospital

Colchester Garrison Hospital, closed 1977, demolished 1990s

Halstead, Greenstead Hall, a Red Cross convalescent home/auxiliary hospital

Halstead, Moyns Park, a Red Cross convalescent home/auxiliary hospital

Harlow, Hillingdon Hall, a Red Cross convalescent home/auxiliary hospital

Newport, Shortgrove Park, a US 280th station hospital

Stansted Hall, a Red Cross convalescent home/auxiliary hospital from 1945-2000

Braintree, HMS *Cicero*, Royal Navy Orthopaedic Rehabilitation Centre from 1947-8

Wethersfield airfield, a designated emergency mortuary, 2000

Appendix Nine: Military Airfields

Drawing or Type Numbers used in several places show sequence/year of production: the Watch Office for All Commands was built to the 343rd design to emerge from the Air Ministry drawing office in 1943 – hence 343/43.

Airfields marked L also appear in the London volume of this series.

1. ANDREWSFIELD (Great Saling): The first airfield to be completed by US Army engineers, it was named for an air force general killed in an accident in Iceland. It was of conventional utility design with three runways, two T2 hangars, a technical area with the standard mix of tb and Nissen huts, and dispersed living sites for 2,800 personnel. Initially home to VIIIth USAAF bombers, it was soon taken over by a IXth USAAF Bomb Group raiding Continental targets with B26 Marauders. Following D-Day, redeployments saw RAF fighters move in. Early in 1946 flying ceased and the airfield had been returned to agriculture by 1953, with a grass private flying strip operating from 1976. The two hangars and a Braithwaite tank remain.

2. BIRCH: Opened in 1944 as the last airfield built by the US Army engineers for the VIIIth USAAF, it suffered immediately from subsidence and was never used for its planned purpose as a bomber station, alternating between VIIIth and IXth USAAF occupancy. Used for a while for glider training and storage, it closed in 1944 and has now disappeared through gravel extraction.

3. BOREHAM: Operational as a bomber base for only five months, it became home to the USAAF unit processing and evaluating captured enemy equipment. It had the standard layout, and was built by the US Army Engineer Corps. The watch office is home to the Essex Police Helicopter Unit.

Figure 14 Map to show military airfields in Essex (the First World War landing-fields in italics).

4. BOXTED: Although it opened as a bomber station, it quickly switched to hosting fighter groups of both VIIIth and IXth USAAFs which together accumulated the biggest total of kills, flying bomber protection missions with P51 Mustangs and P-47D Thunderbolts. After the end of the war, the RAF arrived with Mosquitoes and then Meteor jet-fighters, ceasing operations in 1948 whilst retaining an emergency capability as a Standby Airfield under Care and Maintenance. Built as a standard utility airfield, many of the smaller tb structures remain, particularly on the technical site.

5. BRADWELL BAY: The airfield began life servicing the Denghie Flats air-to-ground firing range, and work commenced early in 1941 to build a fighter satellite station. Fighter squadrons were based here as bomber escorts, and to intercept enemy bombers and V1s. It continued in use for squadrons using the ranges, and for refuelling during escort operations. It was the only fighter field to be provided with FIDO. Right up until 1955 there were plans to reopen the airfield as a fighter station with Rivenhall as its satellite, but none was implemented and it shut in 1960. A number of local buildings were requisitioned for RAF use. The watch office (12096/41 for night fighters) has been converted into a house. Aircraft were dispersed in a mixture of Blister hangars, hard-standings and protected pens.

6. BROOMFIELD: A landing ground during the First World War.

7. BURNHAM-ON-CROUCH: A landing ground during the First World War used by No. 37 Squadron, it measured 750 by 600 yards.

8. (L) CHINGFORD: Used mainly for training throughout the First World War, becoming No. 207 TDS. It closed in 1919, and most of the site now lies under the Lea Valley reservoirs, but recent investigations have shown that traces of surviving structures remain under the grass apron.

9. CHIPPING ONGAR: As one of the earliest stations to be built by the USAAF, it opened in mid-1943, for bombing operations against airfields and rocket-sites. After supporting ground operations following D-Day, the airfield was used for storing gliders. After 1945, it was speedily returned to agriculture. The south wing of Blake Hall had earlier been gutted for an RAF operations room, superseded by the purpose-built operations block which survives, along with a stand-by-set house and a Blister hangar used as a free-gunnery trainer.

10. DEBDEN: Commenced building in 1935, opening in 1937, flying Gladiators as an Expansion Scheme airfield and becoming, in 1939, an 11 Group Sector Station with Hurricanes and Blenheims. In 1942 the Debden Spitfire Wing was operating, followed in 1943 by the 4th Fighter Group VIIIth USAAF with P-47 Thunderbolts, escorting bomber operations, within 65th Fighter Wing, with its HQ in Dame Bradbury's School, Saffron Walden. Although Meteors had flown here in 1944 as a tactical development exercise, it only returned to the RAF after the war, passing to RAF Technical Training Command until 1960 after which it remained the RAF Police Depot until closure in 1975. A typical Expansion Scheme airfield, it had three C-type hangars, a Fort (207/36) watch office and all the usual technical, administrative, training, and domestic buildings. It was rebuilt in 1940-1 by W. and C. French Ltd, who laid two concrete runways of 4,800 and 3,950ft (1,477 and 1,215m) adding one Bellman and eleven Blister hangars, along with fourteen twin blast pens, and sixty-four PSP or steel mat standings. From 1975 the station has been Carver Barracks. Although the hangars and watch office have been demolished, many of the original buildings remain, including the operations block, station HQ, guardroom, officers' mess and main stores. The runways and perimeter track survive with a number of pillboxes, whilst, south of the road, three Blister hangars remain.

11. EARLS COLNE: Built by US army engineers, it opened in mid-1943 as a bomber station flying sorties in B26 Marauders against targets in France, Belgium and Holland. When the US fliers moved south to support D-Day, 38 Group RAF, with its HQ in nearby Marks Hall, returned with airborne units, Horsa gliders towed by Albemarles, as well as missions supporting SOE operations. After brief use by Meteors, the airfield was placed under Care and Maintenance from 1946 until it was eventually judged surplus to requirements in the 1960s. It had a standard layout and buildings with two T2 hangars and a watch office (343/43). The hangars appear to survive, much altered, in the present industrial estate.

12. (L) FAIRLOP (Hainault Farm): Established in 1915 as a Home Defence fighter airfield, continuing as such, as No. 54 TDS, until it moved to London Colney

(Hertfordshire), and then as a sub-station of No. 207 TDS at Chingford, until closure in 1919. Earmarked in abortive plans for a City of London airport in 1930, it was rebuilt as a fighter station in 1940, serving as such until 1944 when it became No. 24 Balloon Centre, closing in 1946. Surviving buildings include twin aeroplane sheds (56/17), and two groups of 1855 farm buildings, used as accommodation and messes.

13. FYFIELD: A landing ground during the First World War, it was on or near the site of Chipping Ongar, the Second World War airfield.

14. GOLDHANGER: It served as an operational Home Defence fighter station during the First World War. St George's church, Heybridge Basin, was the sergeants' mess, re-erected there in 1920.

15. GOSFIELD: Opened in autumn 1943, the fighters of IXth USAAF commenced operations only in February 1944, closely followed by several different units flying A20 Havocs, against invasion targets. When the US bombers moved to France, 38 Group RAF moved in carrying out airborne operations, closing in late 1945. It was a standard bomber airfield with two T2 hangars and a general purpose watch office (343/43), which remains in use as offices.

16. GREAT DUNMOW: In autumn 1943, a IXth USAAF bomb group arrived with B26 Marauders, to take part in joint operations with the RAF on D-Day-related targets. At the end of the year the RAF brought Stirling squadrons for supply dropping, and – after a period of re-training – bombing missions, as well as glider-towing. Flying ceased in 1945 but the airfield remained in Care and Maintenance, in use as a USAF supply depot into the 1960s. It had a standard layout with a watch office (343/43) and two T2 hangars. A cluster of Nissen huts represents the HQ and administrative site, with a Blister hangar and stand-by set house nearby.

17. GREAT SAMPFORD: Opened in 1942 as a satellite for Debden's Spitfires, this was a grass field, 4,800 by 3,150ft (1,477 by 970m) with a 1,000-yard Sommerfield Track runway. When the 4th USAAF Fighter Group, with P-47 Thunderbolts, took up residence in 1943, they found the flying area unsuitable, confining use to dispersal and emergency landings. It then operated as a RAF Regiment Battle School until late 1944. For a short while prior to D-Day there were practice landings by Horsa gliders, followed by a spell in Balloon Command combating V1s. It closed in early 1946. Its rudimentary fighter satellite watch office (17658/40) had never been replaced, and its only hangars were Blisters, supplemented by dispersal pens and hard-standings. Some of the communal site buildings remain, notably a group of Handcraft huts.

(FOR HAINAULT FARM: see FAIRLOP)

18. (L) HORNCHURCH: Known as Suttons Farm in the First World War, it had operated as a Home Defence squadron base, and was demolished in 1918. It was rebuilt

from scratch in 1928, as a fighter station, some distance to the west of the earlier air-field, with A- and C-type hangars, and a Fort-type watch office without the tower (2062/34) operating up to mid-1944. Its final role was training and aircrew selection, until 1962. Surviving buildings include the officers' mess (Astra Close), similar to that at North Weald, extensive housing and married quarters, and fighter-pens and defences around the airfield perimeter. It is now a country park.

19. LITTLE WALDEN (Hadstock): Used by IXth USAAF bombers on pre-D-Day operations, then by fighter squadrons of the VIIIth USAAF flying Mustangs, flying escort and ground-attack missions. Although flying ceased at the end of 1945, the station continued in RAF use into the 1950s. There survive some fine examples of buildings from a typical airfield of this period including the watch office (12779/41), T2 hangars, parachute store (11137/41) and dinghy store (2901/43), the Gas Defence Centre (12408/41) and a Blister hangar used as the Free Gunnery Trainer (7810/42).

20. MATCHING: One of the last airfields built for the USAAF, it opened early in 1944 for bombers of the IXth USAAF operating against pre-invasion targets, V2 sites, and then for RAF glider tows for Operation Varsity, the Rhine crossing. After desultory occupation in 1945, the airfield was run down. The watch office (343/43), now used for radar trials, still stands along with part of the adjacent technical site. A very extensive communal site retains the Braithwaite tank, rows of Romney and Nissen huts including those used by the US engineers who constructed the airfield.

21. NORTH BENFLEET: A landing ground during the First World War.

22. (L) NORTH WEALD (BASSETT): Starting life as a Home Defence station throughout the First World War, it was completely rebuilt in 1926. Ad Astra House, built in 1908 and requisitioned as Station HQ in 1916, was one of the few survivors from the early days, and new buildings included two A-type hangars. It operated as a Fighter Sector Station in the Battle of Britain, suffering bomb damage. In around 1952 a new control tower was added, but flying ceased in around 1965, and it was finally disposed of in 1979. Surviving buildings include Ad Astra House, the officers' mess, one A-type hangar, the 5223a/51 control tower, and the operations block, updated for use as a nuclear bunker.

23. ORSETT: A landing ground used by 78 Squadron RFC on Home Defence duties from 1917-9, with only tented accommodation.

24. PALMERS FARM (Shenfield, Brentwood): A First World War landing ground. (N.B.: another Palmers Farm exists next to the Second World War airfield at Birch.)

25. RIDGEWELL: Opened in 1942 as a satellite of the 3 Group RAF bomber station at Stradishall, flying Stirlings on large-scale raids over Germany. In May 1943 the VIIIth USAAF moved in, flying bombing missions over France, Germany and

Norway. After the war the RAF used it as a Maintenance Unit HQ, and there was a stores depot serving Wethersfield up until 1967.

26. RIVENHALL: Operations only commenced here in late February 1944, when a fighter group of the IXth USAAF arrived to fly escort and ground-attack missions. They were soon replaced by bombers targeting lines of communication behind the German defences prior to the invasion. From October 1944, 38 Group RAF organised drops to French resistance groups, and glider-towing for Operation Varsity using Stirlings. Following its use as a camp for displaced persons, the airfield was taken over by Marconi in 1956. Two T2 hangars and other buildings remain along with traces of radar tower bases from the Marconi days.

27. ROCHFORD: Identified in 1914 as a Home Defence aerodrome, the RFC moved in a year later eventually flying Sopwith Pups, SE5As and Camels, alongside a depot squadron carrying out pilot training. By 1920 it had been derequisitioned and returned to agriculture. In 1935 the airfield had been resurrected as Southend's municipal airport with a resident flying club, and within two years the RAAF had formed No. 34 ERFTS operating Tiger Moths, which closed on the outbreak of war. The airfield became first a satellite of Hornchurch, and then a free-standing station, operating fighters during the Battle of Britain and throughout the war. It was returned to civilian flying in 1946, finally receiving paved runways in 1956. The airfield had two Bellman hangars, three Blister hangars and six of the larger-size fighter dispersal pens for Blenheims. No watch office appears on the 1945 Air Ministry plan and it would appear that it relied on temporary Flight Office buildings.

28. SIBLE HEDINGHAM: A landing ground during the First World War.

29. STANSTED: Except for a brief period from March to September 1944 when operational bombers were based here, the airfield functioned exclusively as a USAAF Air Depot, repairing and servicing aircraft. After the war it served briefly as a USAAF transit centre, then a RAF MU, and then in 1949 the Civil Aviation Authority took over. Whilst in most respects it was a standard bomber field with the usual 343/43 watch office and mainly tb and Nissen buildings, it had two extra T2 hangars. As an Air Depot there were two further T2 hangars, and the close-on 3,000 personnel based there were in communal sites dispersed over a wide area. One such site, west of the M11, has only recently been demolished.

30. (L) STAPLEFORD TAWNEY: Opened in 1934 as a base for civilian services, it was taken over as an ERFTS in 1938, becoming a satellite for North Weald's fighters in 1940. Late in 1943 it was transferred to US 2nd TAF, who left in 1953. Since then it has reverted mainly to club flying. Surviving buildings include the large steel and asbestos hangar, and the smaller hangar/armoury/office, officers' mess, NAAFI and other timber huts.

31. STOW MARIES: An operational Home Defence fighter aerodrome throughout the First World War, many of whose buildings are undergoing restoration at Flambirds Farm. These include workshops and stores, MT garages, station offices and HQ, the Institute, the officers' mess and living quarters. In the Second World War it was included in the proposed VIIIth USAAF airfield site at Cold Norton, but not taken up.

(SUTTONS FARM see HORNCHURCH)

32. THAXTED: A landing ground during the First World War.

33. WESTPOLE FARM: A landing ground during the First World War (not located).

34. WETHERSFIELD: Operational for only nine months in 1944 when the IXth USAAF flew A20 Havocs against D-Day targets. The RAF returned with airborne units flying Stirlings and C47 Dakotas for the Rhine Crossing, Operation Varsity. After the war, runway extensions enabled their use by jet fighters of 3rd USAF with temporary use by a RAF FTS. Super Sabres and Thunderstreaks carrying nuclear weapons were based here and the facilities were constantly being improved into the 1970s. The USAF stayed until 1991 when it became the MOD Police Depot.

35. WORMINGFORD: The site of a First World War landing ground, this standard layout airfield became operational as a IXth USAAF fighter base early in 1944. Flying Thunderbolts and Lightnings (!) as bomber escorts and as tactical ground support, its planes stayed until the war's end. After a brief occupation by the RAF, the airfield closed early in 1948.

36. WRITTLE: A First World War landing ground covering 22 acres (9ha), and used from 1914 to 1916 by No. 1 Reserve Aeroplane Squadron RFC; occupied the site of the Napoleonic Camp (TL680065).

Other premises occupied by RAF, USAAF, etc.

Bobbingworth, Blake Hall: south wing gutted for RAF Chipping Ongar Operations Room.

Bradwell: East Wick and Weymarks House: Station HQ; Bradwell Lodge: officers' mess; Peverills and Down Hall: officers' quarters; The Holt: WAAF officers' quarters; Tudor Hall: WAAF quarters and MT park; Highfields: twenty-bed sick quarters; St Cedd's: senior NCOs' quarters; Yacht Club: RAF Regiment HQ.

Chigwell: No. 4 Balloon Centre, RAF; closed 1958, demolished 1968.

Clacton-on-Sea: airstrip for US 987 Field Artillery Battalion aerial ops.

Earls Colne, Marks Hall: HQ 38 Group RAF.

Great Dunmow: the entire Easton Lodge estate was requisitioned by the Air Ministry in 1939, but there is no evidence that the house, which was demolished in around 1950 after a fire, was occupied by either the RAF or the USAAF.

Rochford: Station HQ at Greenways, Hall Road; then at Earls Hall School (late 1940).

Saffron Walden, Dame Bradbury's School: HQ and operations room, 65th Fighter Wing, US VIIIth Air Force.

Airfields projected during the Second World War, but never built:
Beaumont, Bulphan, Burnham, Castle Hedingham, Cold Norton (Stow Maries), High Roding, Ingatestone, Little Clacton, Maldon, Southminster and Weeley.

Appendix Ten: Drill Halls in Post-1974 Essex

Italics are used for sites which have been destroyed.

Braintree
★1. *Corn Exchange* used prior to 1911

★2. Victoria Street, drill hall, 1911; two-storey, T-shaped front block with hall attached; sold in 1963 and now a community centre; Nos 18 and 20 opposite, with Essex crests, were staff houses

★3. *Coggeshall Road*, acquired 1939 for site of new TAC, never built; hutted camp used by TA after 1963; now demolished for Kilkee Lodge nursing home; ACF uses garage (1980) and Nissen hut small-arms range on site.

In 1914, base for B Sqdn Essex Yeo., for F Coy 5 Bn Essex Regt, and drill station for C Coy 8 (Cyclist) Bn Essex Regt; in 1950, R Bty 646 LAA Regt (ex-5 Bn Essex Regt) + WRAC (Victoria Street) and 313 Sqdn, 134 (Essex) Construction Regt RE (Coggeshall Road)

Brentwood
Chestnut Grove, drill hall, 1935, sold for redevelopment 1985; new TAC at Warley incorporating former Depot officers' mess, now Blenheim House.

In 1914, drill station for D Sqdn Essex Yeo.; HQ 4 Bn Essex Regt and base for G Coy 8 (Cyclist) Bn Essex Regt; in 1950, Q Bty 304 Fd. Regt RA (Essex Yeo.) and HQ R Bty 563 LAA/SL Regt

Brightlingsea
★1. Sydney Street, Foresters' Hall, in use *c.* 1914; gabled, brick hall, two-storey cross-wing to Tower Street

★2. High Street, drill hall, pre-First World War; lately YMCA.

In 1950, detachment of Q Bty 530 LAA Regt

Burnham-on-Crouch
High Street, drill hall, built as chapel, mid-nineteenth century; subsequently drill hall, auction-house, snooker club, now sail-maker and shops; used by Home Guard

In 1914, drill station for F Coy 4 Bn Essex Regt; in 1950, detachment of B Coy 4 Bn Essex Regt

Canvey Island
Runnymede Road, TAC, demolished 1987, new ACF centre

In 1950, P (Essex) Bty 415 Coast Regt RA (TA)

Chelmsford

*1. *Market Road*, militia storehouse built in around 1855 for West Essex Militia, super-seded by drill hall 1902; demolished 1994; a sign is incorporated in present gate

*2. London Road, RE drill hall, around 1930s; used by GPO into 1980s, now church; front block with porch, hall behind; large yard, whose east wall was the inner wall of the indoor range, (lead staining); 1950s garages in commercial use

*3. *Broomfield Road*, RE unit here 1947–61; pair of instructors' houses, now private dwellings

*4. Springfield Lyons, TAC, built 1994; two large, linked blocks of two storeys and garage block; main façade has elements of traditional drill hall; original foundation stones by gate

*5. 250 Springfield Road, Springfield Tyrells, 1888, HQ RFCA East Anglia; large, three-storey detached mansion, built as home for Ridley, the brewer, surrounded by temporary government office buildings in the Second World War

*6. Pitfield House, *c*. 1900, near Army and Navy roundabout, last used by RN Reserve; two detached officers' houses, bungalow last used as cadet centre, all now private dwellings

In 1914, drill station B Sqdn Essex Yeo.; HQ and Battery plus Sub-Section Ammunition Column Essex RHA; HQ No. 1 Electric Lights Coy RE (Fortress), HQ, A and B Coys 5 Bn Essex Regt (drill station at Broomfield); Eastern Mounted Bde. Transport and Supply Column ASC

In 1950, HQ and P Bty 646 LAA Regt plus workshop units, 855 Fire Control Bty (Essex Fortress), 1563 Tipper Coy RASC, 3 Essex Platoon, WRAC (Market Road), 304 Field Regt Essex Yeo. (London Road) and 313 Field Sqdn (one troop) of 134 Construction Regt RE (Broomfield Road)

Clacton

26 Rosemary Road, Osborne Hotel/drill hall, *c*. 1880s; mentioned in 1902 as base for Essex Volunteers, and as the venue for the Shooting Club; still in use 1915, but prob-ably not after 1918; hotel, now Sandles, is three-storey Victorian build with Italianate tower and hall behind with skylights

In 1914, base for H Coy 5 Bn Essex Regt; in 1950, Q Bty 530 LAA Regt

Colchester

*1. *Stanwell Street*, 1855, storehouse of East Essex Militia, drill hall from 1887; demolished 1983.

*2. 17 *Sir Isaac's Walk*, HQ Essex Yeo. in 1914; redeveloped as shops *c*. 1980s

*3. Reed Hall Camp, TAC; in use 1950

*4. Butt Road, TAC; late 1960s, three-storey, flat-roofed, concrete-framed building for TA but use brief

*5. Circular Road East, TAC, 1984, in use; long, two-storey admin block, two large halls and garages; this replaced huts at junction of Circular Road East and Napier Road

*6. 8 *Head Street*, HQ Eastern Mounted Bde (1914); redeveloped pre-Second World War

In 1914, HQ and A Sqdn Essex Yeo.; No.1 Section Bty and A sub-Section Ammunition Column, Essex RHA; C Coy 5 Bn; HQ and A Coy; 8 (Cyclist) Bn Essex Regt

In 1950, HQ and P Bty 530 LAA Regt (Stanwell Street); P Bty 304 Field Regt (Essex Yeo.), RE, REME, Royal Signals, RASC, RAOC and WRAC TA units (Reed Hall Camp)

Coggeshall
King's seed warehouse, at corner of The Gravel opposite Kings Acre, adapted as *drill hall*; demolished post-First World War; now a public garden

In 1914, base for H Coy 8 (Cyclist) Bn Essex Regt

Great Dunmow
High Street, drill hall, 1927; single-storey front block with hall behind

In 1914, drill station C Sqdn Essex Yeo.; F Coy 5 Bn Essex Regt; and C Coy 8 (Cyclist) Bn Essex Regt; in 1950, detachment R Bty 646 LAA Regt

Epping
Hempnall Street, drill hall, only garage remains as cadet centre

In 1914, drill station for G Coy 4 Bn Essex Regt; in 1950, base for C Coy 4 Bn Essex Regt

Grays
★ 1. Brook Road, drill hall, in use First World War; 1960s replacement TAC on site.
★ 2. *2 High Street*, in use 1950

In 1914, drill station for D Sqdn Essex Yeo.; 3 Essex Bty 2 E Anglian Bde. RFA (artillery drill hall); drill station for H Coy 6 Bn Essex Regt; in 1950, 534 Coy RASC, (2 High St) and R Bty 285 Airborne Light Regt (Brook Rd)

Great Bardfield
Dunmow Road, '*Drill Hall House*', (*c.*1950) drill hall demolished

In 1914, drill station for F Coy 5 Bn Essex Regt

Halstead
Pretoria Road, drill hall, *c.* 1920s, single-storey block with hall to rear, now Jehovah's Witnesses' Kingdom Hall

In 1914, drill station for B Sqdn Essex Yeo.; base E Coy 5 Bn Essex Regt; in 1950, detachment of R Bty 646 LAA Regt

Harlow
Old Road, drill hall, 1947, two-storey offices on right of yard, plus hall and garages

In 1914, drill station for G Coy 4 Bn Essex Regt; in 1950, R Bty 304 Field Regt (Essex Yeo.)

Harwich

Main Road, Dovercourt, drill hall, pre-First World War; E-plan building with two-storey wing at one end, and single-storey at other; small hall in centre, and annexes behind; HQ of Essex and Suffolk RGA, inscription over doorway with stone canopy and mouldings; large corrugated-iron-clad hall alongside, now Park Pavilion community centre; ACF building on site

In 1914, drill station for A Sqdn Essex Yeo.; HQ + 1 Coy Essex and Suffolk RGA-Defended Ports; in 1937, Suffolk Heavy Bde RA (TA)

Ingatestone

Fryerning Lane, drill hall, pre-Second World War; two-storey front block, with hall behind; porch added; engineering workshop, now nursery

In 1914, drill station for No. 2 Section Essex Bty RHA; in 1937, HQ No. 4 Essex Group AA Searchlights; in 1950, 3 Coy 10 Para Bn TA and detachment R Bty 563 LAA/SL Regt

Leigh-on-Sea

Eastwood Road, *drill hall*, built 1937, demolished and redeveloped 1996; garage forms part of new cadet centre

In 1950, Q Bty 482 (M) HAA Regt; Q Bty 517 LAA Regt

Little Waltham

Tufnell Village Hall, drill hall of *c.* 1913

In 1914, drill station for A Coy 5 Bn Essex Regt

Maldon

Tenterfield Road, drill hall, pre-First World War; ACF use garage/range block; two-storey gabled-front block now private residence, remainder demolished

In 1914, base G Coy 5 Bn Essex Regt and drill station C Coy 8 (Cyclist) Bn Essex Regt; in 1950, detachments of P Bty 646 LAA Regt; P Bty 304 Field Regt (Yeo.)

Manningtree

Mill Lane, drill hall, *c.* 1930s; hall/offices with small-arms range built on one end; blocked tall, garage-type opening in end wall, possibly gun store

In 1914, base for D Coy 5 Bn Essex Regt; in 1950, detachment of R Bty 530 LAA Regt

Ongar

*1. High Street, Wren House with drill hall of 1873 to rear, in use as offices

*2. Coopers Hill, *drill hall*, *c.* 1935; latterly known as The Haunt, demolished early 1980s for Coopers Mews; ACF hut

In 1914, base for G Coy 4 Bn Essex Regt; in 1950, detachment of Q Bty 304 Field Regt Essex Yeo.

Saffron Walden
Station Street, *drill hall*, demolished *c.* 1990
>In 1914, base for D Coy 8 (Cyclist) Bn Essex Regt
>In 1950, Q Bty 646 LAA Regt

Shoeburyness, Horseshoe Barracks, in use 1856-1986
>In 1950, WRAC units (TA)

Southend-on-Sea
★1. East Street, Prittlewell, drill hall, 1930, two-storey T-shaped block and garages.
★2. East Street (west side), drill hall, formerly Recruiting Office, electrical and auto businesses; two-storey front block with elaborate Essex crest on gable to street; large hall behind; in use pre-1914-2000
★3. Prince Avenue, *drill hall* in use in 1950, demolished
★4. York Road, *drill hall*, in use pre-1914 to 1950, demolished.
>In 1914, base for D Sqdn Essex Yeo. (Prittlewell); No. 3 Coy Essex and Suffolk RGA Defended Ports (York Road) H Coy 6 Bn Essex Regt; A and B Sections 3rd East Anglian Divisional Field Ambulance RAMC and C Section drill station (Prittlewell); in 1931, 175 (Essex Heavy) Bty RA (TA); 414 Bty of 104 Field Bde (Essex Yeo.) RA (TA) (both York Road); D Coy 6 Bn Essex Regt and 54 East Anglian Coy Royal Signals (both Prittlewell); in 1950, P Bty 600 HAA Regt (Prittlewell); detachment Q Bty 304 Field Regt Essex Yeo.; R (Essex) Bty 415 Coast Regt (Prince Avenue) 314 Sqdn 134 (Essex) Construction Regt RE (York Road); 536 GT Coy RASC and 133 (TA) Field Security Section (East Street, Prittlewell)

Southminster
★1. South Street, Parish Room, possible Volunteer Armoury
★2. Queenborough Road, *drill hall* and house, demolished for housing 1990s; in use by 1914, in 1937, by Home Guard in the Second World War, and in 1950
>In 1914, base for F Coy 4 Bn Essex Regt; in 1950, detachment of B Coy 4 Bn Essex Regt

South Ockendon
Buckles Farm Camp, *hutted camp* in use 1950, redeveloped
>In 1950, WRAC Unit (TA); 43 Med. Workshops, REME

Stanford-le-Hope
Corringham Road, *drill hall*, demolished
>In 1950, No.1932 Coy RASC (Tractor)

Thaxted
No dedicated building located
>In 1914, drill station for F Coy 5 Bn Essex Regt

Thorpe-le-Soken

High Street, Women's Institute Hall, *c.* 1914; used by volunteer units

In 1950, R Bty 530 LAA Regt

Vange

Brickfield Road, *hutted camp* used by TA 1981-96, demolished for housing

Waltham Abbey

★1. *Church Street* (next to Lloyds Bank) Yeomanry Stores, in use 1914

In 1914, base for C Sqdn Essex Yeo.; in 1950 detachment of R Bty 304 Field Regt (Essex Yeo.)

Warley

Clive Road, TAC, 1989, in use

Witham

Guithavon Road, *drill hall*, demolished 1974

In 1914, drill station for G Coy 5 Bn Essex Regt; in 1950, detachment P Bty 646 LAA Regt

Drill stations for TF/TA units in post-1974 Essex:

Althorne, Ardleigh, Billericay, Bocking, Boreham, Bradfield, Bradwell, Broomfield, Coggeshall, Danbury, Dedham, Earls Colne, Felstead, Great Bardfield, Hatfield (Heath, Broad Oak, or Peverel?), Hedingham, Maplestead, Mountnessing, Orsett, Pebmarsh, Stansted, Terling, Thaxted, Tillingham, Tiptree, Tollesbury, Walton-on-the-Naze, Wickford, Wickham Bishops, Witham, Wivenhoe, Writtle, Yeldham

Bases★/drill stations for TF/TA units in historic Essex now Greater London:

Abridge, ★Barking, Becontree, Buckhurst Hill, Chingford, Dagenham, ★East Ham, Harold Wood, ★Hornchurch, ★Ilford, ★Leyton, ★Loughton, ★Manor Park, Newbury Park, Rainham, ★Romford, Silvertown, ★Stratford, Upminster, ★Walthamstow, Wanstead, ★West Ham, Woodford

Bibliography

Alexander, C., *Ironside's Line*, Storrington, 1998

Appleby, D., 'Colonel William Maxey: an Essex Cavalier' in English Civil War, *Notes and Queries* No. 50, n.d.

Appleby, D., 'Essex Men at the Battle of Worcester', *English Civil War Times*, No. 52, n.d.

Appleby, D., 'Manchester's Essex Dragoons', *English Civil War Times*, No. 56, n.d.

Bettley, J. and Pevsner, N., *Essex* [part of the 'Buildings of England' series], 2007, New Haven and London

Boustred, R.E., *Last Stand for the King*, Colchester Borough Council, 1974

Bowyer, M., *Action Stations 1: Military airfields in East Anglia*, Wellingborough, 1979 and 1990

Bowyer, M., *Action Stations Revisited 1: Eastern England*, Manchester, 2000

Brown, M and Pattison, P., *Beacon Hill Fort, Essex*, Cambridge, RCHME, 1997

Brown, M and Pattison, P., *Coalhouse Point: Archaeological features in the inter-tidal zone*, East Tilbury, Essex; Cambridge, EH, 2003

Campbell, D., *War Plan UK*, London, 1982

Campbell, D., *The Unsinkable Aircraft Carrier*, London, 1984

Clements, B., *Martello Towers Worldwide*, Barnsley, 2011

Cocroft, W. and Menuge, A., *Buildings of the Electronics Industry, Chelmsford*, Cambridge, RCHME, 1999

Cocroft, W., *Dangerous Energy*, EH, 2000

Cocroft, W. and Thomas R., *Cold War, Building for Nuclear Confrontation 1946-89*, Swindon, EH, 2003

Crummy, P., *City of Victory*, Colchester, 1997

Dietz, P. (ed), 'Colchester' in *Garrison – Ten British Military Towns*, London, 1986

Dobinson, C., *Twentieth Century Fortifications in England*, York, CBA, 1996/2000, various

Dobinson, C., *Fields of Deception*, London, EH and Methuen, 2000

Dobinson, C., *AA Command*, London, EH and Methuen, 2001

Dobinson, C., *Building Radar*, London, EH and Methuen, 2010

Douet, J., *British Barracks 1600-1914*; Norwich, HMSO, 1998

Essex County Council, *Essex Archaeology, 10-15* and *Essex Past and Present, 1-7*, Chelmsford, 1993–2005

Faulkner, N. and Durrani, N., *In Search of the Zeppelin War*, Stroud, 2008

Foley, M., *Essex in the First World War*, Stroud, 2009

Foot, W., *Beaches, Fields, Streets and Hills*, CBA Research Report 144, York, 2006

Foynes, J.P., *The Battle of the East Coast 1939-1945*, published by the author, 1994

Francis, P. and Crisp, G., *Military Command and Control Organisation*, Swindon (in CD form for EH), 2008

Francis, P., *Airfield Defences*, 2010, Ware

Free, K., *Camp 186: The lost town at Berechurch*, Chalford, 2010

Gilman, P. and Nash, F.: *Fortress Essex*, Chelmsford, 1995

Goodwin, J., *Military Signals from the South Coast*, Midhurst, 2000

Hedges, J., 'Essex Moats', in Aberg, F.A. (ed), *Medieval Moated Sites*, CBA Research Report No. 17, London, 1978

Hill, Major A.S., unpublished notes on Shoeburyness School and ranges, 1995

Kent, P., *Fortifications of East Anglia,* 1988, Lavenham

Kent, P., 'East Anglian fortifications in the Twentieth Century' in *Fortress 3*, Liphook, 1989

Kenyon, J., *Castles, Town Defences and Artillery Fortifications in the United Kingdom and Ireland: a Bibliography 1945-2006,* Donington, 2008

King, D.J.C. and Alcock, L., 'Ringworks of England and Wales' in Taylor, A.J. (ed) *Chateau Gaillard III*, Chichester, 1966 and 1969

King, D.J.C.: *Castellarium Anglicanum* (index and bibliography), New York, 1983

Liddiard, R., *Castles in Context*, Macclesfield, 2005

Marshall, P., 'The internal arrangement of the donjon at Colchester in Essex: a reconsideration', in Guy, N. (ed), *CSG Journal* No. 23, Daventry, 2010

McCamley, N., *Cold War Secret Nuclear Bunkers*, Barnsley, 2002

Mount Bures 2011 excavation, www.arch.cam.ac.uk/aca/mountbures.html

National Trust's Rayleigh Mount Local Committee, *Rayleigh Mount*, Rayleigh, 1965

Osborne, M., *Defending Britain*, Stroud, 2004

Osborne, M., *Always Ready, The Drill Halls of Britain's Volunteer Forces,* Leigh-on-Sea, 2006

Osborne, M., *Pillboxes in Britain and Ireland*, Stroud, 2008

Oswald, A., *Anti-Aircraft Batteries Bowaters Farm, East Tilbury, Essex;* Swindon (RCHME), 1994

Pattison, P. and Guillery, P. *Purfleet Gunpowder Magazines, Thurrock, Essex*, Cambridge, RCHME, 1994

Saunders, A., *Tilbury Fort*, London, EH, 1960 guidebook (revised 1980)

Saunders, A., *Fortress Builder Bernard de Gomme, Charles II's Military Engineer*, Exeter, 2004

Smith, V., *Defending London's River*, Rochester, North Kent Books, 1985

Tendring District Council, *Beacon Hill Ancient Monument, draft action and management plan*, Tendring DC, 1989

Trollope, C., 'The defences of Harwich: 1983', in *FORT 11, Liverpool*

Warlow, Lt Cdr B., *Shore Establishments of the Royal Navy*, Liskeard, 1992 and 2000

Webster, G., *The Roman Invasion of Britain*, London, 1993

Wood, D.A., *Landguard Fort,* Felixstowe, 1982

Wright, A.C., 'Essex and the Volunteers', in *Essex Journal VII*, 1972

Index